THE SOMME

THE SOMME

The Epic Battle in the Soldiers' own Words and Photographs

Richard van Emden

Pen & Sword
MILITARY

First published in Great Britain in Paperback in 2016 by
Pen & Sword Military
an imprint of
Pen & Sword Books Ltd
47 Church Street
Barnsley
South Yorkshire
S70 2AS

ISBN 978 1 47389 364 1

A CIP catalogue record for this book is available from the
British Library

Typeset in Ehrhardt by
Mac Style Ltd, Bridlington, East Yorkshire
Printed and bound in the UK by CPI Group (UK) Ltd,
Croydon, CRO 4YY

Pen & Sword Books Ltd incorporates the imprints of Pen & Sword Archaeology,
Atlas, Aviation, Battleground, Discovery, Family History, History, Maritime,
Military, Naval, Politics, Railways, Select, Transport,
True Crime, and Fiction, Frontline Books, Leo Cooper, Praetorian Press,
Seaforth Publishing and Wharncliffe.

For a complete list of Pen & Sword titles please contact
PEN & SWORD BOOKS LIMITED
47 Church Street, Barnsley, South Yorkshire, S70 2AS, England
E-mail: enquiries@pen-and-sword.co.uk
Website: www.pen-and-sword.co.uk

Title Page: *Captain Ormonde Whiteman looks through a periscope. He was killed in November, 1917.*
Frontispiece: *An officer of the Royal Engineers stands on the ruins of in La Boisselle Church, July 1916.*

*To the memory of Sapper Norman Ralph Skelton, 1898–1988
103915, Wireless Section, Royal Engineers*

and

*Alicia Wilson, aged 104, daughter of Captain Hugh Russell Wilson,
C Coy, 1/5th Durham Light Infantry, killed in action
11 September 1916, buried Bécourt Cemetery, Somme*

My dear George and Alicia

Thank you both so very much for sending me such nice photographs, you are kind and you do look well and pretty. I am having such a nice birthday. I got up at 6 o'clock and went for a ride on a mule, or as we call them, a Moke. It is half a horse and half a donkey and is called Billy. I am going to a party tonight and hope to enjoy myself. There are lots of guns round about us and they do make a row, I'm sure they would wake you up if you had them going off near you in the night. Daisy is quite well but she will gallop so and it makes her far too hot. I hope you enjoy Harrogate. Mind, be kind to Granny and Grandpa and be good children.

Your affectionate
Daddy

[Captain Hugh Wilson, written on his 38th birthday, 2nd August 1916]

CONTENTS

Opposite:
Officers and men of the 8th East Lancashire Regiment in the waterlogged trenches near Foncquevillers, winter 1915.

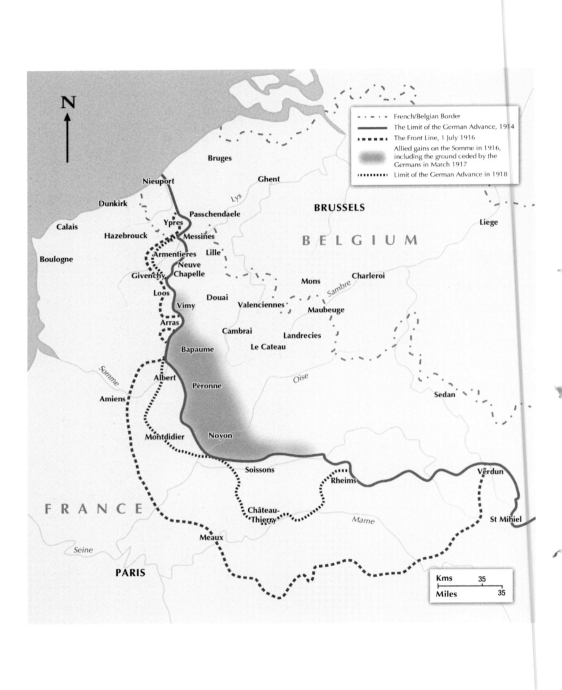

N

French/Belgian Border
The Limit of the German Advance, 1914
The Front Line, 1 July 1916
Allied gains on the Somme in 1916, including the ground ceded by the Germans in March 1917
Limit of the German Advance in 1918

Bruges

Nieuport   Ghent

Dunkirk   BRUSSELS

Calais   Ypres   Passchendaele   Liege

Hazebrouck   Messines   BELGIUM

Boulogne   Armentieres Lille

Givenchy Neuve
          Chapelle   Mons   Charleroi

Loos   Douai   Sambre

Vimy   Valenciennes   Maubeuge

Arras   Cambrai   Landrecies

Bapaume   Le Cateau

Albert   Oise

Amiens   Peronne   Sedan

Montdidier   Noyon

FRANCE   Soissons   Verdun

                        Rheims

Château-
Thierry   Marne   St Mihiel

Meaux

Seine

PARIS   Kms   35
                                 Miles 35

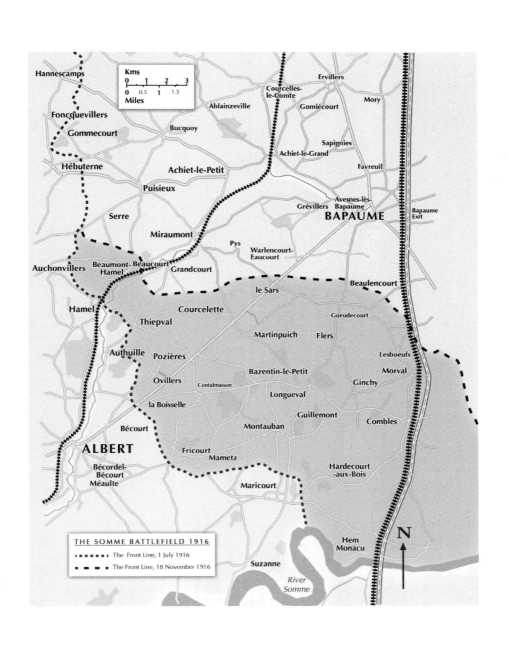

Hannescamps

Foncquevillers

Gommecourt

Hébuterne

Auchonvillers

Kms
0   1   2   3
0   0.5   1   1.5
Miles

Bucquoy

Puisieux

Serre

Miraumont

Achiet-le-Petit

Ablainzeville

Courcelles-
le-Comte

Ervillers

Gomiécourt

Mory

Sapignies

Achiet-le-Grand

Favreuil

Grévillers   Avesnes-lès-
Bapaume

BAPAUME   Bapaume
Exit

Pys

Warlencourt-
Eaucourt

Beaumont-   Beaucourt
Hamel   Grandcourt

le Sars

Beaulencourt

Hamel

Thiepval

Courcelette

Gueudecourt

Martinpuich   Flers

Authuille

Pozières

Ovillers   Contalmaison

Bazentin-le-Petit

Longueval

Lesboeufs

Morval

Ginchy

la Boiselle

Guillemont

Combles

Bécourt

Montauban

ALBERT

Fricourt   Mametz

Bécordel-
Bécourt
Méaulte

Maricourt

Hardecourt
-aux-Bois

Hem
Monacu

N

Suzanne

*River
Somme*

THE SOMME BATTLEFIELD 1916
▪▪▪▪▪▪▪ The Front Line, 1 July 1916
▬ ▬ ▬ The Front Line, 18 November 1916

Introduction

'There was no mistaking the importance of this
enormous struggle [on the Somme], for the roads
were almost jammed with night traffic for many miles,
and vast stores of shells lay in the fields. Burdened
ration-carts rumbled by. Guns each drawn by a team of
straining horses, thundered on. Officers in flowing rain-
cloaks and mounted orderlies clattered along the stony
sidewalks. Infantrymen, grey with mud, tramped with
pick and spade. Cyclist orderlies threaded a perilous way,
like Cockney youths rushing evening papers through the
streets.'

Sergeant William Andrews, 4/5th The Black Watch

———————

'Idealism perished on the Somme,' according to the historian A.J.P.
Taylor. 'The enthusiastic volunteers were enthusiastic no longer. They
had lost faith in their cause, in their leaders, in everything except loyalty
to their fighting comrades. The war ceased to have a purpose. It went on
for its own sake, as a contest of endurance.'

In recent years, the views of A.J.P. Taylor have fallen victim to a new
and vigorous revisionism, and his sentiments, honed in the 1960s, now
seem too crude and subject to the prevailing attitudes of the time: that
the war was a hopeless slaughter prosecuted by British generals who were
in the main rotten and out of their depth. Most historians would now
question whether indeed the war had ceased to have a purpose in soldiers'
eyes, or whether these young men had really lost faith in their leaders
and the cause. But in one way his sentiments still strike the right note:
the Somme changed the mindset of those who fought. This battle brought
home to the men – and senior officers too – the blunt understanding that
to beat Germany would require an attritional campaign over an extended

*Opposite: Horses belonging to the 116th Seaforth Highlanders are taken through a
village on the Somme, summer 1915.*

period, and at terrible cost to all sides. Germany had to be beaten on the Western Front: expensive sideshows, such as the campaign on the Gallipoli peninsula, had proved that there was no cheap and easy alternative. In that sense, the fighting did continue as a contest of endurance while enthusiasm was replaced by a stubborn and resigned determination to win. Before the Somme, there was still public optimism that the war could be won with one great masterstroke, men borne to victory on a tide of enthusiasm rather than professionalism, and so, in that narrowly defined sense, idealism did perish on the Somme.

This is not an exhaustive study of the campaign, analyzing the progress of the battle wood by wood, valley by valley, trench by trench. I, for one, find this history wearying, not because the witnesses are not remarkable diarists or correspondents, but because it is possible to suffer a reader's form of battlefield fatigue, battered by descriptions of brutality and increasingly impervious to the human cost. The losses of the first day of the Somme, 20,000 killed and 40,000 wounded, are, in theory, staggering but they are the most commonly used statistic of the Great War and have now lost almost all their power to shock, leave alone visualize. This book is not then a blow-by-blow account of the fighting but rather a detailed impression of what it was like to serve on the Somme.

The Somme is a special place for me, and for this reason my introduction is more personal in style than the introductions to my other books. It was the first Great War battlefield that I visited back in 1985, and it is still my favourite place on the Western Front; I have returned at least once every year since and I intend to be there for the 100th anniversary this year. I have seen the number of visitors grow exponentially, inspired by writers such as the historians Martin Middlebrook and Lyn Macdonald and by the general reinvigoration of interest in the Great War, including the establishment of organizations such as the Western Front Association, inaugurated on 11 November 1980.

In 1991, on the 75th anniversary of the battle, I stood at the impressive Lochnagar Crater, blown at 7.28 on the morning of 1 July 1916, two minutes before the infantry attacked. There were perhaps 300 people there, including a small band of veterans. The priest who took the service noted out loud the large number of visitors and recalled a similar number who had attended the commemorations there in 1986. And then he commented that he had also been there at the crater in 1976. Back then he had been entirely alone.

It is ten years since the last soldier who fought on the Somme died, and yet interest has continued to burgeon. With the new visitors has come a proliferation of hotels, battlefield visitor centres and memorials. Another sign of the growing interest has been the upgrading and widening of the small D roads in France – roads that wound their way round farmers' fields and woods. Many new houses have been built in recent years, and Albert, the main town behind the British lines, has seen significant expansion around the fringes. Even so, the Somme retains its backwater character. The villages were rebuilt and the woods were reborn on precisely the same spot where they had been in 1916; the roads, now metalled, run on the same routes along which the soldiers marched. The sunken roads of 1916 are by and large sunken still; the valleys retain their characteristics of a hundred years ago.

The Somme: The Epic Battle in the Soldiers' own Words and Photographs is published to mark the centenary of the battle that raged for four and a half months in Picardy. But the Somme is more than an offensive: it was home to a million or more British servicemen for an extended period. The British began to arrive in Picardy in the second half of July 1915, taking over the line north of the river Somme, a gesture symbolic of Britain's expanding commitment to the struggle. They left the area only after the Germans' dramatic retreat to the newly constructed Hindenburg Line about 25 miles to the east, a move forced upon them after their unsustainable losses at Verdun and the Somme, and an associated need to shorten their lines. The British were on the Somme not for the four and a half months of battle but for twenty months, and this book will reflect that stay, examining what it was like to serve there in the quieter times as well as in direct conflict with the enemy.

As with two of my previous books, *Tommy's War* and *Gallipoli* (the second written with co-author Stephen Chambers), the story of conflict, this time of the Somme Battle, will be told through soldiers' diaries, letters and memoirs, and just as importantly through the photographs that these men themselves took on their own illegally held cameras.

*The post-war
note slipped
into Richard
Hawkins' Somme
photograph
album..*

These images, the vast majority never published before, will give a different perspective of the war, a fresh view and not one necessarily held by the two official photographers. Too often, a book's narrative *is* the sole story and any images are selected almost as an afterthought. The same official photographs appear again and again and as a result their impact is greatly diminished. In *The Somme*, the images are as important as the narrative, indeed at times I have specifically chosen a soldier's memories to fit as closely as possible to the images that I have found.

Pages 1 to 11   No 1

All these photos were taken by me on a Vest Pocket Kodak in France, 1915-16 Remainder were taken on Salisbury Plain, London, Eastbourne & Bedford about the end of 1916 I sent the camera home because cameras were really forbidden & if I was lucky enough to be wounded I did not want it to be found in my valise. The films were all lost or stolen in the post.

The cameras that the fighting men carried in 1916 were far fewer in number than in 1914 and early 1915. The army banned their use just before Christmas 1914 when it was discovered that soldiers, mainly officers, were selling their photographs to the British press. Newspapers were starved of images owing to the failure by politicians and soldiers alike to grasp the importance of propaganda photographs. The order banning cameras was reissued in March 1915 and, as fear of enemy spies working in and around the British trenches grew steadily, so the army issued threats of severe disciplinary action against anyone found with a camera. In the weeks before the British offensive at Loos in September 1915, the army again rammed home its hostility towards privately held cameras, at which point most of those serving soldiers still in possession of photographic equipment finally buckled and sent their cameras home.

By 1916, no man could claim ignorance of military law and should he be caught out, there could be no room for a plea of mitigation at a court martial: an officer could be cashiered from the army; an other rank risked several months' hard labour in prison. In a telling note inserted many years later into Richard Hawkins' own photograph album, the former lieutenant, who served with the 11th Royal Fusiliers, explained that he

Sergeant Huborn Godfrey, Royal Garrison Artillery, leans over his Vest Pocket Kodak to look down the viewfinder,

was well aware of the legal position. 'I sent the camera home [around September 1916] because cameras were really forbidden and if I was lucky enough to be wounded I did not want it to be found in my valise.'

Men stopped taking pictures not simply for fear of army retribution, but because they were increasingly tired of the war. They had lost that sense of adventure and excitement that had encouraged so many to take their cameras in the first place. Residual enthusiasm and optimism, held by many men prior to the Battle of the Somme, were eroded in the first days and weeks of the offensive as expectations of a breakthrough were dashed. Soldiers were not inclined to record this war for their families or even for themselves and their mates. They no longer thought of a future when they might want to sit down and look at their wartime snaps as others might do after a holiday. They would, by and large, want to forget. There were perhaps 400,000 men on the Western Front in May 1915, but we get many, many times more pictures of that period of the war than we do scenes from the Somme or from later battles such as the Third Battle of Ypres when there were 2 million men in France and Flanders.

Fortunately for posterity, cameras were still kept by a small number of officers and even fewer other ranks. In the main, private photographs were not taken in moments of critical danger – men had other more pressing issues to take care of. There were some exceptions. A few pictures were taken during the intense fighting at Schwaben Redoubt where the 36th Ulster Division was in action on 1 July, but the majority of photographs taken that first day were snapped on the southern flank of the attack where the British had some success around the villages of Montauban and Mametz. These include a series of pictures taken by Lieutenant Anthony Nash, serving with the 16th Manchester Regiment. His battalion had gone over the top in a second wave, advancing at 8.30 am. In his memoirs he noted how:

'As we approached Train Alley, I took a snapshot of our men approaching it and later I took a photograph of Montauban itself as we were advancing on it. I had carried for long a small VPK [Vest Pocket Kodak] camera in my hip pocket. The snaps are not very good as I could not ask the troops to stand still and look pleasant!'

Photographs taken during the fighting are poignant, for the subject of the camera's eye did not always survive the month and sometimes not

Exhausted officers of the 9th Rifle Brigade, August 1916. From L to R: Lt Elliott, killed 20/11/1916, Lt Kirkpatrick, wounded, Captain Garton, killed 15/9/1916, Lt Southwell, killed 15/9/1916, 2nd Lt Kiek, wounded 27/4/1918.

even the day. In these cases, prints could be made and sent to relations of the fallen. After Anthony Nash was wounded on 8 July and returned to hospital in England, he wrote to Agnes Johnson, the mother of a fallen fellow officer, Captain William Morton Johnson.

My dear Mrs Johnson

I have at last received my camera from France, and am sending you four copies of the last photograph ever taken of Morton. As a likeness it is bad, but it will show you that he was happy – he is distinctly smiling. You will notice that he is wearing Tommy's clothes, and his glasses. The trench is 'Montauban Alley', which we consolidated and held after the capture and during the defence of Montauban.

On the right you will see round recesses in the side of the trench. These go back under the earth for 6 feet, and are supported by galvanized iron; the Germans used them for shelters. On the ground at the foot of them you will see some German equipment thrown hastily out. The cloth thing hanging from the side of the trench is a German India rubber ground sheet. The floor of the trench is of wood. On the left, is a trench ladder.

Morton and I had just been up to the extreme end of the trench to see if any Germans had been left in dugouts.

The photograph was taken at about 12 noon on July 1st, 1916, and Morton went then to hold the right of the line, leaving me to hold the left.

Yours ever affectionately

Anthony Nash

How do privately taken pictures differ from those taken by the official photographers? Private pictures were taken by keen amateurs, are unposed, and can feel more natural and less 'artistic' than images taken by a professional. Those photographed are usually among friends and such familiarity permits them to appear more relaxed. Two official photographers on the Western Front in 1916 could not hope to capture the variety of incidents that soldiers could with their cameras, albeit cameras diminished in number. And most importantly, the official photographers were not concerned with a man's identity. Hardly any official photographs include the names of the men featured, and even locations were often only vaguely given, whereas private images are often annotated in detail and names put to faces. Knowing who a man was and knowing what might have happened to him, and those around him, can turn an ordinary looking image into one of the deepest poignancy.

The images you will see in this book tell a remarkable story, revealing the land lush and green in 1915, moving gradually to a moonscape scene more in tune with public perception of a Great War battlefield. The pictures published are overwhelmingly British. However, on a few occasions I have decided to use collections of German images to give an alternative view of the war and in one case, the fighting around Thiepval, I have used extended extracts of a German soldier's diary written during his service in August and September 1916.

The pictures have come from a variety of sources, from online auctioneers to regimental museums; direct from the families of the men who fought, to well-known repositories such as Imperial War Museums. Sometimes they have come to me loose or in small bundles, unloved and with no attribution. More often they appear as a few snaps in an album of domestic life, but then there are albums crammed with images, an album dedicated by the soldier entirely to his wartime service. Some pictures are unidentified but show known locations on the Somme. Other images have brief descriptions; some, when removed from albums, have fascinating information written on the reverse.

I have sought to link the images with the appropriate text so that photographs appear broadly in date order. Pictures and text are generally linked in time and place, but this is not always possible, and so, for example, a reference to Shelter Wood, near the village of Fricourt, is illustrated with an image taken in the wood, albeit not at precisely the time described. NO PICTURES appear in this book unless I am certain that they were taken on or just behind the fighting lines in late 1915, 1916 or early 1917.

The first veteran I ever met on the Somme was Norman Ralph Skelton, an underage volunteer who served with the Royal Engineers. Born in October 1898, he served on the Somme in 1916 aged 17 until he was wounded in the village of Le Sars that autumn. He was sitting by the Lochnagar Crater watching as volunteers tidied the crater for the following day's 70th anniversary of the first day of the battle. I was fortunate to chat to him – and to visit him again at his home in New Malden – and to talk too with many of the veterans who were on tours of the battlefield that year. Of the thousands of civilians who were there at the same time, I would guess few of us truly appreciated just how fortunate we were to mingle with these men and to be in such close physical contact with history.

Richard van Emden
January 2016

Overleaf:
*Damaged houses
in the summer of
1915, probably
in Albert.*

I Live and Let Live

'I must confess that I was far from happy at being expected to project my head well above the parapet ... When, however, the French officer escorting us did this with complete sangfroid, honour compelled me to do likewise. When he came to the end of our part of the front line he suddenly mounted the fire step, and with a wave of his hand towards the Boches, exclaimed 'Voila! C'est chic', a somewhat surprising epithet to apply.'

Lieutenant Victor Eberle, 2nd Field Company, Royal Engineers

———

The names of dead and wounded soldiers published daily by *The Times* newspaper brought home to the British people the bleak reality of international war. But while the lists appeared painfully long, the numbers were relatively small, indeed insignificantly trivial when placed beside the catastrophic losses that Britain's ally France had suffered on the Western Front in 1914 and 1915. Right from the start, the German army had unleashed its might against French and, to a much lesser extent, Belgian forces, while the British had been important but little more than peripheral participants. Mons, Le Cateau, the First and Second Battles of Ypres, Neuve Chapelle, Aubers Ridge, Loos were all names that would burn themselves into the British consciousness, but context is everything. The British at Mons lost about 1,600 men killed, wounded and taken prisoner; the previous day, 22 August, the French had suffered 27,000 dead. British soldiers might fight and die in what had appeared to be bewildering numbers, but in reality the French army took the brunt of the fighting.

The small but highly efficient British Expeditionary Force of regular soldiers was dispatched to the Continent in August 1914 and had been quickly augmented by the embarkation of the Territorial Army, a home defence force, swiftly utilized to help shore up the front line. It would be many months before a new army could be sent overseas, an army of volunteers drawn from the civil population who responded with overwhelming enthusiasm to Secretary of State for War

Opposite: *Men of the 116th Seaforth Highlanders relax in the Somme village of Bouzincourt.*

Lord Kitchener's appeal for 100,000 men. By the end of 1914, 1.1 million men had volunteered but it would take time and scant resources to mould them into a worthy fighting force. Meanwhile, the French continued to take the strain, an arrangement of enforced circumstances that would wear thin, very thin, in 1915. The French wanted, indeed desperately needed, the British to rapidly expand their commitment to the war; the Battle of Loos had been the first joint Allied offensive in September, but this battle and other earlier offensives had proven inconclusive at best, utter failures at worst. In the summer of 1915, and as a signal of London's willingness to shoulder more of the responsibility, British troops marched south from Ypres, from Ploegsteert, and from Festubert, to take over French positions north of the river Somme, an unspoilt and relatively peaceful rural backwater where German and French troops had cleverly learnt to avoid unnecessary antagonism.

Second
Lieutenant
George Webb,
1st Dorset
Regiment

31 July, 1915

Dear Mother

We have reached our new destination and are now no longer in Belgium but are in the depths of France. … We are at present in a delightful little village some way east of Amiens. In a few days I expect we shall move up nearer the firing line as we are going to relieve the French in this district.

The inhabitants seem delighted to see us as there have been no British troops here for a very long time, not since the retirement, I believe. The country is simply superb. I have never seen anything in England to compare with the valley of the Somme. It is one mass of lakes and fords in a broad valley for miles and miles and the woods are beyond all description. … How I wish I was here for a pleasure trip instead of on this beastly job. It seems so foolish to set about destroying everything that is beautiful, all because a few people are objectionable.

Private James
Racine, 1/5th
Seaforth
Highlanders

After two or three days' [rest] we entrained and, after a fourteen-hour journey, reached the Somme area. The transport was unloaded at a place named Corbie and we were marched to Pont Noyelle[s]. Windows of houses were raised and the inhabitants gazed at us as we passed by in the

dark of the night. We were now about 15 miles from the front line and
speculated what kind of sector we would be called upon to hold. ...

On the top of a hill near the village, I visited the monument which
had been erected to commemorate the Franco–German war of 1870. I
entered into conversation with two aged inhabitants of the village and
they informed me that the Uhlans had visited that part in the early days of
the [current] war and they remembered the Germans being there during
the 1870 war; bullet marks in the door of their house were pointed out in
confirmation.

Two days later, we commenced a 15-mile march towards the front line
and, during the journey, the field kitchens prepared food for us to have
during one of the short rests.

*The harvest
is gathered in
behind the front
lines: Bouzincourt,
September 1915.*

Second
Lieutenant
Frederick
Roe, 1/6th
Gloucestershire
Regiment

In view of the almost daily marches, very serious attention had to be given to care of the feet and legs. As often as possible, clean socks had to replace the dirty wet ones, and boots and puttees had to be dried out. We soon found out that drying out the leather too near a fire quickly killed its suppleness. … Puttees became sodden daily in the rain and, if unattended to, quickly brought trouble to the skin of the legs. Taking off and putting on wet and muddy puttees which had to be wrapped carefully round the leg and finished off with not-too-tight tapes below the knee was a most distasteful job. Feet blisters were considered to be bad soldiering but they were something inevitable and gently pricking the blisters and disinfecting was all too familiar a task. …

Sometimes we were lucky to get two nights and the day between as a rest either in a farmhouse or in a barn full of lovely soft dry straw. This leisure was a real luxury and gave the men a chance to clean and oil their rifles thoroughly. Socks could be mended from a 'housewife' which was our sewing kit. The thick grey army issue socks were indisputably without rival for warmth and good wear. Meals could be leisurely. From time to time we were sent to a real farmhouse. One I remember was run by an elderly couple. Madame was the undoubted commander. She was a strong well-built formidable lady with a husband called Jules, a name she pronounced with a high-pitched short sharp hiss. The British soldiers would call him a would-be scrounger and he was literally hounded by Madame and on the run all the hours of daylight.

Three of us subalterns set up a temporary officers' mess in the kitchen of a much larger house nearby. After supper when I returned to my billet where Madame had given me a bedroom, I found that it was a miniscule glory hole. Worse still was the fact that the only way I could get into it was through the bedroom occupied by Madame and Jules, both sound asleep. They both woke up when I clumsily tried to tiptoe through, feeling thoroughly embarrassed. He greeted me however with a cheery, '*Bon soir, Monsieur, et bonne nuit.*'

Captain Francis
Smith, 1st Royal
Scots

In the afternoon [we] met a lot of French troops on the march. … They look very fit but not in the least smart, and all wear the very long light blue overcoat, with the skirts folded back. They have either light or dark blue trousers – no red now. Their transport is funny – any old farm cart laden up in the most extraordinary way, and we met a cab – an actual cab, also laden with stores, following behind a battalion!! They keep little or no march discipline and just struggle along with no attempt at step or keeping in fours. Apparently they don't believe in it. …

The country rolls in great waves and the roads are all white with chalk and great chalky clouds of dust are kicked up by any traffic.

French roads were mostly cobbled across the crown leaving 4 or 5 feet of soft going on either side. When marching in fours and keeping to the right of the road, two men of each four would be on the cobbles, number three would have one foot on cobbles and one foot on soft ground and number four would be altogether on the soft going. A halt was called at the end of every hour and a changeover made, the outside man went to the inside and the other moved up a place.

Private Victor Cole, 7th Royal West Kent Regiment

After one night at Bray-sur-Somme we pushed off by road and duckboard track to a strongpoint called 'The Citadel' near Carnoy Farm. This sector was being held by the First Battalion, and we, the Seventh, were to go in with them for instruction in trench warfare. For the signal section this meant telephone maintenance and line laying under actual combat conditions.

I was posted to a nice snug signal dugout and slept comfortably in a wire netting bed until early morning, when, with a sudden rush of sound, four shells burst in rapid succession just outside the door. They made a great deal of noise and splinters whined all over the place. This seemed to be the cue for everybody to wake up and get on with the war, for within moments our guns had opened up, firing over our heads towards Fricourt and Mametz. The Germans, not to be outdone, then lobbed a lot of heavy stuff over in the direction of Albert.

The country is at its best now; a distant view of two small towns – one in German hands [Bapaume] and the other immediately behind our trenches [Albert] – is lovely; the red tiles of such houses as still have a roof, the deep blue sky, the green trees and green and brown earth, with huge patches of yellow turnip flower, forming a kaleidoscopic landscape;

Gunner Cecil Longley, 1st South Midland Brigade Royal Field Artillery

Swimming in the river Ancre near Aveluy, after a stint in the front line trenches.

but a closer inspection of these little towns and villages is a horror that will haunt all who see them to the end of their lives. Towerless churches, streets pockmarked by heavy shellfire into craters that would hide a dozen men. Here is to be seen a disembowelled house, with carpeted floor bared to the sky, there a roof resting on chipped walls, with nothing underneath it but a mass of crushed bricks and household furniture – not a whole house or a living soul to be seen; everywhere one turns there are shell-rent buildings, roofs shattered and twisted into every conceivable shape, with jagged rafters pointing up into the heavens, as witnesses to God of the havoc around, which is one of the brands burnt by a cultured Christian Power into the face of a little brother nation.

Private James Racine, 1/5th Seaforth Highlanders

We came to rest in the village of Authuille, which is situated at the foot of a hill just behind the line. We were the first division of British troops to relieve the French on the Somme.

The sector was extraordinarily quiet, especially in comparison with Festubert and, although the village was in such close proximity to the front line trench, it had been very slightly damaged. Several estaminets still dispensed their refreshments.

Here we found large dugouts and the French troops had evidently believed in comfort, for they had constructed beds, made from struts and covered with wire netting, which were very comfortable. They had also constructed rustic tables and chairs. In an old house I found a very much out of tune piano and accompanied a mixture of French and British troops in a sing-song. The French troops gave us a hearty welcome and informed us that the sector was extremely quiet and that only eight light shells a day were fired into the village. They were sent over in pairs at the following times 11.00 am, 2.00 pm, 4.00 pm, and 8.00 pm, and the French artillery replied similarly.

At the times stated, the trench troops had gone into the dugouts while the shells burst, and returned to the estaminets at the conclusion of the comic bombardment. We thought this to be an extraordinary way of carrying on war but were prepared to enjoy our improved surroundings. We were also informed that, previous to our arrival, the enemy had shouted across to the French that they were being relieved by Scottish troops and the French had ridiculed the idea. The secret intelligence of the enemy was extraordinary and he seemed to know, in detail, the movements of our troops. ...

At dawn on the first day, we found on our barbed wire entanglements a piece of paper on which was a written request that two or three of our men would, at a given time, proceed halfway across no-man's-land and meet a similar number of Germans in order to exchange periodicals and souvenirs, as the French had been accustomed to do.

After a consultation, our interpreter and two men agreed and, at noon, met the enemy halfway; the heads of the troops on each side were above the parapets and no firing took place. Later, when we left the trenches, we were paraded before the Commanding Officer and severely reprimanded. He stated that 'it was impossible to fight a man with one hand and give him chocolates with the other.' We were given to understand that any similar action in the future would be severely dealt with.

Private Victor
Cole, 7th Royal
West Kent
Regiment

I was sent to do duty at a small telephone post dug into the side of the trench and here for the first time I began to realize what I had let myself in for. Fritz was throwing over *Minenwerfers* [mortars]. The blast from these things almost stopped one's breath and usually the telephone line would go dead, necessitating an exploratory trip along the wire to find and repair the break.

Battalion Headquarters at Bécourt Chateau was much knocked about but still habitable on the ground floor and in the cellars. A shell-burst in the small library had scattered books all about the place. They were torn and dusty but one could see amongst them the beautiful bindings of old volumes inscribed on flyleaf or cover with the name 'Comte de Valmont'. A little chapel adjoined the chateau. It was almost undamaged but there were graves of French soldiers in the garden and the water supply in the well was found to be poisoned. The circular carriage drive in front of the chateau we labelled 'Piccadilly Circus' and from it communication trenches led away down the hill through a small copse to the front line. From the chateau roof one could just see the 'Hanging Virgin' crowning the ruined basilica at Albert.

In the chateau salon was an old piano, played now and again by some happy warrior to the accompaniment of shells passing overhead and the

The damaged chateau at Bécourt, a mile behind the lines at La Boisselle.

clack-clack of machine-gun bullets through what was left of the roof. In the sunken road behind Battalion HQ we kept the drinking water cart. I nipped down there one quiet night to fill my water bottle. Suddenly a machine gun opened up and a shower of bullets smacked into the ground all round the cart – then silence. A man beside me groaned and went down. A stretcher-bearer came up at the run and we found that a bullet had entered the poor bloke's back in the lumber region and it had come out just above his left knee. When bandaged he seemed to be all right and went off on a stretcher smoking a cigarette.

Sleep in the family vault of the Comte de Valmont, in company with three other runners and seven closed coffins. Slept well for all that, however. This chateau has been a beautiful place and situated in very nice surroundings, in the heart of a wood, from which it derives its name. Remains of several houses around. It is a very sad spectacle but I am getting used to it. Such a sight does not impress us now, as it would have done two months ago, nevertheless a lump forms in our throats when we consider what the place was like, and what it is like now.

Private Robert Cude, 7th the Buffs (East Kent Regiment)

The German trenches opposite were an unusually great distance away, about 500 yards. In [this] sector both French and Germans had been opposite each other for a long time and both sides had adopted the policy of live and let live. To us who had been in the Ypres Salient trenches and the first gas attack this seemed unnaturally and most reprehensibly quiet.

Second Lieutenant Frederick Roe, 1/6th Gloucestershire Regiment

The area was solid chalk; in the sun sometimes dazzlingly white but perfectly damnably messy and intractable when trying to shovel it after rain. My working parties were unanimous in loathing the extremely heavy chalk stuff to put down on the roads behind the line for the never-ending road repair.

The trenches were very deep and dry with wide walkways between parapet and parados with very few traverses to make fire bays. The dugouts were large and deep and often dug under the parapet. As there was no constant vigilance, the fire steps were not well maintained and therefore not continuous.

Looking from a freshly dug trench towards Albert and the town's damaged Basilica.

Within the chalk wall at the entrance to my dugout was the top of a human skull which the French officer I relieved told me was so white and shiny because the French officers had got quite fond of it – they called it François and used to stroke it as they went in and out of the dugout. It had been taken from the skeleton of a French soldier they dug up when first making the dugout and they had incorporated into the trench wall.

The dugout itself was carefully lined on all its walls with rabbit wire netting and this kept in place an inch-thick lining of very dry grass and dead weeds, presumably for warmth. But it was absolutely alive with countless hordes of vigorously active fleas and the morning after moving in I tore down the whole abominable contraption, rabbit wire and all, and soaked every inch of the dugout, including walls, floor, and ceiling, with a very strong solution of creosote. This was not the end of the matter though, for well after the war was over my wife told me that the next few letters I sent home from the dugout were so impregnated with the smell of the creosote that she had to cook them in the oven to make them readable.

Gunner Cecil Longley, 1st South Midland Brigade, Royal Field Artillery

The dugouts are rather dirty, as are most French positions we take over, and there is just room for six men to sleep and to work the switchboard and instruments. The outlook is gorgeous, and judging from tonight we are going to have some lovely sky effects, having such a large view, only bounded on the horizon all round by small villages in woods. The wind and open air are lovely, and if you don't look at your frowsy khaki or at the guns, you could imagine yourself getting a sea breeze on the Towyn sand dunes!

Our observing station is in a hefty trench that runs parallel to our position about 500 yards in front. The dugouts there are 12 feet below the surface and smell very poor after eleven months' French occupation, but their environs are – like most of France that we have been through – lovely. The trench takes the line of a road, and as you walk along your head is on a level with what was the bottom of the ditch at the roadside, the bank being one mass of wild flowers, the prevailing colours suggesting to the fanciful an irregular series of Allied flags, from the clumps of red poppy, white meadowsweet and blue harebells. Poke your head over the thrown-out soil on the other side of the road, and it is a welter of rusty bins, old respirators, broken bits of equipment and a second-hand wardrobe of French garments in all stages of decay. During an 'off' time I trudged along this trench for a mile to what is left of a village on our left front, which we drove out of the other day; every wall chipped and cracked in a thousand places with bullets and shrapnel, all houses loopholed, and the trench I was in took me bang through a house, through the dining room and kitchen, and on a level with my head was the dresser with the earth thrown up all round and on it. I felt quite a qualified looter when I scrambled out of the trench and 'wangled' a pocketful of apples from the orchard. Must go on duty now. All quiet at present, though we tickled them up with our new guns today!

British soldiers were generally unimpressed with the quality of French trenches, and particularly their ongoing maintenance, normally deemed sloppy. By contrast, each British regiment prided itself on the good order in which the line was left when handed over to an incoming unit. Outgoing battalions returned to billets in villages that were still inhabited by civilians who chose to live on with the dangers of desultory shelling.

I have just returned to billets – a barn – from a lonely but enjoyable stroll across fields in the stillness of the evening to the hills above the town [Etincham] from which there spreads a beautiful view of the long valley lined with trees threaded by a large river [the Somme]. Directly below where I was, there were the stone walls of an old windmill and further on, the whitewashed houses and barns of the town nestling round its church. I stayed long enough to see all but the spire vanished in a white mist rising

Signaller Cyril Newman, 1/9th London Regiment (Queen Victoria Rifles)

from the river. On my way back I came across an old French peasant pulling up turnips and carrots from a field. Women in France do much outdoor work on the farms. Yesterday I saw one ploughing. This peasant was shrunken and wrinkled like most peasant women I have seen. We talked – more than once I had to gasp '*Non compris*' – and I carried her large bundle of vegetables to a house for her. I felt glad at doing a 'good turn'.

Second
Lieutenant
Frederick
Roe, 1/6th
Gloucestershire
Regiment

I saw coming towards me an elderly woman. She was dressed in the traditional Sunday black clothes which were covered by a large apron. She was hatless and her hair was in disarray. Her face was heavily blacking with the grimy dust from the shelling which filled the air with a thick haze, as the bombardment was still going on. As we approached each other I was surprised to see that she had made a container of the skirt of her apron and that she was carrying something rather heavy in it. She slowed down and I stopped and asked her what had happened. With slow tears filling her eyes and travelling down her begrimed face she told me that her house and all she possessed had been destroyed in the bombardments.

On examination I found to my intense surprise that she was carrying half a dozen bottles of wine which proved to be Chambertin. I can only suppose that some desperate desire to salvage something she could carry away made her choose the burgundy. I have wondered since if she might have been the proprietress of the small bistro of the village. The least I could do was to offer to buy the wine at the price she asked as bargaining in the circumstances would have been churlish. She was most grateful to be relieved of the burden and to receive in return something much more easily portable. She thanked me with a sad dignity and went on her way down the road. I have often wondered where she went and how she fared. Her little world and security had vanished as she walked out of Hébuterne on the afternoon of its destruction.

Gunner Cecil
Longley, 1st
South Midland
Brigade, Royal
Field Artillery

I [have] astonished myself by the ease with which I can converse with the natives and understand them, and they are as pleased as a dog with ten tails when they find a soldier who can understand them as well as talk to them, and needless to say not a shred of what I learned at school has been of the remotest use, for so far I haven't had occasion to ask the

keeper of a general store if she 'has the pen of the gardener's aunt.' If I had
I would bet a gunner's pay she would answer, 'No, but I have some food of
the grandchild of my husband's brother.' And how could one keep up an
entente cordiale on that sort of thing? ...

It is a penny scream to go into an *épicerie* and listen to 'Tommy' buying
his groceries. I usually perhaps chaff the woman a bit and give her a few
sentences of my best French in the vain hope that she'll think I know what
the prices of things really ought to be, and will consequently take a franc
or so off the price of a small tin of fruit; but it is never any use, and I have
to pay two francs for a 10½d. tin of fruit and one franc for a 3½d. tin of
sardines. A Tommy hearing me babbling wildly in what he takes to be
French, first looks at me to see if he should salute, and then probably says:
'Ere choom, watter they call them there things in them tins?' Of course
I generally do the whole deal for him, but often I don't, so as to enjoy an
inward chortle on hearing him – prompted by myself – ask for '*serrisses
ong boyt*' [*cerises en boite*] or '*botool der vynn-blong*' or even '*vin blank*'!
Sometimes he will come in with a worried but defiant look on his face and
ask in a loud tone, '*Pang?*' – '*Unn* loaf, yer know, *Maddermessel*,' at the
same time probably wishing he could make a noise like a piece of bread

*Second
Lieutenant
Eric Anderson,
the battalion
billeting officer,
116th Seaforth
Highlanders,
ingratiating
himself with
French civilians in
Bouzincourt.*

for her behoof. The answer is generally the loaf and a murmured '*Quatre vingt, M'sieu.*' 'What the blank, blank, does she mean by that?' 'Ere, take it outer this, ma cherry. Blimey, they'll diddle yer any road,' – addressing me and the woman alternately.

Captain Francis Smith, 1st Royal Scots

There is only one shop in the village and food is hard to get. We had a great time buying hens to cook, and now they cost five francs each. We four armed ourselves with sticks, called on a terrible old lady who owns a big farm here. After great argument she let us buy a chicken provided we caught it ourselves. Several French labourers and a beautiful French maiden and a farm boy all joined in the chase and we fairly 'strafed' the cock and all his family and eventually caught and slew one of his wives. It was really funny. Harris fell full length into a heap of unpleasant stuff in the farmyard in the course of operations, to the delight of the assembled multitude. We had a great argument about the price and Harris offered the old lady two francs – her only answer was to aim a shrewd blow at his head. We gave her a five franc note and she refused to give us any change. ...

This is a very queer country. Everyone says we shall all go mad if we stay here long. We did a three hours' march for the whole battalion yesterday. The pipers have got their kilts on again and this excites mingled feelings in the country people here who have never heard the pipes or seen a kilt before, for we are the first British troops they have met. It is rather amusing marching through the old tumbledown villages to the 'Cock of the North' etc. ...

The country here is thickly strewn with crucifixes and shrines. They put a big cross on any little bit of high ground. They have all got five trees planted in a semi-circle round so close, that all their leaves and branches grow together and form one thick clump. Bell and I were passing a lonely place where four roads meet and there was a crucifix, but in front of it on the stone steps where the people kneel to pray, sat two cavalrymen (English) and between them a fire was burning and their supper cooking in a vulgar looking pot, and behind, tethered to the cross, their two horses stood and munched in their nosebags and blinked their eyes in the firelight. It seemed a little incongruous!

10 August: We were warned during the day that we were to go into the line that night. Many of the men who were fond of 'booze' indulged in what they no doubt thought might be their last 'bust-up', and when the time drew near, when we were to parade, several were well 'oiled'. One man in our section was quite maudlin, and wandered round the billet repeating, at short intervals, 'Might as well die 'appy if gotter die', and shedding bitter (or beery) tears. He paraded with the rest of us at 5.30 pm, as if he were a martyr going to execution. We marched off at 6.00 pm, full of natural curiosity, and wonderment as to what we were to experience 'in the line'. We marched across the Amiens–Albert road, then by a very roundabout route about 10 miles in length, eventually reaching the southern outskirts of Albert soon after dark. Marched through to the road to Bécourt–Bécordel, halting when a short distance beyond Albert, to wait for 'guides'. While waiting, we were warned not to smoke, as the striking of matches would be certain to draw enemy shellfire. When the guides arrived, we started off again in single file, halting once more in a wood, where the German bullets were buzzing about, and smacking into the trees all around. After a few minutes, on we went again, now feeling very 'windy', and soon found ourselves in a communication trench, and then in the firing line at last. The trenches had no 'duckboards' in them at this time, and were drained by sump holes dug into the sides, at the bottom. As we were quite inexperienced, we were continually slipping into one or another of these holes up to a knee in water. The sides of the trench were in some places strengthened with wire netting, which was forever getting attached to a buckle or a button. The only light we had was from the occasional flare sent up from our own or the German lines, and … we had a strong tendency to crouch in the bottom of the trench when these flares shone out. This was due to our ignorance of the measure of protection given by the trenches against the bullets which continually whined and cracked overhead. We found that the troops holding the line here were the 7th Gordons, who had recently come down with other troops from Festubert, and had taken over the line from the French.

There was a lot of rifle and machine-gun firing on both sides, especially when a flare went up. The Germans had no doubt discovered that they were now faced by the 'Englanders', and were telling us what they

Private Sydney Fuller, 8th Suffolk Regiment

thought of us all, and we were making a suitable reply. We (the Suffolks) were distributed, a few men here and there, amongst the Gordons, to learn what real war was like. I was sent with O. Brown and one of the Gordons to a 'listening post' or 'sally port'. We crept along a shallow trench which ran forward from the front line, under the barbed wire, and found at the extreme end, at the front edge of our barbed wire, a short cross-trench just large enough to accommodate the three of us. This was the post. It was roughly concealed, as was the trench leading to it, by a partial covering of wire netting, which was in turn covered with rough grass. We were informed that our job was to keep a sharp lookout, and our ears open, for any signs of a possible attack or raid by the enemy. If anything suspicious was seen or heard one of us was to go back to the firing line and report the circumstances, while the other held on. There was a wooden loophole in the parapet, and I got quite a shock while looking through it. A large rat crept into the front end of the loophole, during one of the dark intervals between flares, and, as I was already a bit jumpy, I quite thought it was a Fritz.

Private James
Racine, 1/5th
Seaforth
Highlanders

We returned to the front line at La Boisselle, only 15 yards separated the enemy trench from our own. It had been comparatively quiet and the Germans and men had exchanged souvenirs by simply tossing them from one trench to the other.

One day, however, one of men shouted out, 'I'm sending over a present, Fritz.' Instead of throwing a souvenir, he threw a live bomb. From that time onwards, the place was a little hell to occupy and each side periodically exchanged huge trench mortar bombs throughout the day and night and, added to that, mining and counter-mining took place. As soon as the trench was built up, it was smashed down again.

It became impossible for either the enemy or ourselves to occupy that part of the trench during the day but at night, sentries had to crawl out to watch and listen. The slightest sound caused the enemy to open fire with his trench mortars and casualties mounted up quickly while we held this part.

The sentries were relieved every half an hour and glad they were to rejoin their company, for they never knew during their turn of duty, when a bomb might blow them to pieces. The trench and dugouts were smashed flat and it was useless to repair them.

Our artillery had, by then, become exceedingly expert and were supported with guns of a large calibre and a more plentiful supply of ammunition. On one occasion, the enemy had troubled us with a rather large number of his heavy mortar bombs, thus causing considerable damage, and our artillery was telephoned to reply and silence them. We were instructed to withdraw from the front trench to the support line, and a battery of our artillery opened fire with very large shells. I looked over the top of the trench and watched them exploding on the enemy trench, blowing a timber and sandbags into the air. The result was apparently satisfactory, for we had a rest from the bombs.

A deep winding communication trench followed its way to the front line; this we appreciated after being used to taking a chance over flat open country.

I had been kept busy with casualties. One night, when a traverse of the trench was occupied by three of the New Army who had come up for instruction, an enemy mortar bomb landed amongst them. I hurried to their assistance and found the trench completely knocked in and the men partially buried.

It was pitch dark and I was handicapped by being unable to show even a glimmer of light, or a machine gun would have immediately opened fire upon that part of the trench which now had a big gap in it. Groping in the mud, I discovered that one man had been killed but that the others were living.

Left: *German trenches outside La Boisselle village. The building in the middle distance was destroyed in underground fighting in 1915.*

Right: *La Boisselle village from the German perspective looking west.*

Overleaf: *The 116th Seaforth Highlanders near Thiepval. Private Adam Wood is reading the* Daily Sketch *newspaper.*

The two survivors I managed to drag into a small dugout nearby and after carefully screening the doorway with sacks, lit a candle stump and proceeded to render all assistance possible.

One man had a leg blown away and the other was peppered all over with small wounds. The former, after attention, was taken to the dressing station but the latter died in my arms. I felt particularly sorry for the poor fellows because it was their first visit to the line and they had only been in the trench for about hour. Added to those casualties were eleven men of the Engineers who were gassed while engaged in digging a mine.

Private Sydney
Fuller, 8th Suffolk
Regiment

11 August 1915: No-man's-land was just ordinary farmland, grown wild since the trenches were dug. There was a field of mangel, which had run to seed, and so made good cover for patrols. In one place was a four-cylinder 'flat' roller, not far from our trenches. This was often fired on, as it was thought possible that a German sniper might have concealed himself behind it overnight. In another place was a cultivator, standing just as it had been left by the farmer when the Germans came. It was queer, seeing all those miles of trenches in front of us, showing not a sign of life, and yet swarming with the enemy.

Captain Francis
Smith, 1st Royal
Scots

The trenches are very deep and therefore safe, but in an awfully bad state. The French have just left them and an enormous amount of work and material is required to make them decent. The French miners are here still and wander about, tinkering at their mines. There are eight mines ready to touch off on our company front, so the whole German line could be put off in the air any time. The French miners sit along the long galleries all day and night, listening with a special stethoscope apparatus, for sounds of the Germans working, but there are no signs of that. I was right out this afternoon along one of the mine galleries right under the German trenches about 80 yards away. We had to be fearfully silent. The long galleries are lit by little candles at intervals and you have to stoop all the way, at the end it breaks into four sapheads, branching out in different directions. I listened again today myself with the stethoscope but could of course hear nothing. The French miners all wear the new steel cap, shrapnel-proof helmet – it gives a very tawdry appearance for it is painted light blue to match their

coats. They have also nearly all got beards – several enormous ones, so they look weird and wild. …

I now possess a French poodle and I call him Roger! What started the idea was that this place is overrun by rats. We were warned of this by the Leinsters before we came in, so Bell said he strongly advised us all to get cats and take them into the trenches with us to protect us. Our servants scoured the village and we actually bought a kitten for two francs. The other cats escaped, but the kitten was duly carried up to the trenches that long 10 miles and lives in his dugout. But it has not 'strafed' any rats yet. In fact the rats don't think much of it (it is smaller than they are). A couple of rats actually performed the feat of careering right over Bell's bed, over Bell himself, and his kitten. Bell is disappointed in the cat! Roger, on the other hand, has been quite a success. He has killed one rat at least and spends the whole day hunting them. He is shaved in the best poodle fashion and he's an enormous tuft on the end of his tail.

Bored and uninterested, these men appear indifferent to the cameraman.

We are attached as artillery signal service men, two from each battery going into the trenches covered by the zone of their fire, four hours off and four on daily day and night for four days; it is a bit of a strain for two men. At present I am off duty and they are shelling us here heavily with HE [high explosive] gas shells – awful choking chloriney stink, but not bad enough for the smoke helmet, which is simply a flannel helmet with eyeholes and sprayed with a chemical. We look like Inquisition devils when in them. Where I am now we are quite – as it were – safe from the shell fragments unless they pitch down the steps, the bottom one of which I am sitting on.

Gunner Cecil Longley, 1st South Midland Brigade, Royal Field Artillery

This is a German trench captured a few weeks ago, and shows the sort of thing we have to smash up and conquer; the trench, of course, is as usual, the water and mud being kept *in* it and from drowning out the dugouts by a high wooden step at the top of each one. The latter go down fifteen 9-inch steps, and are at frequent intervals all along the trenches; so here we are 12 feet below the surface and 6 feet of earth and trunks above that, with walls, roof, etc., made of 3-inch planking, so that each dugout reminds me of nothing so much as the descent into the Underground or Twopenny Tube while the workmen were still excavating. No fires allowed, therefore nothing to drink but cold water, and of that, one water bottle per day per man and a 2-mile tramp through the communication trenches to refill at night. No water for washing; mud always ankle-deep in long stretches of anything from 1 to 500 yards, the water is just above knee-deep; trenches narrow, floor thereof holey and slippery; so you can imagine what we look like … I haven't had dry legs day or night for five days; but all are the same, only I'm just giving my experiences. Our clothes, hair and hands are grimed and caked with mud, or rather clay, for it is all clay here.

Yesterday our wire from this infantry headquarters back to the battery was smashed by a shell. I ran along to mend it; on climbing out of the communication trench where the break was I had to work the job close against where a dead German was, just lightly covered with soil but feet sticking out; but it has long been a common sight, and sometimes the earth even gets all washed by rain or blown away by shell. All around was debris, French and German equipment, clothing, tools, etc., and burial places – one can't say graves. I was fortunate with the mending, though the same place was spattered by a distant high explosive shell just after I had jumped into the trench again, luckily without breaking the wire. I was hidden from view of the near enemy's firing trenches by the irregular ground, luckily, otherwise their rifles might have made it a warmer job. Nothing makes you feel madder than being deliberately fired at when doing a job that has to be done slowly and carefully, such as insulating the wire after baring the cable and joining the ends. A man who has been fouled at footer has the same feeling.

Today one of us – during his off four hours – will have to go back to the battery to draw rations again, and the other during his time will draw water, as we don't draw from the regiment we are attached to for the time being. Our triumphal entry into the trenches the night before last played havoc with yesterday's and today's rations in a sack on shoulder! The one loaf was a wet mass mostly muddy, from constant fallings upon and wild lashings of the sack to preserve balance! But we have been able to live the two days on one or two of the less dirty lumps of it dried by a candle. Cheese started in a lump, but we now peel it off the bully tins, and one wedge has got driven into a little tin that held our tea; just as well, as we cannot boil water to have the tea, and to see usable tealeaves without being able to use them would be pure aggravation. *Compris*? The infantry, poor beggars, are often worse off, though; yesterday those here had only

A sniper of the 1/4th Royal Berkshire Regiment takes aim. A pair of binoculars are to his right.

one tin of jam to every seventeen men, instead of one between four. That – considering there is no such thing as butter, and jam is the only thing besides cheese that one really eats, as no one can stand bully beef now – I thought was a real hardship!

But all round, the infantry get it worse than we do; the only pull they have over us is that they move by day and we always by night. A lot of them have cut their trousers off just above the knee and go about in boots and socks under that arrangement of clothing! If the trenches are as bad as this now after four weeks' rain, heaven help us in the 'swellings of Jordan' or when the winter comes on. And still – after seeing men hit out here and there and seeing the poor beggars of infantry enduring these conditions – we read in the paper, 'There is nothing doing on the Western Front'. But although it seems as if we are doing nothing, we are never at rest. Infantry, cavalry, sappers, artillerymen, are always digging, draining, making or mending dugouts, trenches, drains, gun positions, dummy trenches and positions, laying wires and taking them up again and relaying elsewhere, carrying materials and food about, all of them doing each other's jobs. Infantry making an observing station for artillery, artillery laying or burying perhaps a wire for the infantry or digging a trench for them. Yet through it all we fire a good deal, though the infantry don't; it is mostly artillery here.

Private Sydney Fuller, 8th Suffolk Regiment

3 September: Came off duty at 'stand down' – 4.45 am. During the afternoon I saw my first German. He was working in their trenches to the left of us, apparently building up or repairing the trench with sandbags. I had a good look at him through a telescope I had with me. He was a tall, thin man, wearing a dark grey or green uniform and it was noticeable that he sported 'sideboards'. We judged the distance to be about 1,400 yards, and set our rifle sights for that distance. Our shots had no effect beyond making him stop work and glance up every time a shot was fired. Later on, the machine gunners used their rangefinder, and the distance was found to be only 800 yards. A Lewis gun was used shortly afterwards, at this range, when three or more Germans were visible at the spot. This, one of the machine gunners told me, made them move very quickly. A 'miss' was signalled by one of them, with a piece of board, as soon as they were under cover.

September: You'd like to hear about our billet. It is a small cottage in an orchard with the typical ladder up from the hall into the garret where, according to French and Belgian custom, all disused clothes, old books, stores of corn and rice, articles of household and agricultural furniture and anything else in the house that is frowsy, decrepit or broken is stored, and where the cats and the rats struggle for supremacy. The southern end of the roof is sheared off by a shell, and there is only one pane in the windows and a few tiles on the roof, most of the woodwork and the windows being 'concussed' out as well as the glass, and the wall against which I sleep is slit from top to bottom at each of two corners and leans drunkenly outwards. The brick floors, however, are intact, and, in spite of the slight coating of deceased beetle that won't brush away, form a dry if springless bed. There is a shell hole in the garden which saved us the trouble of digging a rubbish and tin pit.

Gunner Cecil Longley, 1st South Midland Brigade, Royal Field Artillery

Today I am sitting in the orchard writing this, and the Germans are getting busy. To get an idea of the effect, sit in our orchard and imagine first a shell bursting on the lawn, another in the air over the stables, with the bits dropping all round beyond one, another on the house and in the duck pond. There! that last was a close one, about 20 yards away; it has brought down a pear tree, but it is really safer outdoors than in. I would rather risk being hit by a piece of shell than crushed in a building. They are putting us through it today (and yesterday). One of our men was hit above the knee yesterday. Lucky beggar; that will mean England for certain.

We are still resting here and we sleep in what was a sort of commercial hotel and have a bed each, which is luxury – we look out on the princely main street. There is a lunatic here who gibbers and moans all day. There is also an old man of 83 who is stone deaf. The Prussians hit him over the head when they were here last August, and made him deaf. There is also an orphan niece, who does all the housework and periodically the others throw pots and pans and things at her, and then they all weep together. But they seem to get on fairly well on the whole. When the Huns were here, all the inhabitants who could walk fled, but the old man's wife couldn't walk and hid in a cave for four days. There was quite a big battle all over the village and fields during the great retreat of the French after Mons

Captain Francis Smith, 1st Royal Scots

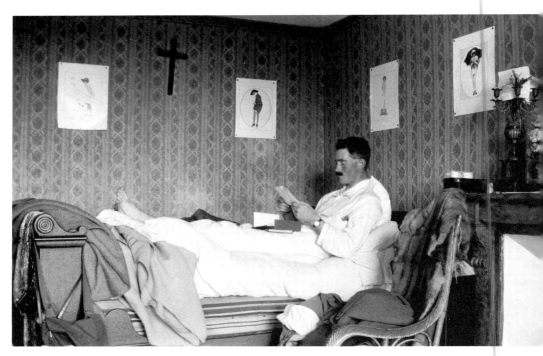

and Charleroi. The fields are all studded with graves, some with big iron crosses and immortelles on them, but others with only small little wooden crosses and one or two have a soldier's 'kepi' hanging on the cross.

Gunner Cecil Longley, 1st South Midland Brigade, Royal Field Artillery

September: You would laugh to see us now: no leather visible on boots, or cloth on puttees or breeches till about 4 inches above the knee, all caked in mud, shoulders too, from scraping past men in the trenches. The infantry generally have a word to say to us about it, such as 'Yo ain arf a putten 'em thro' it now, choom,' or 'Yo artillery blokes is injiyin' yerselves now.' They know us as artillery by cap, badge, etc., but most of us signallers are pretty well known personally in many regiments, and have many good friends humble and otherwise amongst them. What silly details my letters must seem to give you dear home people who are looking for big results, and moves of miles by army corps, and who cannot realize, as we can and

do, what it means to gain even a short length of the enemy's front line
trench, what organization, what preparation, what buzzing of thousands
of Morsed messages over the 'phone or by lamps or helio[graph] (only
used in emergencies). We may not get your letters for a week now, though
you'll get ours, I hope, as the transport goes back from the front empty
more or less. I washed my hands in my mess tin with a cupful of water,
otherwise I could not have written, being plastered with mud. Water is a
jewel of rarity; it is a 2-mile walk each way, through the communication
trench, to fetch it, though as the crow flies ten minutes' walk would do
the trick; we can only fetch it at certain times. Food also has to be fetched
from the same dump behind the trenches, though one of our wire patrols
was good enough to bring ours today – a tin of Maconochie [stew] and
three-quarter loaf of bread for three signallers here, plus dry rations of
tea and sugar for twenty-four hours' food!! No jam today – we are on our
quarter rations again – but I was lucky enough to be able to go to a village

Opposite: Lieutenant Herbert Preston, 120th Battery, Royal Field Artillery, reads a letter in his billet in Suzanne village, summer 1915.

2 miles in rear of our guns yesterday, before
coming here, and got a precious tin of pears
and some chocolate, so we are the envy of the
infantry signallers. One of the latter yesterday
was hit by a shell full in the back and killed
instantly. But the greatest difficulty is dealing
with the badly wounded – e.g. this morning
a man had his leg torn from thigh to ankle.
It is very awkward to carry such cases out,
poor beggars; the labour is enormous, almost
killing to the stretcher-bearers. I helped to
carry a man at Neuve Église across the open
for a short mile, and shall never forget it; here
it is over 2 miles of torturous trench – slipping
and inches of mud at that.

Falling earth: a small calibre shell explodes in a muddy trench.

Dead silence has rent the air for the last ten
minutes. As the rain is so thick, no observing
can take place, but there is an earth-trembling
sort of rumble that shows there is heavy firing
going on somewhere, up or down the line 15

or 20 miles away. Everybody is wonderfully cheerful and smiling, as is ever the case whenever there is any chance of strafing the Hun heavily, and it bucks you up and makes you think we shall finish them off before Christmas! But as we tell one another, the first seven years of a war are the worst, so we expect an easier time after 1921!!!

'Great Scott!' We had a bang then from a German heavy gun, burst about 100 yards away, dirt and bits falling in all directions, and shook the ground. There's another! I must go now on duty at observing station about 100 yards off, but it is seven minutes' walk, scramble, slither and slush along the fire trench. …

The sixth heavy shell has fallen since I wrote 'Great Scott!' Could someone kindly send a pair of bootlaces, some shaving soap and some disinfecting soap for washing clothes and self? No. 7 just burst. Here's No. 8! Our poor ears; we shall be deaf. (No. 9!) They are firing quickly now from heavy howitzers. (No 10! No. 11!) A battery of heavies, evidently. (No. 12!) Cheer oh! See you for Christmas (No. 13!), I hope. Excuse writing (No. 14); they'll be on now all night with a field gun accompaniment.

Private Sydney Fuller, 8th Suffolk Regiment

21 September: One C Company man was killed in the morning – Lance Corporal C. Sheldrake. He and another man were taking turns at 'sniping' at various objects in the enemy lines, through one of the wooden loopholes in the parapet which has been left by the French. At the time the casualty occurred, the other man was firing, and Sheldrake was looking over his shoulder to see where the bullet struck, when a German bullet came through the loophole, passed by the firing man without touching him or his rifle, and struck Sheldrake in the head, killing him instantly. The man who was firing did not hear the bullet pass (it must have come through the loophole at the instant he fired), and, as Sheldrake did not say whether he had hit what he was aiming at, the man turned to ask, and found Sheldrake lying dead in the trench. Shortly after this, as a result of similar occurrences, these loopholes were covered up or removed, as it was found that the enemy used to put their crack shots on these loopholes, and when a shot or shots were fired through them, they would fire through them themselves, and they did not always miss. The loopholes were therefore, more or less, deathtraps.

11 October: Moved at 2.15 pm, taking over the front line on the left of La Boisselle. (This was the position of 'Centre Company' – at this time the battalion held this sector with three companies in the front line, and one in support.) Brown and myself were, with four other men, put on duty, in a listening post – two men being on duty at one time, two-hour shifts, thus, two hours duty, four hours off. This listening post was situated well out in no-man's-land, in front of our wire, and was, with the trench leading to it, entirely underground. The post was a small chamber, just large enough for two men to sit in, and a small circular hole had been made in the roof (which was about 18 inches thick), and the rank grass above had been pulled over the hole, effectively concealing it. Being in front of our wire, we could not have a light at night, and dare not talk, as an enemy patrol might 'spot' us by these signs, in which case we should have had a rapid introduction to enemy bombs.

We were severely strafed by the Hun with *Minenwerfers*, and an enfilade fire from 4.2-inch howitzers all at one time. Five of my platoon went to hospital suffering from shock. Two are back again, but the other three have been sent down the line and two were simply jabbering idiots when they left here. One fellow began shrieking and mouthing and screaming. I just seized him by the shoulders and shook him with all my strength and yelled into his ear about six times, that there was nothing the matter with him. He had just been blown along the trench by a *Minenwerfer* and then buried by the earth. ... He kept screaming and pointing up to the sky and then flinging himself on the ground. I never saw anyone making such faces. I was violently assisted along the trench and flung down by the same explosion – but I was further away.

When I got up, I found a great lump of stone had fallen within an inch of my nose. The men were rushing up and down the trenches, not knowing which way to turn, you see you can see the *Minenwerfers* coming, and special men are on the lookout with whistles and everyone flies for his life, from the place they think they are going to land. There were tremendous stampedes. Such silly things happen – Lance Corporal Castell flung himself flat in the narrow trench and about ten people who were rushing behind all fell over on top of him, so that there was a solid

Captain Francis Smith, 1st Royal Scots

Bécourt Cemetery, 28 or 29 August 1915, three weeks after it was
opened. Twenty men are already buried and almost 700 more would
follow them, including the father of Alicia Wilson.
Inset: *Private James Jack, killed while on a working party and buried in*
Bécourt Cemetery. His grave was ornately decorated by the men of his
platoon.

struggling mass, blocking the trench almost to the top of the parapet, with
old Sergeant Samuels on the top of the heap. Castell has gone down the
line suffering from shock, but whether it was the *Minenwerfer* or all the
people falling on him, I really don't know. It was quite funny, especially
Samuels' face of mingled rage and alarm, from the top of the heap. It made
me laugh at the time. I was in front – going like blazes – but we never got
far in one direction for another would be going the other way again, as
our bit of trench was only 150 yards long and we only had that spear to
stampede in.

The British Army was woefully unprepared for the onset of winter weather. The troops shuddered in their trenches, trenches often without duckboards of any sort to help men keep their feet out of the muck, and there were few pumps to clear the water. There were too few goatskin jerkins to go around and many men relied on gloves, mittens and balaclavas being sent from family members back home along with pots of Vaseline for abrasions and sores. Scores of men had to be evacuated from the front line suffering from exposure and frostbite.

My little trio is again in the fire trench for its four days, and a rare old time we have been having in this deep, dark, dank dugout. After these weeks of rain alternating with hard frosts the state of what is left of the trenches is indescribable. We have all given up using communication trenches to get over the crest a mile away, and all walk in and out of the fire and reserve trenches over the land after dark, falling into shell holes and tripping up over smashed barbed wire and half-filled-in and disused trenches and frequently bodies and impedimenta, and mounds of earth that half conceal bodies, all of which mark the battlefield of Hébuterne, which the French lost so heavily in taking, about two months before we came here. Starlights keep on going up, and we have to freeze until the few seconds of brilliance are over. The German 'typewriters' [machine guns] and trench sentries' shots you have to risk; they are intermittent all through the night, and generally catch a few of the infantry ration parties coming in overland.

Private Sydney Fuller, 8th Suffolk Regiment

One beast of a 'typewriter' is laid on the parapet of our dugout, and he 'tanks' away all night; I fancy he can see with glasses in the day that a sort of scramble path exists up out of the trench and over the top of the dugout, and hopes to catch someone using it. Where our dugout emerges from below onto the trench bottom we have a dam either side. One side is 2½ feet of water and another of mud, now all frozen, but not hard enough to bear; and the other is about a foot deep. But for these dams the water and mud would just flow down the steps and fill up the dugout. As it is, a constant trickle comes down and we have a huge sump at the bottom, which has to be laboriously baled; I say laboriously, because we cannot stand upright in the dugout, and when going up the stairs we have to bend double, as the roof follows the stairs at a height of about 3½ feet. Now the wretched stairs are beginning to fall in, which means constant digging to keep ourselves from being buried all alive.

Second Lieutenant Frederick Roe, 1/6th Gloucestershire Regiment

The German choice [of the high ground] naturally ensured that all the surface waters in rainy weather and throughout the winter drained downhill into our trenches because there was nowhere else for it to go. Devices called sump pots had to be dug into the floor of the trench whenever the water level permitted. These sump pits were covered at the top with duckboards, which were slatted wooden covers to make possible movement up and down the trench line. This was fine but very often the sump pit filled with water so that the water spread over the rest of the trench and the duckboards floated away from the top. In the dark especially it was impossible to watch every step we took, and many times the sump had to be negotiated when only one end of the duckboard was on the trench floor. Stepping on the other floating end meant that it went down into the water, the other end came up smartly and gave a good bang on the face or head – down went the victim into the sump where the water was very cold and muddy.

Gunner Cecil Longley, 1st South Midland Brigade, Royal Field Artillery

Opposite: *Major Beauchamp Magrath, 8th East Lancashire Regiment in a communication trench near Fonquevillers, winter 1915.*

You will have seen from my last letter how the communication and other trenches are; well, they are worse now and simply don't exist in places for yards. This slippery clay slides on itself and carries the strongest engineering works bodily with it; revetting, sandbagging, posts and dugouts all slide in towards one another from both sides of the trench, which, in places, is 6 to 8 feet deep in sticky slime; in no place from here back to Hébuterne (which is a mile across country and two through the communication trenches) is the mud or water less than knee-deep. Coming in, as we did on Monday, by day, we had to use them, clambering out over the top for the deep bits, lying flat when spotted and the shots began to sweep over; but there are so many folds in the ground, shell holes and disused bits of trench, that we were always able to get cover, except when hopping over the parapet and back, or crawling along the ground. To do this with your bed on your back, and with haversack, waterbottle all full, smoke helmets, revolver, and nosebag filled with two days' rations, takes such strength and agility as has made me bless my gymnasium days

many a time. You slip, slither, and fall and trip over old unseen tripwires in the grass so that anyone who hadn't learned how to fall would break limbs and strain muscles all day long!

Meanwhile, the three who were already in the trenches were waiting patiently to be relieved. We were two and three-quarters of an hour getting in! One of my little squad, Gunner [Reginald] Neems, got stuck once; the mud was well up his thighs and very sticky. [William] Ferrar and I were a yard or two in front, panting hard after our exertions in getting through a bad bit and glad to stand in water for a change to get less resistance. We called him all sorts of names as soon as breath would allow, but all to no purpose. He struggled and wrenched, and we went back and tugged at him and got our arms up to the shoulder in mud in getting a grip of his knees; but he was exhausted, and after great struggles to get ourselves out we got a spade or two, and with the help of two infantrymen in a working party round the next traverse we laboriously dug him out, the job taking three-quarters of an hour; so you can imagine our state on getting here. For two days, luckily, no trench observing had to be done, and we stayed down here just with the telegraph duty and lived in our blankets and shirts.

Second Lieutenant Anthony Nash, 16th Manchester Regiment

The First Field Dressing Station at Hébuterne was slightly below the level of the ground, being approached by seven steps down from the road outside. It was a cellar in a demolished house. It was badly lit by a hurricane lamp suspended from the ceiling. In the centre stood a rough deal table under the flickering light; on this table were placed in turn the wounded. Two doctors with their tunics off and shirtsleeves rolled up were working with quick desperation on each case as it was placed on the table. The perspiration was streaming from them. Whenever a shell burst near the cellar outside, the force of the concussion put the light out. There were rows of stretcher cases awaiting attention, some were brought in only to be covered with a blanket and carried out again to await burial. Groups of walking wounded were also waiting their turn. The smell of mingled blood and anaesthetic pervaded the atmosphere.

On 13 December we went into the trenches again. This in and out business was very trying but owing to the appallingly wet state of the line the troops had to be relieved frequently. While we were in this time, Greg and Captain Clarke were sitting in the Company Headquarters dugout when one of our Manchester lads appeared at the top of the slippery steps leading into this dugout, proudly carrying an unexploded shell rather gingerly in his hands. Had he slipped and dropped it we should all have gone to perdition. It was explained to him in forcible language that dud shells, like sleeping dogs, are best left undisturbed.

The Brigadier made a tour of inspection of the front line. This particular sector was quiet, which would no doubt account for the appearance of the General and his Staff, for they generally kept well to the rear when any activity was evidenced. The General passed along the trench, halted, and having enquired as to whether it was safe to look over, he gingerly hoisted himself onto the firing step, looked over the top and took a hurried glance at the enemy trench opposite.

Private James
Racine, 1/5th
Seaforth
Highlanders

He stepped down into the trench not having been fired upon during the moment he had looked over the top, informed the Captain of my company that as it was so quiet, it was possible that the Germans were not occupying their front trench and that, as a test a tunic and cap were to be placed on a rifle and held just above the top of the trench, while he continued his inspection of the sector. Upon his return, we would examine the tunic and, if found to be riddled could be safely assumed that the enemy had not forgotten the war and gone home.

We knew quite well that the enemy occupied his trench in an exceedingly efficient manner, by reason of the rapid fire to which we had been subjected.

However, as soon as the General had passed on and the tunic and cap had been exposed as ordered the Captain whispered hurried instructions to several of the men to open fire on the tunic with their rifles; when the Staff returned, ample evidence was afforded of the activity of the enemy. The Captain knew perfectly well that, had the clothing by some unforeseen chance not been bullet ridden, parties would have been detailed to go over to the enemy trench after dark and investigate. None of us were exactly excited at the prospect.

Second
Lieutenant
Anthony
Nash, 16th
Manchester
Regiment

At half past eleven on the night of Christmas Eve, a fire broke out at No. 15 Platoon's billet, and the alarm was sounded. The cause of the fire was never discovered but its effect was to arouse the entire battalion to put it out. There was only a very old hand fire engine in the village and this had to be filled with buckets of water passed up by a living chain from the nearest pond.

The inhabitants insisted on interfering and created a certain amount of confusion during which someone wiped out a grudge against the battalion interpreter by dropping a brick on his head and one gay lad turned the hose onto the mayor of the town, thereby giving him the first bath he had had for a long time. Knowles did yeoman work in getting the chickens and pigs out of harm's way. It was not until noon that we had got the fire really in hand and by that time we were all very tired and very dirty.

There were innumerable courts of enquiry afterwards and the general impression was that the blaze had been started by a match thrown into the straw. As all lights were strictly forbidden in these barns it seems unlikely, and my own idea remains that the fire was purposely started by the owner of the barn in order to secure excessive compensation.

Gunner Cecil
Longley, 1st
South Midland
Brigade, Royal
Field Artillery

Someone was asking me if there was going to be a sort of Christmas truce. I am glad to say there is not; strict orders have been issued that there is to be no such waste of kindness towards the enemy that has caused us so many losses and used the foulest of means of securing those losses. Also, if we are spending 5 million pounds a day on the war and every day makes it harder for the Germans, why waste 5 millions and slacken the awful 'tanking' they are getting? We want to make them fed up, not to give them opportunities of feeding up, and if they send a shell or two over into our infantry trenches on Christmas Day, as they most certainly will (probably two or three hundred will come over, or at the batteries, and observing station and villages we occupy), I believe we are to respond with a searching and unceasing bombardment of their trenches, first line and reserves of Essarts, Puisieux, and Serre woods and villages that will break up their Christmas parties.

31 December: The trenches began to show signs of improvement due to the continual baling and pumping. From the signs which we saw everywhere, the Lancs Fusiliers must have been a bright lot. We heard that they were in the habit of leaving the trenches without permission, going down to Albert whenever they saw fit. In the mud were found great quantities of stuff that they had abandoned. There were dozens and dozens of gumboots, and even a dead man. One of their Lewis guns was found in the mud <u>under</u> a duckboard (or 'sump ladder', as we called them), and it must have been deliberately hidden there. In the mud on the dugout floors were found many blankets, waterproof sheets, sets of equipment, and even <u>unopened</u> jars of rum. If Fritz had known how things were, he might have marched up the road to Albert, while the Lancs Fusiliers were asleep or running away.

A mine was fired by our side in the 'Glory Hole', at 11.45 am, result unknown. The enemy fired one at 4.55 pm, and then fired several trench mortars, but I did not hear if they did any damage. About 11.00 pm the enemy opened out with a lot of machine-gun fire and a few whiz-bangs. This we took to be some sort of New Year's greeting, 'Shoot out the Old, shoot in the New', as it were. At midnight several heavier shells were fired, which sounded as if they dropped in Albert.

Private Sydney Fuller, 8th Suffolk Regiment

Overleaf: *German troops stroll through the village of Beaumont Hamel, several months before the British assault.*

2 Bedding-In

'I saw about fifty German prisoners marched through the village. Three officers were in front – white, broken muddy, and one of them wounded. Most of the men were very boyish and intelligent looking, but one officer, who looked about 20, was one of the noblest looking men I have ever seen. He held his head up and looked so proud that I could have wept.'

Captain Theodore Wilson, 10th Sherwood Foresters

It must not be imagined that I at once grasped all the essential details of our trench system. On the contrary, it was only very gradually that I accumulated my intimate knowledge of our maze of trenches, only by degrees that I learnt the lie of the land, and only by personal patrolling that I learnt the interior economy of the [mine] craters. At first the front line, with its loops and bombing posts, and portions 'patrolled only', its sandbag dumps, its unexpected visions of Royal Engineers scurrying like bolted rabbits from mine shafts, its sudden jerk round a corner that brought you in full view of the German parapet across a crater that made you gaze fascinated several seconds before you realized that you should be stooping low, as here was a bad bit of trench that wanted deepening at once and had not been cleared properly after being blown in last night – all this, I say, was at first a most perplexing labyrinth. It was only gradually that I solved its mysteries, and discovered an order in its complexity.

Lieutenant Bernard Adams, 1st Royal Welch Fusiliers

I think my first impression was of the difficulty of finding one's way about in a maze of muddy ditches which all looked exactly alike, despite a few occasional muddy notice boards perched in odd comers: 'Princess Street', 'Sauchiehall Street', 'Manchester Avenue', 'Stinking Sap', 'Carlisle Road', and the like. I had a trench map of the sector, but it seemed to me one never could possibly identify the different ways, all mud being alike, and

Anonymous letters of a New Army (Kitchener) Officer

Opposite: *January 1916: view snapped by Lieutenant Richard Hawkins on his Vest Pocket Kodak. Using a metal stylus, he opened a small flap on the rear of his camera to reveal backing paper attached to the negative on which to scratch in details of the picture. F**c***t is Fricourt village.*

*A company of
the 11th Royal
Fusiliers making
their way through
the winter snow
of 1915/16.*

no trench offering anything but mud to remember it by. In the front or fire
trench itself, the firing line, one can hop up on the fire step, look round
quickly between bullets, and get a bearing. But in all these interminable
communication and branch trenches where one goes to and fro, at a depth
varying from 6 to 10 or 12 feet, seeing only clay and sky, how the dickens
could one find the way?

And yet, do you know, so quickly are things borne in upon you in this
crude, savage life of raw realities, so narrow is your world, so vital your
need of knowing it; so unavoidable is your continuous alertness, and so

circumscribed the field of your occupation, that I feel now I know nothing else in the world quite so well and intimately as I know that warren of stinking mud: the two sub-sectors in which I spent last week. Manchester Avenue, Carlisle Road, Princess Street, with all their side alleys and boggy byways! Why, they are so photographed on the lining of my brain that, if I were an artist (instead of a very muddy subaltern ex-clerk) I could paint the whole thing for you – I wish I could. Not only do I know them, but I've merely to shut my eyes to see any and every yard of them; I can smell them now; I can feel the precise texture of their mud. I know their hidden holes and traps, where the water lies deep. I know to an inch where the bad breaks are in the duckboards that you can't see because the yellow water covers them. Find one's way! I know them far better than I know the Thames Embankment, the Strand, or Brixton Hill! That's not an exaggeration.

It had frozen again, and an inch of snow lay on the ground. It was a sunny morning, and from the new post all Fricourt lay in full view before me. How well I remember every detail of that city of the dead. In the centre stood the white ruin of the church, still higher than the

A view across Fricourt and the trenches crossing the La Boisselle spur. Although this was taken from German lines, Adams' view across the valley here was not very dissimilar.

Lieutenant Bernard Adams, 1st Royal Welch Fusiliers

houses around it, though a stubby stump compared to what it must have been before thousands of shells reduced it to its present state. All around were houses; roofless, wall-less skeletons all of them, save in a few cases, where a red roof still remained, or a house seemed by some magic to be still untouched. On the extreme right was Rose Cottage, a well-known artillery mark; just to its left were some large park gates, with stone pillars, leading into Fricourt Wood; and just inside the wood was a small cottage – a lodge, I suppose. The extreme northern part of the village was invisible, as the ground fell away north of the church. I could see where the road disappeared from view; then beyond, clear of the houses, the road reappeared and ran straight up to the skyline, a mile further on. A communication trench crossed this road: (I remember we saw some men digging there one morning). With my glasses I could see every detail; beyond the communication trench were various small copses, and tracks running over the field; and on the skyline, about 3,000 yards, away, was a long row of bushes.

And just to the left of it all ran the two white lace borders of chalk trenches, winding and wobbling along, up, up, up until they disappeared over the hill to La Boisselle. Sometimes they diverged as much as 300 yards, but only to come in together again, so close that it was hard to see which was ours and which the German. Due west of Fricourt church they touched in a small crater chain.

It was a fascinating view. I could not realize that there lay a French village; I think we often forgot that we were on French soil, and not on a sort of unreal earth that would disappear when the war was over; especially was no-man's-land a kind of neutral stage, whereon was played the great game. To a Frenchman, of course, Fricourt was as French as ever it had been. But I often forgot, when I watched the shells demolishing a few more houses, that these were not German houses deserving of their fate. Perhaps people will not understand this: it is true, anyway.

I was drawing a sketch of the village, when lo! and behold! coolly walking down the road into Fricourt came a solitary man. I had to think rapidly, and decide it must be a German, because the thing was so unexpected; I could not for the moment get out of my head the unreasonable idea that it might be one of our own men! However, I soon got over that.

'Sight your rifle at 2,000 yards,' said I to Morgan, who was with me. 'Now, give it to me.'

Carefully I took aim. I seemed to be holding the rifle up at an absurd angle. I squeezed, and squeezed. The German jumped to one side, onto the grass at the side of the road, and doubled for all he was worth out of sight into Fricourt!

I went out towards Aveluy with Syd Harris, looking for more shell noses. We worked over the ground, finding several 'noses' and were suddenly made aware that we had got into full view of the enemy, by a rifle bullet, which went so close to my ear that the 'crack' of it deafened me. We did not stop long enough for Fritz to fire another shot – we just fell into the trench. After this little reminder, we were not so keen on souvenir hunting.

Private Sydney Fuller, 8th Suffolk Regiment

Normally a man felt safe enough in villages behind the front and support lines. He might feel safe in the trenches too, but such were the twists and turns in opposing trenches, rising up and over ridges, that it was not always possible to remain immune from enemy observation, as 19-year-old Vic Cole discovered. As a signaller, he had the freedom to roam more freely than an infantryman.

I was making my way along a much battered and little used trench endeavouring to trace a broken telephone wire, when, taking a look over the top to see where I was, I saw a German about 300 yards away digging at the back of a trench parados. I watched him for a moment and thought, 'Well, I'm entitled to have a shot at him.' I aimed, pulled the trigger and saw a piece of cloth or leather fly off the side of his coat – he disappeared – did I wound him? I shall never know, but it was my first shot at the enemy. …

Private Victor Cole, 7th Royal West Kent Regiment

Being a signaller, I had a leather frog with a pair of wire cutters on my belt as well as a little bag full of wire prongs for fixing the wire to the side of the trench. When you laid a new telephone cable, you laid it along the side of the trench and held it with the prongs knocked into the back wall about 10 yards apart. It was my job day today to check they were all right.

Along the trench were other wires placed for the Royal Engineers' Signal Company. They always had superior thicker cable than ours, and another wire was dug in for the artillery spotters. So there were three wires: our thin black D3 cable, and below that a thicker red cable for the artillery observation post, and below that a thicker black cable of the Signal Company.

I carried a D3 telephone with me and if the wire was broken, I could put the bare end round the terminal and turn a little handle and try to get through to make sure the rest of the line was intact before fixing the break. However, sometimes when we got into the line I found that the first chap to lay the wire had done it at night and instead of going around the trench, he had gone over the top. This meant that if the line was broken I might have to climb up and look around. Zzzzp, a bullet, so back down I'd go again, cut a new piece of wire, strip off about 2 inches of insulation at the end of a wire, tie a reef knot, put a bit of insulation tape round and peg it round the trench instead of the line going over the top.

I enjoyed signalling. All the time I could go where I wanted, but the infantry, the poor buggers, couldn't move. Instead, they had little niches in the side of the trench to avoid the shrapnel, while those who weren't resting were on the fire step for hour after hour. I felt sorry for them.

Second Lieutenant Anthony Nash enjoyed a certain freedom, too. Appointed to be the battalion's intelligence officer, he was to oversee the job of enemy surveillance, noting anything and everything observed of enemy activity from the arrival of ration parties to the time that sentries were relieved, from noting fresh trench workings to the position of enemy machine guns.

Second Lieutenant Anthony Nash, 16th Manchester Regiment

It was fine to have a roving commission, answerable to no one but the Colonel, and not tied down to one small section of the trenches. I used to set out in the morning in my little cut-down Burberry, the tails cut off to be out of the mud, thigh gum boots, a gas helmet over one shoulder and binoculars over the other, pockets stuffed with maps and notebook and a stray piece of chocolate for lunch, a long trench stick, revolver, trench gloves and shrapnel helmet. I used to feel like a country squire going round my estate. There they were, my trenches, mine because I knew them as no one else had a chance of knowing them. Every sandbag and loophole

had its own history and I used to feel the pride of proprietorship as I gaily went on my rounds. Going up and down the battalion front and in and out of the trenches was of course slightly more risky than staying put in one place, but it was vastly more interesting and at 21, danger was the spice that enabled one to beat the monotony of trench warfare.

I know nothing whatever about psychology but I do know that life was very full of zest in those days. There was a thrill in walking with death at one's elbow. There was immense satisfaction in taking what was perhaps a totally unjustifiable risk and getting away with it. It was rather fun to be sniped at, and just missed, and when a shell burst very near or overhead and you listened to the bits of shrapnel coming down, it was distinctly exhilarating. There is a phrase about the 'joy of battle'. I have appreciated this to the full, but I wonder whether I shall be believed when I say that this feeling of joy and lightheartedness does not come from any pleasure in killing – that's the rotten part – but in the risk of being killed. My days in the trenches were days of utter content; I cannot explain why, even to myself. It is not a case of looking back when everything in the past is wonderful and nothing is so depressing as the present and future; my actual notes of the time are full of happiness and joy. The natural sadness of losing one's dear friends was mitigated by knowing that one shared the same risks and would probably meet a similar fate tomorrow.

Lieutenant Ronald Beloe, 8th East Lancashire Regiment, in the trenches near Fonquevillers, winter 1915.

Not everyone shared Nash's unbounded joy of trench life.

Lieutenant
Bernard Adams,
1st Royal Welch
Fusiliers

A shell has splinters that spread far and wide; a trench mortar is a clumsy monster with a thin skin, no splinters, and an abominable, noisy, vulgar way of making the most of itself. 'Sausages' were another but milder form of the vulgar trench mortar; aerial torpedoes were daintier people with wings, who looked so cherubic as they came sailing over, that one almost forgot their deadly stinging powers; they, too, were a species of trench mortar.

It is natural to write lightly of these things; yet they were no light matters. They were the instruments of death that took their daily toll of lives. …

Sometimes we forgot it in the interest of the present activity; sometimes we saw it face to face, without a qualm; but always it was there with its relentless overhanging presence, dulling our spirits, wearing out our lives. The papers are always full of Tommy smiling: [Bruce] Bairnsfather [the war cartoonist] has immortalized his indomitable humour. Yes, it is true. We laugh, we smile. But for an hour of laughter, there are how many hours of weariness, strain, and grim agony! It is great that Tommy's laughter has been immortalized; but do not forget that its greatness lies in this, that it was uttered beneath the canopy of ever-impending Death.

2 Feb: In the trenches. Everything very quiet. We are in support, in a place called Maple Redoubt, on the reverse slope of a big ridge. Good dugouts, and a view behind, over a big expanse of chalk downs, which is most exhilarating. A day with blue sky and a tingle of frost. Being on the reverse slope, you can walk about anywhere, and so can see everything. Have just been up in the front trenches which are over the ridge, and a regular, or rather very irregular, rabbit warren. The Boche generally only about 30 to 40 yards away. The trenches are dry, that is the glorious thing. Dry. Just off to pow-wow to the new members of my platoon.

3 Feb: Another beautiful February morning. Slept quite well, despite rats overhead. O'Brien and Dixon awfully dull and heavy; can't think why. Everything outside is full of life; there is a crispness in the air, and a delightful sharp shadow and light contrast as you look up Maple Redoubt.

6 Feb: Yesterday was a divine day. I sat up in 'the Fort' most of the day, watching the bombardment. Blue sky, on the top of a high chalk down;

Dugouts behind the line near Fricourt occupied by men of the 11th Royal Fusiliers in the winter and early spring of 1915/16. The contemporary caption notes that they were 'not very shell proof!'.

larks singing; and a real sunny dance in the air. We watched four aeroplanes sail over, amid white puffs of shrapnel; and a German plane came over. I could see the black crosses very plainly with my glasses. Most godlike it must have been up there on such a morning. I felt very pleased with life, and did two sketches, one of Sawyer, another of Richards. A dull thud, and then 'there goes another' shouts someone. It reminds me of Bill the lizard coming out of the chimney pot in *Alice in Wonderland*. Everyone gazes and waits for the crash! Toppling through the sky comes a big tin oil can followed immediately by another; both fall and explode with a tremendous din, sending up a 50-foot spurt of black earth and flying debris, while down the wind comes the scud of sandbag fluff and the smell of powder.

Trench life on the Somme, as elsewhere, was exhilarating to those new to the line, but interminably dull to those who had been there month after month. It was punctuated by moments of intense excitement and fear, but in the main it was characterized by stifling boredom, days passing slowly in an endless and repetitive round of duties. In dugouts, weary officers sought what rest they could in cramped and verminous conditions. Receiving letters and writing home was one avenue of mental escape, with some men more adept correspondents than others.

Anonymous letters of a New Army (Kitchener) Officer

'Dugout' is the only word for it. I don't know who did the christening, but it is, like so many words and phrases adopted without question by Tommy at the front, the one proper, exact, and adequate name for the places we inhabit in the trenches. The particular dugout I have in mind is a Company Headquarters, situated, like a good many others, in a loop trench, perhaps 70 to 100 yards long, which curves round at a distance of 20 or 30 yards in rear of the fire trench. … It happens that my picture of this Company Headquarters dugout is a three o'clock in the morning picture: moonless, and the deadest hour of the night, when Brother Boche is pretty generally silent.

As one gropes along this ditch one comes to narrow gaps here and there in the side farthest from the enemy. These lead to all kinds of odd necessary places: the homes of signallers, runners, and others, refuse pits, bomb and trench stores, and so on. Presently, a thin streak of light shows like a white string in the blackness. This is one of the gaps, about 4 feet high and 18 inches wide. A dripping waterproof sheet hangs as a curtain over this gap: the white string is the light from within escaping down one side of the sheet. Lift the sheet to one side, take two steps down and forward – the sheet dripping on your neck the while – and you are in the Company Headquarters dugout: a hole dug out of the back of the ditch, its floor 2 feet below the level of the duckboards outside, its internal dimensions 10 feet by 8 by 6.

At the back of this little cave, facing you as you enter – and unless you go warily you are apt to enter with a rush, landing on the earthen floor in a sitting position, what with the wet slime on your gum boots and the steps – are two bunks, one above the other, each 2 feet wide and made of wire netting stretched on rough stakes fastened to stout poles and covered more or less by a few empty sandbags. One of these is the bunk of the OC Company, used alternately by one of his subalterns. In the other, a platoon commander lies now asleep, one gum-booted leg, mud-caked well above the knee, dangling over the front edge, a goatskin coat over his shoulders, his cap jammed hard down over his eyes to shut out the light of the candle which, stayed firmly to the newspaper tablecloth by a small island of its own grease, burns as cheerily as it can in this rather draughty spot, sheltered a little from the entrance by a screen consisting of a few tins half full of condensed milk, butter, sugar, and the like. The officer in the bunk is sleeping as though dead, and the candlelight catching the mud-flecked stubble on his chin suggests that his turn in the trenches should be at least half over. Another few days should bring him to billets and shaving water. ...

The table – say, 30 inches by 20 inches – was made from a packing case, and is perched on rough stake legs against the earthen side of the dugout, with a shelf over it which was formerly a case holding two jars of rum. On the shelf are foodstuffs, Very lights, a couple of rockets, a knobkerrie, a copy of *Punch*, a shortbread tin full of candles, a map, an automatic pistol, and, most curiously, a dust-encrusted French cookery book, which has taken on the qualities of an antique, and become a kind of landlord's fixture among trench stores in the eyes of the ever-changing succession of company commanders who have taken over, week in and week out, since the French occupation in '14.

Hung about the sides of the dugout are half-empty canvas packs or valises, field glasses, a couple of periscopes, a Very pistol, two sticks caked all over with dry mud, an oilskin coat or two similarly varnished over with the all-pervading mud of the trench, a steel helmet, a couple of pairs of field boots and half a dozen pictures from illustrated papers, including one clever drawing of a grinning cat, having under it the legend, 'Smile, damn you!' The field boots are there, and not in use, because the weather is of the prevalent sort, wet, and the tenants of the place are living in what the returns call 'boots, trench, gum, thigh'.

Overhead is stretched across the low roof tarred felt. Above that are rough-hewn logs, then galvanized iron and stones and earth: not shell-proof, really, but bullet- and splinter-proof, and for the most part weatherproof – at least as much so as the average coat sold under that description. The trench outside is very still just now, but inside the dugout there is plenty of movement. All round about it, and above and below, the place is honeycombed by rats – brown rats with whitish bellies, big as young cats, heavy with good living; blundering, happy-go-lucky, fearless brutes, who do not bother to hunt the infinitely nimbler mice who at this moment are delicately investigating the tins of foodstuffs within a few inches of the head of the OC Company. The rats are variously occupied: as to a couple of them, matrons, in opposite corners of the roof, very obviously in suckling their young, who feed with awful zest; as to half a dozen others, in courting, during which process they keep up a curious kind of crooning, chirruping song wearisome to human ears; and as to the numerous remainder, in conducting a cross-country steeplechase of sorts, to and fro and round and round on the top side of the roofing felt, which their heavy bodies cause to bulge and sag till one fancies it must give way.

There is a rough rickety stool beside the table. On this is seated the OC Company, his arms outspread on the little ledge of a table, his head on his arms, his face resting on the pages of an open Army Book 153, in which, half an hour ago, he wrote his morning situation report, in order that his signallers might inform Battalion Headquarters, nearly a mile away down the communication trench to the rear, with sundry details, that there was nothing doing beyond the normal intermittent strafing of a quiet night.

The OC Company is asleep. A mouse is clearing its whiskers of condensed milk within 2 inches of his left ear, and the candle is guttering within 2 inches of his cap peak. During the past few days he has had four or five such sleeps as this, half an hour or so at a time, and no more, for there has been work toward in the line, involving exposure for men on the parapet and so forth, of a sort which does not make for restfulness among OC companies.

There comes a quiet sound of footfalls on the greasy duckboards outside. Two mice on the table sit bolt upright to listen. The cross-country meeting overhead is temporarily suspended. The OC Company's oilskin-covered shoulders twitch nervously. The mother rats continue noisily suckling their young, though one warily pokes its sharp nose out over the edge of the felt, sniffing inquiringly. Then the waterproof sheet is drawn aside, and the OC Company sits up with a jerk. A signaller on whose leather jerkin the raindrops glisten in the flickering candlelight thrusts head and shoulders into the dugout. 'Message from the Adjutant, Sir!'

It was in the dugout that officers' servants would bring meals, served up with as much formality as was possible in the circumstances.

Behind the curtain there was a great business. Lewis and Brady had brought up the rations; Gray was busy with a big stew, and Richards was apparently engaged in getting out plates and knives and forks from a box; Davies was reading aloud, in the middle of the chaos, from the *Daily Mail*. Sometimes the Mess-president took it into his head to inspect the servants' dugout; but it was an unwise procedure, for it took away the relish of the meal, if you saw the details of its preparation. So long as it was served up tolerably clean, one should be satisfied.

Lieutenant Bernard Adams, 1st Royal Welch Fusiliers

Richards' procedure at half past seven was first to take all articles on the table and dump them on the nearest bed. Then a knife, fork, and spoon were put to each place, and a varied collection of tin mugs and glasses arranged likewise; then came salt and mustard in glass potted meat jars; bread sitting bareback on the newspaper tablecloth; and a bottle of O.V.H. [whisky] and two bottles of Perrier to crown the feast. All this was arranged

Dishing out the rum on a cold morning. The letters SRD, which ubiquitously appeared on the side of jars, stood for Supply Reserve Depot.

with a deliberate smile, as by one who knew the exact value of things, and defied instruction in any detail of laying a table. Richards was an old soldier, and he had won from Dixon at first unbounded praise; but he had been found to possess a lot too much talk at present, and had been sat on once or twice fairly heavily of late. So now he wore the face of one who was politely amused, yet, knowing his own worth, could forbear from malice. He gave the table a last look with his head on one side, and then departed in silence.

Lieutenant Richard Hawkins, 11th Royal Fusiliers, left, in a dugout with Lieutenant Richard Vaughan-Thompson.

Colonel Weber, the Chief of our Divisional Staff, came up to have a look around the front line and I was deputed to show him round. He was immaculately dressed, nicely cleaned and polished, and I thought of the conditions under which the men in the line were living. So I thought that I would show him all that there was to be seen. I took him through the muddiest of trenches and nearly drowned him; I led him past every dangerous corner there was, pointing out the German sniping posts after we had passed each one; I finally got him back to Battalion Headquarters simply smothered with mud and with all the curiosity sweated out of him. I will say that he bore no malice and frequently during our journey expressed anxiety for my safety, not entirely disinterested in his own perhaps; however, he never forgot me or his remarkably hectic outing and we were always very good friends although he never asked me to take him round those trenches again. Few lads of 20 had such an opportunity of making their mark on the Chief of Divisional Staff.

Second Lieutenant Anthony Nash, 16th Manchester Regiment

War is indescribably disgusting. Any man who has seen it and praises it is degenerate. I had a long time to think, by myself, on that fatigue job – under the stars, and please God I'll live to put some of it in print, one day, but I can't write it in a letter. The rats interrupted me. They are fat and grey and bold. One came and looked at me and squealed at about three o'clock in the morning when I could see no prospect of going to bed ever, and so infuriated me that I slashed at him with my stick and splashed my whole face so with mud that I had to spend the next hour or so trying to get a lump of it out of my eye. I missed the rat, and imagined him with a paw to his horrible nose – laughing at me.

Captain Theodore Wilson, 10th Sherwood Foresters

The rats were getting really beyond all bearing. They used to parade regularly for rations and if the ration party were late in getting up for supplies, these fat monsters would get terribly angry and run about making the most indignant noise. Every evening at more or less the same time the battalion transport section would bring up the next day's rations – sacks of bread, bacon, butter and cheese and so forth. These would be put down at Battalion Headquarters or any other convenient dump and would be collected by the ration carriers from each platoon, who would take their respective shares up

Second Lieutenant Anthony Nash, 16th Manchester Regiment

to the trenches. It was the job of the Quartermaster Sergeant to apportion these rations and naturally there would be crumbs spilt and little bits of fat bacon occasionally. Hordes of rats would appear as punctually as the platoon ration carriers and await the arrival of the battalion transport and the subsequent division of food. The ground around would be just one moving mass of rats, great fat fellows the size of small cats, with red tusks and very vicious habits, beasts which battened on the corpses and which would attack without fear even the wounded if they were isolated.

After completing a turn in the trenches, typically three days in the front line, three days in close support and three days in reserve, a battalion would be withdrawn and billeted for a number of days in one of the many villages close to the front line but not normally under fire. On the Somme, villages such as Suzanne, Morlancourt, Millencourt and Colincamps were extensively utilized over a long period of time. Billeting officers would automatically go ahead of the battalion, agreeing deals with local people for rooms in homes, barns and stables, chalking up the details on walls or doors, allocating accommodation so that troops would not be held up for too long on arrival. Most other ranks found themselves in farms close to but not in the villages while officers were in private homes.

Anonymous letters of a New Army (Kitchener) Officer

When I mention billets you mustn't think of the style in which you billeted those four recruits last spring, you know. By Jove, no! It is laid down that billets in France mean the provision of shelter from the elements. Sometimes it's complete shelter, and sometimes it isn't; but it's always the best the folk can give. In this village, for instance, there are hardly any inhabitants left. Ninety per cent of the houses are empty, and a good many have been pretty badly knocked about by shells. I have often laughed in remembering your careful anxiety about providing ashtrays and comfortable chairs for your recruits last year; and the trouble you took about cocoa last thing at night, and having the evening meal really hot, even though the times of arrival with your lodgers might be a bit irregular. It's not quite like that behind the firing line, you know.

In some places the men's billets are all barns, granaries, sheds and stables, cow houses, and the like. Here, they are nearly all rooms in empty houses. As for their condition, that, like our cocoa of a night, and cooking generally, is our own affair. In our division, discipline is very strict about billets. They are carefully inspected once or twice during each turnout by the Commanding Officer, and every day by the OC Company and the platoon commanders. We have no brooms, brushes, or dusters, except what we can make. But the billets have to be very carefully cleaned out twice a day, and there must be no dirt or crumbs or dust about when they are inspected. Even the mire of the yards outside has to be scraped and cleared away, and kept clear; and any kind of destruction, like breaking down doors or anything of that sort, is a serious crime, to be dealt with very severely. The men thoroughly understand all this now. ...

In the first convenient archway handy to our billets you will find the company's field cooker. You have seen them trailing across the Plain down Salisbury way on field days – the same old cookers. The rations come there each day, from the battalion QM store, 3 miles away; and there the men

Left: Rue de Villers in the village of Morlancourt, a 'home' used by many British soldiers while out on rest.

Right: Lieutenant Richard Vaughan-Thompson, 11th Royal Fusiliers, standing at the door of his billet.

draw them in their cooked form at mealtimes. In every village there is a canteen where men buy stuff like chocolate, condensed milk, tinned cafe-au-lait, biscuits, cake, and so forth.

In the daytime, when there are no carrying fatigues, we have frequent inspections, and once the first day out of trenches is past, every man's equipment has to be just so, and himself clean-shaven and smart. We have a bathhouse down near the river, where everyone soaks in huge tubs of hot water; and in the yard of every billet you will find socks, shirts, and the like hanging out to dry after washing. By 8.30 at night all men not engaged in carrying fatigues have turned in. During the week out of trenches we get all the sleep we can. There are football matches most afternoons, and sing-songs in the early evenings. And all and every one of these things are subject to one other thing – strafe; which, according to its nature, may send us to our cellars, or to the manning of support trenches and bridgehead defences.

With regard to the officers, our batmen cook our grub, moderately well or atrociously badly, according to their capacity. But, gradually, they are all acquiring the soldierly faculty of knocking together a decent meal out of any rough elements of food there may be available. More often than not we do quite well. Our days are pretty much filled up in looking after the men, and in the evenings, after supper, we have their letters to censor, our own to write, if we are energetic enough, and a yarn and a smoke round whatever fire there may be before turning in; after which the Boche artillery is powerless to keep us awake. At this present moment I doubt whether there's another soul in A Company, besides myself, who's awake, except the sentry outside Headquarters.

Lieutenant Bernard Adams, 1st Royal Welch Fusiliers

Behind the lines at rest, Morlancourt. I had to pass from one end of the village to the other. The orderly room was not far from our company 'Mess' and was at a crossroads. Opposite, in one of the angles made by the junction of the four roads, was a deep and usually muddy horse-pond. … As I walked along the streets I passed sundry Tommies acting as road-scavengers; 'permanent road fatigue' they were called, although they were anything but permanent, being changed every day. Formerly they had seemed to be engaged in a Herculean, though unromantic, task of scraping great rolling puddings of mud to the side of the road, in the vain hope that the mud would find an automatic exit into neighbouring gardens and ponds; for Morlancourt did not boast such modern things as gutters. Today there were large pats of mud lining the street, but these were now caked and hard, and even crumbling into dust, that whisked about among the sparrows. The permanent road fatigue was gathering wastepaper and tins in large quantities, but otherwise was having a holiday.

Women were working, or gossiping at the doorsteps. The estaminet doors were flung wide open, and the floors were being scrubbed and sprinkled with sawdust. A little bare-legged girl, in a black cotton dress, was hugging a great wide loaf; an old man sat blinking in the sunshine; cats were basking, dogs nosing about lazily. A party of about thirty bombers passed me, the sergeant giving 'eyes right' and waking me from meditations on the eternal calm of cats. Then I reached the headquarter guard, and the sentry saluted with a rattling clap upon his butt, and I did my best to emulate his smartness. So I passed along all the length of the shuttered houses of Morlancourt. 'A great day, this,' I thought, as I came to the small field where B Company was paraded; not 250 men, as you will

Martinsart Wood: a camouflaged tent used by officers of the 36th (Ulster) Division. The picture was taken by Colonel R.D. Perceval-Maxwell.

doubtless assume from the textbooks, but some thirty or forty men only; one was lucky if one mustered forty. Where were the rest, you ask? Well, bombers bombing; Lewis gunners under Edwards; some on 'permanent mining fatigue', that is, carrying the sandbags from the mineshafts to the dumps; transport, pioneers, stretcher-bearers, men under bombing instruction, officers' servants, headquarter orderlies, men on leave, etc. etc. The Company Sergeant Major will make out a parade slate for you if you want it, showing exactly where every man is. But here are forty men. Let's drill them.

Half were engaged in arm drill under my best drill sergeants; the other half were doing musketry in gas helmets, an unpleasant practice which nothing would induce me to do on a sunny May morning. They lay on their fronts, legs well apart, and were working the bolts of their rifles fifteen times a minute. After a while they changed over and did arm drill, while the other half took over the gas helmets, the mouthpieces having first been dipped in a solution of carbolic brought by one of the stretcher-bearers in a canteen. These gas helmets were marked DP (drill purposes), and each company had so many with which to practise. …

The rest of the morning we spent 'on the range', which meant firing into a steep chalk bank at a hundred yards. Targets and paste pot had been procured from the pioneer's shop, and after posting a couple of 'look-out' men on either side, we started range practice. The men are always keen about firing on the range, and it is really the most interesting and pleasant part of the infantryman's training. I watched these fellows, hugging their rifle butt into their shoulder, and feeling the smooth wood against their cheeks, they wriggled their bodies about to get a comfortable position; sometimes they flinched as they fired and jerked the rifle; sometimes they pressed the trigger as softly, as softly … and gradually, carefully, we tried to detect and eliminate the faults. Then we ended up with fifteen rounds rapid in a minute. The 'mad minute' it used to be called at home.

Not every soldier appreciated the natural desire of officers to keep their men occupied while out of the line.

We are so messed about and badgered from pillar to post that I hardly know which way to turn; but it's all so childish and farcical that you can't help laughing at it when you can spare the time from swearing! I told you that we expected to move from the valley and looked forward to a short march of 3 or 4 miles; but they sprang another 17 miles on us. It's really extraordinary how the rumour of these things runs through the battalion. I was lying on the grass, writing on the previous afternoon – sun shining, birds singing, 'everything in the garden lovely' – when a man passed and remarked '*Compris* 17 miles tomorrow.' 'Nonsense, where did you hear it?' 'Oh, Price (the Adjutant) told the chaps who were playing football not to exert themselves, as we had to do at least 17 miles tomorrow.' 'I don't believe it – tell it to the marines.' But the nasty seed of unrest was planted and the sun didn't seem to shine so brightly. Then someone else strolled along, 'Heard that we're moving tomorrow? 20 miles, the signallers say.' And so on, until by the time I reached my billet everybody had it in varying forms although the powers that be made no sign until the order for an emergency sick parade in the evening settled the question in favour of a long march.

Lance Corporal James Parr, 1/16th London Regiment

You've no idea of what a rush it is to get off in the morning of a long march. Reveille 5.30, blankets to be rolled in bundles of ten and stacked at a certain place by 6, washing bowls, spades, lamps to be collected from the barns and taken somewhere else by 6.30 (L/Cpl Parr to be responsible for this). Breakfast 6.30, barns to be thoroughly cleaned and tidied by 6.45, battalion parades ready for marching at 7 – and then is generally kept waiting for an hour before it starts. (L/Cpl Parr spent half an hour looking for a measly bowl, irredeemably perjuring his soul in the process.) Well, we started at last. I've never dropped out of a march or avoided one since I joined the army but they nearly did it on me this time. To begin with, I had not been feeling up to the mark all the time I had been in the valley – the sudden change from the heights and frost to the valley and heat I suppose – and I had a blister on my heel, so I started with the expectation of going till I dropped – and you don't get much sympathy for dropping out, you're generally only blamed for not going sick before the march. And quite right too; your dropping out is only a nuisance to the battalion and spoils the marching reputation. Still, I didn't think I should finish that march. It was boiling hot and mostly uphill in the morning, climbing up out of the valley, struggling on from one halt to another, very often just as much as some of us could do.

We march for fifty minutes and halt for ten, regular as clockwork. The halt just pulls you round and the first twenty of the fifty minutes go fairly easily, then time begins to drag and the last ten mins are done by sheer physical force. On and on, till it feels as if your neck muscles were being pulled out with pincers and your boots were soled with red-hot iron. You push your cap to the back of your head and the Colonel, riding down the column, calls out, 'Put your cap on straight, that corporal there!' And all the time you have to smile and joke, because the others are joking round you (when they aren't swearing) and you know that many of them are worse than you. That boy marching alongside you – it is his birthday and he's just 19 – has got a swollen joint in his foot from frostbite last winter and dreads the halts almost as much as the marching because it means the pain of starting afresh; and that bugler in the platoon in front, who is having his pack carried by an officer, is sure to fall out about the tenth mile, for he is flat-footed and that is his limit. The dinner halt is very near now, thank God – only one more hill (and a nasty one) to be negotiated. I have seen nothing of the country, as my eyes have been fixed for the most part on the heels of the man in front.

A final struggle up the hill and just on the crest, the longed-for whistle. Just in time, as most of the men were baked and the column was beginning to waver and sag. Then that blessed hour's rest and tea! Oh, what should we do without our tea here! A million blessings on the head of Sir Walter Raleigh or Isaac Newton or whoever it was that discovered its gorgeous refreshing properties. I was too tired to eat more than a mouthful but just lay and basked in the waves of fatigue that passed through and out of me. Then boots and puttees off, and a change of socks and when we took up our pilgrimage again, I felt a new man. Rather a tottery new man, as my feet were a bit sore, but one among many similar. It was miraculous the transformation caused by the rest and the tea – it was one o'clock when we halted and we had had nothing since a very hurried breakfast at 6.30 and our spirits were further raised by the name of our destination on a signpost with the magic figures '4K'. Of course, signposts in France are very similar in their encouraging lies to those in England, and 4K usually means 6, but it looked good and bucked us up tremendously.

About a mile from 'home', my left leg began to give – I strained a little muscle in my thigh very slightly, but enough to play the devil with my leg in my tired condition. Still, C Co were singing at the back of us and we managed to raise a song to beat them; and then the village in sight and the Quartermaster waiting to guide to billets and then the usual barn – never so welcome – and down on the straw to lie for an hour till I felt I could stand again. I swear I couldn't have done another 100 yards. Then the orderly sergeant, 'Sorry, old man, but you'll have to do the guard tonight, Jones has gone sick.' That meant sleeping in boots and equipment but I didn't mind anything.

Spies were known to be at work in the civilian population and upon our earnest representations all the civilians were evacuated. There was in Suzanne a church with a tower which was visible from the German lines. There was a clock in the tower. Although the clock had stopped it was noticed that the hands of the clock had changed their position. The gentleman who altered the position of the hands had used them to semaphore information to the Huns as to our movements. He was eliminated, not by us but by the French authorities to whom we handed him over. There was also a farm on the top of the hill with a ploughed field and pigeon loft. The farmer excited our suspicion by his erratic ploughing. He did not follow a straight furrow; sometimes too he worked two brown horses: occasionally he worked one brown horse and a white one. The white horse seemed to have an easy life of it but it was remarked

Second Lieutenant Anthony Nash, 16th Manchester Regiment

A French boy taken under armed guard. Fear of spies reached fever pitch prior to major offensives.

The Basilica of Notre-Dame de Brebières. The statue of Mary and the infant Jesus – also known as the Golden Virgin – became an iconic sight for British servicemen on the Somme. It was hit by a shell in January 1915 and remained in this near-horizontal position until March 1918, when it finally fell. The Basilica was rebuilt after the war and a precise replica of the statue was erected.

Opposite Left: *Lieutenant Patrick Robert Koekkoek, Royal Engineers, sits on a steel girder overhanging the river Ancre as it flows under the Albert Basilica.*

Opposite Right: *Shell damage to the Basilica's façade.*

Rifleman Giles Eyre, 2nd Kings Royal Rifle Corps

We swing into the square. On one side a church badly damaged by gunfire, with a tall spire, gapped here and there where a shell has struck, towering up into the gloom, and from the top, bent at right angles and looking down towards the ground, a huge statue of Our Lady with the Infant Christ in her arms: Notre Dame des Brebieres, famed over the whole battlefront.

As we pass by underneath it seems to me as if the Virgin is stretching out and blessing the columns of passing men, giving them assurance that while there is tribulation, strife and death in the world beneath, the gates of Bliss lie beyond our natural horizon.

O'Donnell, reckless as he may be, but a devout Catholic, crosses himself.

We trudge through the dark rubble-covered streets of Albert, half unreal in the darkness, and out beyond, the rain now beating at us and running down in rivulets from our groundsheets, draped round shoulders and heads.

Major Geoffrey Hardwick, 57th Field Ambulance, RAMC

Went into Albert this afternoon with Kilbey on his box-car – it has not been shelled for a week. It is not knocked about as much as one would expect. It must have been a jolly fine town once. The church of St Brebiere is a wonderful sight – very badly smashed about. The great image of he 'Lady' holding out the base is now almost horizontal and with the sun shining on it all golden coloured is certainly marvellous to look at – in fact it fills one with a certain amount of awe wondering how it can still stand there and how it will be before it does fall – it must weigh quite 14–15 tons at least. The place is packed with troops and there are a few civilians still living there….

that it was usually at work when we were due to return to the trenches. This gentleman was also called to account; I have no doubt that his rather overdue account was settled in full.

Private Edward Higson, 16th Manchester Regiment

1 May saw us back in the line again, in our old sector (at Maricourt). Nothing exciting happened until the 25th of the month, when, much to our joy, a few of us were detailed to attend a trench mortar exhibition. The exhibition was to be held about 40 miles behind the line and we were to travel down by motor buses. The trip through the country, in motors instead of having to walk, gave the lucky few a great treat. We stopped for lunch at Corbie, then continued on our journey. We had just pulled up in the village near the exhibition ground, when we were startled by a terrific explosion; shrapnel simply rained down on us. We thought that the Germans had got a long-range gun on us for we could not see any enemy aeroplanes about. On investigation, however, we found that the dump of shells for the purpose of the exhibition had, through somebody dropping a lighted fuse, exploded, killing about six and wounding about thirty. There was nothing else to do but get into our buses and ride back to the line again. Arriving back at Battalion Headquarters I found out I was detailed for a raiding party and was to remain out with fifty other men to practise the stunt. We practised for a couple of days and then six of us went up the line to patrol the enemy sector that we were going to raid. This raid, however, was cancelled by the French who were going to relieve us, on the grounds that they would have to stand the result of it, which in most cases means a counter raid by the enemy after a lapse of a few days.

Signaller Cyril Newman, 1/9th London Regiment (Queen Victoria Rifles)

29 May: Am writing sitting on the floor of a trench part of the front line [Hébuterne]. 'Tis a beautiful morning and the air is full of the restless buzzing of aeroplanes. Not only has the sunshine brought out aeroplanes, but also the small inhabitants of the lower world – ants, huge beetles, things with 'umptun' legs and other creepy-crawly insects found in freshly dug earth. Have just been watching a large greenish beetle trying to scale the walls of the trench. On his hind legs he has a pair of spurs like climbing irons, which he digs into the soil to get a hole. However, either he hasn't learnt how to use them properly or has lived too well and grown fat, for

four attempts have failed. He would doubtless have made many more had
I not had compassion, spread one of your envelopes before him, enticed
him on it and thrown him overboard. Now, was not that kind! The ants are
too industrious; – not content with the trench they must needs crawl over
me – as if I had notions to spare them! There is a nasty, black, jumping
tribe of spiders – I kill any who come near me. I don't like them. ...

(My word! these ants are strong – there are two trying to carry away
a piece of cheese twice their combined size – the front ant is pulling
backwards and seems to be doing all the work, the other ant, supposed to
be pushing, seems to be hanging on and having a ride.)

[To his aunt] 27 April: I'm writing in a trench not very far from the
Germans and I've just heard the first cuckoo! It's blazing sunlight. Behind,
there is a French town – quivering in the heat – chimneys and roofs
apparently intact from here, though the whole place in reality is a mere
husk of a town. Nearer, between the town and us, is a village, which is quite
a ruin – its church spire a broken stump, its house walls honeycombed
with shellfire. Then comes a great blazing belt of yellow flowers – a sort of
[wild] mustard or charlock [mustard] – smelling to heaven like incense,
in the sun – and above it all are larks. Then a bare field strewn with barbed
wire – rusted to a sort of Titian red – out of which a hare came just now,
and sat up with fear in his eyes and the sun shining red through his ears.

Then the trench. An indescribable mingling of the artificial with the
natural. Piled earth with groundsel and great flaming dandelions, and
chickweed, and pimpernels, running riot over it. Decayed sandbags, new
sandbags, boards, dropped ammunition, empty tins, corrugated iron, a
smell of boots, and stagnant water and burnt powder and oil and men, the
occasional bang of a rifle, and the click of a bolt, the occasional crack of
a bullet coming over, or the wailing diminuendo of a ricochet. And over
everything the larks and a blessed bee or two. And far more often, very
high up in the blue – a little resolute whitish-yellow fly of an aeroplane –
watching, watching – speaking, probably, by wireless to the hidden stations
behind the lines; dropping, when he thinks fit, a sort of thunderous death
onto the green earth under him; moving with a sort of triumphant calm
through the tiny snow-white puffs of shrapnel round him. And on the

Captain
Theodore
Wilson, 10th
Sherwood
Foresters

other side, nothing but a mud wall, with a few dandelions against the sky, until you look over the top, or through a periscope, and then you see barbed wire and more barbed wire, and then fields with larks over them, and then barbed wire again – German wire this time – and a long wavy line of mud and sandbags – the German line – which is being watched all day from end to end with eyes which hardly wink. The slightest movement on it – the mere adjusting of sandbag from below – is met with fire. The same goes on of course with our line. Look over the top for longer than two seconds and you are lucky to step down without a bullet through your brain. By day it's very quiet. Some twenty shells or so have come over this morning from the German side. You hear a sound rather like a circular saw cutting through thin wood and moving towards you at the same time with terrific speed – straight for your middle it seems, till you get used to it! It ends in a terrific burst – a shower of earth or bricks or metal, a quiet cloud of smoke – and sometimes a torn man to be put out of sight, or hurried down to the dressing station. Sometimes, but astonishingly seldom with this desultory shelling. Of course a real bombardment, where the sky is one screaming sheet of metal, is hell indescribable.

Lance Corporal George Hackney, 14th Royal Irish Rifles, 36th (Ulster) Division, in a barn in Poulainville, near Amiens. Hackney used a Climax Watch Pocket Camera, a camera that used glass plates and produced better quality images than the roll-film VPK.

This place is very quiet, on the whole. But even the beauty of spring has something of purgatory in it – the sort of purgatory a madman may know who sees all beautiful things through a veil of obscenity. Whatever war journalists may say, or poets either, blood and entrails and spilled brains are obscene. I read a critique of Le Gallienne's out here, in which he takes Rupert Brooke to task for talking of war as 'cleanness'. Le Gallienne is right. War is about the most unclean thing on earth. There are certain big clean virtues about it – comradeship and a whittling away of non-essentials, and sheer stark triumphs of spirit over shrinking nerves, but it's the calculated death, the deliberate tearing of fine young bodies – if you've once seen a bright-eyed fellow suddenly turned to a goggling idiot, with his own brains trickling down into his eyes from under his cap – as I've done, you're either a peacemaker or a degenerate. …

God help us all! I pray, when I fire a rifle myself into the unknown, that if that little singing splinter of metal must kill someone it will a man who loves killing. But I wonder, does it? It may take the life of some Saxon boy who thinks the Kaiser a god, and who has a girl waiting for him at home. All this is what Bismarck would call weakness. … Well, all this is perhaps a little florid. One lives a life of continuous strain and reaction, strain and reaction, and it's difficult to write or think quite quietly.

Much love to you, and many thanks

Jimmy

[To Mrs Orpen] 3-5-16: Every very now and then there comes a sound like a steam saw cutting through thin wood and moving towards you with great speed. It ends suddenly, far off, in thunder. At any minute it may end in thunder close at hand. It is merely an interesting phenomenon to those newcomers who haven't yet seen the work a shell can do. To the rest who have seen, it is a terrible and fiendish thing, which one must keep so to speak, masked – which one mustn't talk too much of! I saw a man today, for instance – No. One can't describe it. Only the memory of things like it makes one see this spring evening's beauty through a sort of veil of obscenity, as a madman may see beauty. For mangled bodies are obscene whatever war journalists may say. War is an obscenity. Thank God we are fighting this to stop war. Otherwise very few of us could go on. Do teach your dear kids the horror of responsibility which rests on the war-maker. I want so much to get at children about it. We've been wrong in the past. We have taught schoolboys 'war' as a romantic subject. We've made them learn the story of Waterloo as a sort of exciting story in fiction. And everyone has grown up soaked in the poetry of war – which exists, because there is poetry in everything, but which is only a tiny part of the great dirty tragedy. All those picturesque phrases of war writers – such as 'he flung the remnants of his Guard against the enemy', 'a magnificent charge won the day and the victorious troops, etc. etc.', are dangerous because they show nothing of the individual horror, nothing of the fine personalities smashed suddenly into red beastliness, nothing of the sick fear that is tearing at the hearts of brave boys, who ought to be laughing, in agony. I can't explain it all without getting into a sort of confounded journalese swing of words, but you'll understand. It isn't death we fear so much as the long-drawn expectation of it – the sight of other fine fellows ripped horribly out of existence by 'reeking shard', as a great war journalist says who spoke (God forgive him) of 'a fine killing' in some battle or other.

Meanwhile there are the compensations of a new sort of comradeship, of new lights on life, of many many new beauties in humanity. I hope I shall come through it alive, though it's doubtful. I hope I shall be a much, much better sort of person for it all though that is a selfish sort of aspect of a huge drama like this. Anyhow I suppose one's friendships don't end here?

Corporal
James Parr,
1/16th London
Regiment

C. had a very narrow escape which I must tell you of, though I don't usually dwell on the casualty side of the picture do I? He, with half the platoon, was supporting B. and the gun in the advanced trench (my day off) when the Huns started trench-mortaring. They're hellish things – so big that you can see them coming through the air – and to give you some idea of the explosive they contain – one of our bombs contains a few ounces of ammonal [explosive]; these trench mortars contain 20 lbs! They will blow a whole traverse in as easily as breaking an eggshell but their effect is so local that if you are in the next traverse, you will probably escape scot-free, barring the concussion. So, as you can see them, you stand a sporting chance of dodging them. Anyway, one of these damned things came over into a traverse on the right where three of our men were posted. C., hearing the explosion, rushed to the spot to see if he could do anything and met one poor devil crawling down the trench. The other two were past help, so C. started to drag this chap into comparative safety. He had got along a traverse or two when he looked up and saw another mortar coming over right at him. He dropped the man and ran (and he blames himself for this) – I think he deserves a DCM for what he did – it was a question only of one life or two if he'd stayed with him. The mortar dropped just behind him, blew him from one end of the traverse to the other, tore his shrapnel helmet off his head and buried it in the clay, the same with his respirator from his shoulder and also buried his rifle. The shock to his nerves must have been terrible but he got up and went back to look for the wounded man, only to find that he had been buried under the earth. Then he went for more help.

They dug the man out and he lived till the next day, but he would have never recovered from his original injuries. They sent C. back to the village but he wouldn't go sick and was put in charge of a digging party within a few hours. And this boy (he's only 21) if there had been no war, would have remained in England, an ordinary tennis party and ballroom nut. Don't tell me war does no good. Someone said to me the other day, 'And after all, what's the use of all this? We lose money, we lose the best years of our lives, we run the risk of losing our lives altogether, at any rate of being incapacitated. And what do we gain? We could live and love and work somewhere in the world whether Germany or England won. What's the use of it all?'

What do we gain? I think we gain the one thing that every man has wanted from his boyhood up – opportunity. Opportunity to show what he is made of. Opportunity to show himself what he's made of, to show that he can be the hero he's always wanted to be from the time when he first made up his mind to be a pirate when he grew up. He may not always know that he wanted it, but to my mind it was the thing missing – the thing that made us at times discontented, moody and unsatisfied. What do we gain? We stand to gain everything and to lose – only our lives. A paltry exchange, if we leave behind a memory that is good. There is a machine gun of ours which fires 'Pom-tiddley-om-pom, Pom-pom' – a quaint idea to think that you might 'go out' to a senseless catchtune played on a lethal weapon! Did I ever tell you that up at Ypres we used to sing and whistle the *Policeman's Holiday* at stand-to and fire our rifles – crack-crack! to emphasize the last two notes?

Second
Lieutenant
Anthony
Nash, 16th
Manchester
Regiment

A dugout collapsed under shellfire, killing three men of D Company – amongst them Corporal Brown. They were buried in the cemetery in Suzanne in pouring rain.

During the more or less stationary period of trench warfare small military cemeteries were concentrated near each sector of trenches and in every village. Sometimes these were entirely apart from the old French civilian cemeteries, occasionally they adjoined them. Whenever possible men who were killed in the front line were conveyed by stretcher-bearers to the rear in order to be buried in one of these cemeteries. It was considered a disgraceful thing to leave one's dead behind one and every effort was made to bring them out.

The grave would be dug by the battalion pioneer section and the body would be sewn in a blanket and carried by bearers on a stretcher draped with a Union Jack to the graveside. The Padre then read a shortened form of the Burial Service, which was usually attended by the man's own officers or particular pals. The service was always reverently carried out, although frequently shells would be dropping around us, and everything was done decently and in order while a note was made of the exact map reference of place of the burial. A bottle containing a slip of paper with the man's name, regiment and rank was usually placed in the grave, and a wooden cross erected straightaway. Most regiments affected their own particular style of cross which of course bore the particulars of the buried man. In the Manchesters we had a cross with an arc of a circle in each right angle.

The first Kitchener divisions had begun to arrive in France in the second half of 1915, while at home British industry had been reorganized to properly supply the nation's troops, after scandals exposed the British Government's hitherto disjointed approach. By January 1916, thirty-eight British divisions were on the Western Front and the Commander-in-Chief, Sir Douglas Haig, was under mounting political pressure at home to co-operate with the French in a joint offensive, an offensive agreed in principle in December between Haig's predecessor, Sir John French, sacked after Loos, and the French Commander-in-Chief, Joseph Joffre. Joffre had unilaterally decided that the offensive would be on the Somme, where British and French forces stood side by side. The British would attack north of the Somme and the French to the south. There was no strategic significance to the Somme; it had been a backwater and Haig, if given the choice, would have preferred to attack in Flanders. However, political imperatives forced his acquiescence.

The Germans had been in occupation of the ground since 1914 and had eighteen months to construct impressive defences, which would now have to be comprehensively breached. That would take months of planning and preparation. These plans were thrown into confusion when, in February, the Germans attacked at Verdun in a deliberate plan to engage and break the French army. The ferocious fighting forced the French to scale back their commitment on the Somme. The offensive, when it came, would be a much more comprehensively British affair, with the French increasingly desperate for the offensive to begin in order to relieve pressure on their forces further south.

Haig handed the intricate task of overseeing the attack to one of his most trusted officers, General Sir Henry Rawlinson. Rawlinson had been appointed to command the Fourth Army, tasked with prosecuting the first stages of the offensive. Rawlinson set about preparing his plans, which would undergo significant revisions over the next two months, not least by Haig, who was concerned by his Army Commander's overcautious approach. In studying the robust and complex German defences, Rawlinson wanted to undertake an initial assault with limited objectives; Haig wanted something more dynamic and thrusting. If a breakthrough could be fashioned and the enemy's first and second lines breached, then war could once again be in the open. The final plan was, if nothing else, ambitious.

I was in the front line again for a spell of duty when I received a written note addressed to me personally. It instructed me to report forthwith to HQ VIIIth Corps. This was most exciting as I took it for granted that at long last it must be something specially connected with my role in forward reconnaissance.

I found out that HQ VIIIth Corps was about 8 miles due west of Hébuterne and housed in Marieux Chateau. Accordingly, dressed in my

Second Lieutenant Frederick Roe, 1/6th Gloucestershire Regiment

trench shabbiness and dirt, I cycled to the chateau in the certainty that I
should at long last have duties so remote from the front line as almost to
be on leave. I had already seen front line service for a full year without
grievous mishap and I honestly believed that I might well be given a stint
of a relatively cushy duty actually at Corps Headquarters.

I arrived in the middle of a glorious spring afternoon. I walked my
bicycle up through the chateau grounds along what seemed an endless
but very well-preserved pavé drive. At the end were some steps leading to
a large patio which was unshelled and in perfect order. When I reached
the top I saw an officer of the Brigade of Guards immaculately dressed
in jacket and trousers, indisputably from Savile Row or Sackville Street,
and with his regiment's arrangements of jacket buttons gleaming in the
sunlight. He was sat on a stool with a painter's palette over his left thumb
and was painting on a canvas which was resting on an artist's easel. My
first reaction was one of resentment but my second was, 'Why not?' If a
Gunners of 120th fighting solder has a discernible philosophy at all it is to eat well and live
Battery, Royal Field as comfortably as possible for as long as possible because round the corner
Artillery, digging will inevitably come some nasty and dangerous requirements.
an emplacement   I stacked my bicycle against the wall of the chateau and found my
for an 18-pounder way to the G (Intelligence) room. I was told that I had been selected to
field gun.   assist in preparation for a forthcoming major offensive against the enemy

and that I would be responsible for VIIIth Corps Forward Intelligence. I was to set up three observation posts sited to cover the whole area of trenches occupied by our troops who were at the bottom of the slope of the valley, but within our support line of trenches, because they must have unimpeded observation of no-man's-land and of the enemy trenches beyond it. The duties would include accurate maps of the whole trench system, getting familiar with the ground details of no-man's-land by regular reconnaissances, including barbed wire entanglements and their access lanes and exits, both our own and the enemy's; shell craters; enemy machine-gun locations; fixed rifle stands and timing and regularity of enemy patrols. I was forbidden to volunteer or be detailed for raids actually into enemy trenches as my responsibility must remain directly with Corps Headquarters as their forward link.

We were to keep as close a watch as possible upon enemy activity behind their front lines, including erection of batteries of heavy guns, reinforcement and relief of enemy front line trenches. The latter duties would necessitate a very close watch on enemy rearward communication trenches and points of assembly, for example of front line ration dumps, shell dumps, and of course of any formation headquarters. Each post was to be manned day and night by one officer and sufficient other ranks, including a senior NCO prepared to take over in the event of the officer becoming a casualty.

11 May: Paraded at 6.45 am, marched to the new model of the German trenches. Practised attacking them. Some men of the Royal Flying Corps were with us, and during the attack they signalled to the aeroplanes, which co-operated with us. The signalling was done with heavy electric lamps, of French makes, and also by flares. There was an aerodrome not far away, and we could see other planes busily firing at targets on the ground while diving. This was all in preparation for the coming stunt, the targets representing enemy troops. The planes used 'tracer' bullets, which could be easily seen, and errors of shooting as easily corrected.

Private Sydney Fuller, 8th Suffolk Regiment

12 May: Paraded at 8.00 am, and practised sending 'DD' messages with discs. A 'DD' message was one which was not answered or acknowledged

by the receiving station. Each word was repeated once – thus a message reading, for instance, 'Short of bombs', would, if sent by the 'DD' method, read 'Short short of of bombs bombs'. The reason for practising these messages, or rather the way of sending, was that, in an actual attack, if a message sent back by visual means from the front were answered or acknowledged in the ordinary way by the station receiving it in the rear, the enemy would be certain to see the answer or received signal, and thereby locate the station, and act accordingly, which would mean, in many cases, the destruction or disorganization of the receiving station, and consequently of communication. The discs were intended for use for such messages, sent from advanced positions, only. They consisted of a disc of tin or sheet iron about a foot in diameter, on a light pole about 4 feet long. The back of the disc, which would be towards the enemy when in use, was camouflage painted, and the front was white, with a black diagonal bar. They were used in the same way as flags.

Second Lieutenant Frederick Roe's three observation posts would be opposite the German-held village of Serre, towards the northern end of the line. He would witness the opening assault from one of these posts. One of the infantry divisions he would watch would be the 31st, composed largely of New Army Kitchener men from the north of England. The 18th Durham Light Infantry, the Durham Pals, was a battalion in this division, and in its ranks served Sergeant Charles Herbert Moss.

Sergeant
Herbert Moss,
18th Durham
Light Infantry

We did not know that we were preparing for an attack, until we had a sort of rehearsal of the plan and method of attack a few weeks before the time to 'go over'.

A miniature copy of the German trenches had been prepared for this purpose on the open country a few kilos behind our billets. A few Brass Hats explained the plan of attack, the timing of the attacking waves, the control of the artillery barrage, and the formation of each battalion's 'wave'. Then each battalion practised their part in it.

The Leeds Pals to be first over the top to capture the German front line, each man a few paces apart, with loaded rifle carried at the 'port' and with bayonet fixed. The Bradford Pals to follow in the same manner and pass over the top of the Leeds Pals to capture the second and third line of trenches. Our battalion was then to follow and make strongpoints to hold the front at all costs against enemy counter-attacks.

I was shown exactly where my Lewis gun post was to be but when I asked the officer what my field of fire would be like he couldn't tell me. I pointed out the sort of country in front was the most vital thing to me to deal with the counter-attack. He resented me calling his attention to this, and all he could say was that I would find out when we got there. I thought that was a poor lookout when so much depended upon this very necessary information, and I told him so.

In the middle of May I paid one of my many visits to Corps Headquarters. I had spent most of the time in earlier months in the trench system between Hébuterne and Beaumont Hamel, the two flanks of the VIIIth Corps front. I was very active indeed and hardly ever free from daily shellfire, the constrictions of trench life and the frequent and regular reconnaissance into no-man's-land. The thing I remember most clearly in this run-up to 1 July was that I was always abysmally tired, so much so that my hands became unsteady and with a tendency to shake. The result was that I couldn't hold steady a filled mug of tea but spilled it so that I had to be content with it being given to me half full. It certainly was not an unusual indication of cold feet and I was more annoyed at this irritating manifestation of excessive fatigue than cast down. On this particular day I was crossing the courtyard of the chateau on my way to my little office when the Corps Commander [Lieutenant General Aylmer Hunter-Weston] came out unaccompanied for once. I wished him good morning, saluted and passed on. After a few paces I heard the General call, 'Boy – come here.' It was then that the unthinkable, unbelievable, happened. When I got back to him he said, 'You are doing a very good job of work but you look pretty well all-in.' A pause, and then the beautiful words, 'How would you like a spot of home leave?'

I behaved like a complete idiot and said, 'But all leave is stopped, Sir!' This was met by a sharp, 'I know that, you stupid boy. How much leave would you like?'

Second
Lieutenant
Frederick
Roe, 1/6th
Gloucestershire
Regiment

Road repairs were a constant chore with the vast increase in traffic. Horses frequently went lame walking on nails dropped by limbers and wagons.

Taking a deep breath, I said, 'If I could have a clear forty-eight hours at home, Sir, I should be most grateful: there is a lot of work still to be done, Sir.'

'You are stupid,' he replied. 'Take a fortnight!' Then he moved on. I remained quite incredulous, barely taking it all in.

There was some prevarication between Joffre and Haig as to the exact timing of the offensive. At a meeting on 26 May, Joffre fervently pressed for 1 July as the latest possible date. Haig, unsure how battle-prepared his men were, especially those of Kitchener's Army, suggested 15 August. Joffre pointed out in rising excitement that the French army would have ceased to exist by that point and so Haig reluctantly fell into line with a date of '1 July or thereabouts'.

Second Lieutenant Geoffrey Fildes, 2nd Coldstream Guards

The month of June had arrived, bringing with it floods of rain. Once more the camp in the wood became a mass of mud, and the roads veritable quagmires. Along with this spell of wet weather came a deluge of rumours. These had one point in common, namely, the prospect of a big attack by our army on this front, but beyond that, most of them were mutually contradictory. Apart from these, however, it was evident to all that something out of the ordinary was impending, for men and guns continued to appear in ever-growing quantities. Valleys that only a week before had been devoid of all occupants now began to assume an aspect of busy preparation. Huts and dugouts were being constantly erected, and the masses of materials assembled for the RE [Royal Engineers] became exceedingly great. Horse lines seemed to spread themselves across every fold in the ground, and batteries to spring from the soil in every direction. Once again, as on the eve of Loos, we lived in an atmosphere of endless speculation.

Certainly, many signs and portents gave credence to our belief that great things were about to happen. The construction of new roads along specially selected routes seemed hardly explicable on any other grounds; also, a new railway was being built across the countryside to the north of us. Though only a single track, it would be a valuable auxiliary to the permanent line down at our present railhead. Every ravine and hollow behind the Fricourt Ridge was being converted into a battery position, and trenching and mining operations were being pushed on at all possible speed throughout the neighbourhood. Miles of wire cables were said to have been laid in trenches 7 feet deep, these being joined up at certain points into a huge telephonic system.

Burdened with a growing atmosphere of tension, the days of June sped slowly by, rumour following rumour. Enormous supplies were now rolling up to the front by day and night. Already events were confirming our anticipations, among which was the fact that our heavy guns had commenced to register their targets. With the certain approach of Fate, a hurricane was brewing in our midst.

By the middle of June, the region about Bray seemed to have grown into a vast encampment, which included not only every branch of the British Army, but also our allies. Below our camp, the flats and roadway of the broad valley swarmed with gangs of French engineers busily constructing a light railway. In addition, several gunboats had crept up the canal, and there was now quite a flotilla of these craft moored along the embankment. Beneath their awnings, one could see large naval guns pointed upward towards the east. In many places the mottled tents of their troops had overflowed the barrier of the river, and were now scattered in ordered fashion upon the British side of the valley.

The French were relieving us of the whole river sector. In the evening … we obtained another view of the Bray–Suzanne road. Flowing in an

Left: *Preparing for future casualties: Grovetown Casualty Clearing Station.*

Right: *'Up-country at last': 4 May 1916, and a motor ambulance convoy arrives at Heilly, a major railhead for supplies and a casualty clearing station.*

endless stream, the same flood of troops and transport rolled on. As far as the eye could reach, the highway surged with men and horses slowly moving in contrary directions. Purring alongside a huge wagonload of bridging materials came a Staff car; inside, seen through the fog of dust raised by the passing men, one noticed the gold-trimmed kepis of its occupants. Then, from the clattering throng emerged a company of French infantry wearing the bright khaki recently issued to some of their army. In one's ears there hummed a multitudinous sound: the tramp of feet, the clatter of hoofs, the groan of labouring wheels. Heralded by a deeper note, there next came a battery of 75s, and here, sitting lazily upon the lofty seats of the wagons or driving the teams, an extraordinary variety of types could be seen. Their chief characteristic was a total disregard for soldierly smartness, both in their persons and in their dress. Dirty and unkempt, their forbidding appearance was intensified by the motley assortment of their uniforms. I could not help contrasting them with the smart figures beside me. No two seemed dressed alike. Here, amid a turmoil of dust, loomed a blue kepi; there, a grey-blue helmet; yonder, a red kepi; and farther off a light-blue forage cap. Some wore dark-blue jackets, others a light-blue greatcoat. Almost every type of kit was represented. It was not a battery, it was a museum. …

Entering Bray at last, we were directed by a British policeman on point duty to a special route through the town reserved for returning motor traffic; otherwise, the congestion through the narrow streets would have been fatal. Here the streams of troops and transport, British almost entirely, caused the walls around to quiver with their echoes.

'Gawd blimey, mate, look at them!' came a whisper from behind me. For a moment there was an amazed silence; even the British soldier was impressed. Then came a storm of hoots, catcalls, and yells, plentifully spiced with the time-honoured epithets of the barrack room. Lumbering down the main road rolled a belching traction engine, drawing in its wake an elephantine mass that rumbled beside the walls of the houses, almost filling the width of the village roadway. To one who had never seen such a piece of ordnance, the sight was almost incredible. Sweeping upward beside the roofs rose its massive barrel, and its giant wheels, huge and ponderous, revolved high above the doll-like forms of men on either flank. The earth quivered beneath its weight, and windows trembled at its approach. Behind it followed another and another behind that.

A glimpse of these vast forms filled every civilian spectator with wonder. To the gaping townsfolk, it must have seemed as if the guns of the British Fleet had entered their midst, like a herd of mastodons.

Speculation on the destination and powers of these enormous howitzers still continued as we drew near the Bois des Tallies. At least the orator of the party knew his own mind.

'You blighters, just mark my words. Them blink-in' things is goin' to punch the Kaiser's ticket!' Whereupon, in order to emphasize his meaning, he spat with faultless aim into the ditch across the road.

15 June: Very increased activity in this area and lorries etc. etc. passing and filling the road at all hours. We have now taken over a big area at Frenchincourt ... also close to the light railway siding and on it are putting up thirty-three big marquees – this is for the reception of wounded sitting cases – they will reach us by motor lorries and go into the tents and we shall pack them into trains at the siding – the CO said today that Burton and myself would take over charge of that place. It ought to accommodate quite 600 at a time. At present there is quite a week's hard work ahead in

Major Geoffrey Hardwick, 59th Field Ambulance, Royal Army Medical Corps erecting marquees and painting them. They each have to be well [sited] etc. as it is fairly open ground, and quite likely to be spotted by aeroplanes, especially as there are many other details fixed up there also. Our division starts moving up today.

Everything seems to be worked out so much better this time as compared to last September [Loos] – at any rate it doesn't seem so amateurish and preparations on a vast scale have been going on for the last three months and this time no news is being told more than necessary, which is a dashed good thing too. The latest rumour is that no letters will be allowed to be written home soon – (i.e.) only Field postcards. Last night 3 solid miles of artillery passed here on its way up, most of it being pulled by caterpillars.

20 June: ... The 19th Division are now in Albert or near it and I hear they are to do the 2nd part of the job – take the 2nd line etc. I am afraid there won't be very many of our division left at the end of all of this – everyone is jolly confident that there is going to be a big success though. The Boche knows all right that something is going soon as he is daily shoving up notices that we had better begin soon or peace will be declared. Also the French civilians know all about it as when buying a barrel of beer for the canteen, we had to pay an extra twenty-five francs for the barrel, making the price of the barrel fifty francs as the girl said, 'There is going to be a big push soon and either the Germans will push you or you will push the Germans – in either case I shall lose my barrel' – some keenness.

Lieutenant Charles Lloyd, D Battery, 81st Brigade, Royal Field Artillery

16 June: Arrived at Abbeville about 12.30. Reported to RTO only to be told that we need not have got out – the train had gone in the meantime. Caught the 4.00 after a futile effort to get some sleep on the floor of the waiting room. Awfully cold. Arrived Amiens about 7.00, changed and arrived at railhead – a place called Méricourt – about 9.00. No one seemed to know where the 80th were. Eventually discovered they were at Heilly, 2 km away. ... Orders to go into action at nine o'clock. We moved out at 6.00, Carver and myself on the limber of No. 1 gun. Progress was slow as the land is hilly and the traffic enormous. If Fritz did not see us he must have been blind as we halted on top of a crest for an hour, an enormously

long column of field guns, heavies and transport, while a Hun balloon looked down on us. There is very little sign of shellfire. It is a wonderful sight to see the batteries and heavy guns moving up from the rear. Every road choked with long columns of artillery. Arrived at our fire position at about 9.00. It is in a place called Happy Valley and is known as Gibraltar. The pits are dug into the foot of a steep forward slope and we have A & B batteries above us. Our dugouts are on the opposite side of the ravine, about 200 yds in front of the guns.

[To his sister] 19 June 1916: As you know from my card, we left the line three days ago and are back where we were before we went in, doing the night digging fatigue again and occasionally some day ones. However, we clear out altogether in a day or two and go back to our last resting place for a breather – after that, *je ne sais quoi*. It is quite on the cards that we shall move to another part of the line or go right back again till we are wanted for some other job. You see we are a kind of flying division to be used anywhere that is necessary and have come up here chiefly to get these new trenches dug. And some fierce work it was (and is) too! I've never seen the battalion worked so hard as when we were in the trenches. Day and night they were at it in constant relays. It was work until a man dropped and then that meant someone else doing a double shift. But the boys kept smiling on the whole and stuck it well, though they were very very tired. I was almost ashamed of myself as I did not do a hand's turn for all that seven days. As I told you, my job was to form part of the covering defensive screen, which meant taking up my position with the gun and two men in the advanced trench nearest the Germans and sticking there for twenty-four hours, supported by half a platoon with an officer and signaller on the telephone at hand. It was a bit of a strain and the monotony was terrible. B. after sitting there for eighteen hours doing nothing, suddenly arose and said to one of his team, 'For Christ's sake turn your face away! I'm sick of looking at it!' …

Oh! I must tell you again of my washout. He is the absolute limit and I loathe him. He's horribly 'windy', selfish, boring and snobbish. Of course, when he heard of that trench mortar business up near the post we were relieving that night, he promptly went sick with a chill. A chill! Ye gods! Also

Corporal James Parr, 1/16th London Regiment

of course he got M & D (medicine and duty) so had to carry on and the chill disappeared like magic. He sits down all day and does not attempt to help in any way except when I tell him to do things. When I ask him to give a hand in cleaning the gun, he says, 'I'll do my part', and his part to his mind consists in taking one small portion of the gun about 20 yds away from the rest of the men, cleaning it very slowly, returning it and going away. He can't forget that once he's been a sergeant. He has a stupid, vacant supercilious face that makes me long to hit him. In fact he's driven me so near insanity that I've spoken to Mr __ about having him removed from the team, but that ___ is afraid to do unless the washout offers to come off and I don't think he'll do that, as although he's terrified to death of the gun, he's still more afraid of work and can see that the gun team at any rate have a decent dugout up the line and get off a lot of fatigues there. To add to my troubles, my No. 1 got a bit of shell in his shoulder the other day so I've lost my best man pro tem, – but I'll shift that snivelling snob out somehow if I die for it.

Second Lieutenant Anthony Nash, 16th Manchester Regiment

On 19 [June] we started to rehearse the part we were to play in the Big Push, namely the capture of Montauban, a strongly held and fortified village 3,000 yards beyond the German front line trenches. A facsimile of the German trenches and of the village itself, roads and church and houses all complete, had been cut out in turf at Briquemesnil, and here we went through all the states of the attack, day by day, explaining carefully to the troops what was happening at each stage and making sure that every man knew his own job.

On [the] 21st we changed billets and moved to Oissy where the Battalion Headquarters were billeted in a magnificent chateau with beautiful grounds and artificial lakes by whose borders frogs croaked all night and most of the day. My bedroom was a sumptuously furnished apartment. On the 22nd the Padre and I rode into Amiens and had a ripping lunch at the Godbert, thinking that it might well be our last, and two days later we had a battalion concert in the grounds of the chateau.

The officers were on the terrace outside the chateau and the men lay at their ease on the green sward that sloped away towards the lake. The flowers were in full splendour and it was a perfect June evening. The scent of bean blossom was reaching us from a nearby field, and the busy hum of the bees was very sweet to our ears. In the old days in England our concert parties were rather noted, and as we listened to Pickering singing *Where my Caravan has rested* and to Healey's favourite song, *I hear you calling me*, we all felt that the concert was almost sacramental. We all knew what was before us, what a welter of mud and slaughter, and it was a heavenly respite to lounge at ease in the sunlight, listening to these silly sentimental songs we loved, and absorbing the sheer beauty of our surroundings.

23 June: Rumours afloat that as soon as we have supplied all batteries with ammunition etc., we move back out of the death trap. For such I am convinced it will be when we start strafing proper on the day allotted.

The morning is beautifully fine. Guns are very quiet. Everyone is making preparations for the coming advance. The Huns put up a board yesterday in their front line trenches and on it was pinned a paper with the following: 'We know you are going to attack. Kitchener is done, Asquith is done. You are done. We are done. In fact we are all done.'

It did not convey much to us. Of course they know the attack is taking place. It is impossible to hide great columns of guns, men, horses and motor lorries, such as have been moving to the firing line during the last fortnight.

Lieutenant Frederick Bursey, 9th Divisional Ammunition Column, Royal Field Artillery

On 24 June, the British began their bombardment of the enemy trenches. The day of the assault had been set for Thursday, 29 June and therefore the artillery assault would last five days, almost around the clock. In the event bad weather ensured a forty-eight-hour postponement, leaving the batteries and trench mortars to continue until the morning of 1 July.

24 June: Called at 4.45, left at 7.00. Dull cheerless day. Arrived at the new OP and tried to make it look its part. Made the telephonist cut thistles and bind them on bits of wood to stick about the parapet for cover. Can get a good view of Fricourt and Montauban, but Mametz is on the other slope. Some French artillery in the signal dugout that we propose to use as a funk hole. At 10.00 a strafe by the heavies took place. This kept up until late pm. Trench mortars also very active and the Hun trenches seemed to go sky-high. Fritz did not retaliate though many 5.9s came over our way

Lieutenant Charles Lloyd, 81st Brigade, Royal Field Artillery

A 60-pounder gun emplacement in Upnor Wood, close to the village of Suzanne. The photographer was Major Colin Borradile who served throughout the Somme Battle.

all through the day – at least 70 per cent duds. I should think they have a very low velocity as one can hear them coming from some distance. Brind came up about 4.00 pm and we watched the strafe together for some time. I came down alone, had tea and Carver and I went to B Battery and saw Hubert. In the evening orders came that we were sending over gas.

Captain Harold Bidder, 1st South Staffordshire Regiment

HQ, MG Coy, 26 June: I think I will describe yesterday. By the time you get this the curtain will have lifted. I spent the morning here in this little town where my HQs are, though some of my guns are up in the line. Our billet (lately an estaminet) has a little court at the back, smothered in roses – standards in the yard, ramblers growing over the iron railings and arched over the gate. Behind again is the garden, tended till a week or two ago, and at the bottom of the garden is the river. This is very like the Upper Thames – flat meadows or marshes on each side, bordered by steepish hills, the edges of the high ground, round which the river bends. Opposite us are clumps of willows to the water's edge. Among these a French band practises, and plays extremely well too.

It was a jolly morning, and the band was playing cheerfully. The water slipped along, unaffected by impending events, and swallows skimmed its surface. A great many mules were brought to the watering place alongside our garden; there was a certain amount of bustle which, with the band, rather gave the impression of Flower Show day in a country town. But the eighteen observation balloons that one could see from our doorstep would have been hard to explain. Also through our garden and all the other back gardens of the street runs a tramway the French have just made; a funny little engine comes puffing along it from time to time. In the afternoon I rode up to the trenches. One goes over a big ridge, and drops into a valley behind the line. There was a good deal of noise going on. We are in a salient here; and on this ridge the trenches surround you to the extent of literally two-thirds of the horizon, at distances of from 2 miles to 6. The German lines on the French side were marked by a continuous line of white and black smoke where the shells were bursting. The rest were not in sight.

Dropping down into the valley, I left the horses and walked on. The din here was incessant. Guns seemed stowed away in every clump of bush, and shells stacked everywhere. Every now and then a big thing would sail across the valley overhead with a humming rush – its parent gun too far back for the discharge to be heard. The Boche was making no reply. I got out of the valley, onto the last ridge, in front of which our trenches lie – beyond the poplar-walled road along the top. In front was a German observation balloon. As I was walking across, I idly noticed a little white cloud to one side of the balloon. Then I saw a spark at the base of the cloud; then a flame; then the balloon began to drop, and as it dropped the flame grew and the pace increased until, one vast sheet of flame, it rushed out of sight, and a thin column of smoke was left. I believe it and another were destroyed by our aeroplanes. There were none left up.

26 June: It's been a rotten rainy afternoon and the camp is in a state of drip. Luckily it has stopped raining now so one can go to sleep without worrying about the rain coming through during the night. Our tent is pretty well watertight and unless a storm of tropical violence (I think that is the right phrase) should break over us we ought to keep

Lieutenant Arthur Terry, 23rd Northumberland Fusiliers (4th Tyneside Scottish)

quite dry. This morning was fine and we went to the crest of a hill to watch the artillery activity which I presume you will have noted in the communiqués. It was really a fine spectacle – nearly all long-range fire and heavy calibre. The bursts carried from white clouds of HE to coal boxes bursting black against the sky and through the glasses one could see the clouds of dust and debris thrown up by the shells bursting on the ground. Clouds of smoke were driven by the wind across the frontage and on the whole I thanked my lucky stars I was at this end of the show and not the other. …

I must tell you one little incident though. I was sitting on my bed reading and happened to look down and there, close to me, was a wee field mouse industriously nibbling away at the grass. I didn't move at first in case I scared it but it seemed so unconcerned that I put my hand out very slowly and began stroking it with one finger. To our amusement it made not the slightest effort to run away but chewed and chewed at the grass as though its life depended on getting through a certain quantity in a given time. Then I tried to lift it up, but it was so small it slipped through my hand and ran off. It hasn't been back since.

Second Lieutenant Frederick Roe 1/6th Gloucestershire Regiment

At a certain stage of prolonged active service in such a totally unnatural environment the average soldier of all ranks, if he remains relatively fit, mentally and physically, learns to take life as it comes. There is such an infinite variety of circumstances waiting round the corner for tomorrow or even in the next hour that nothing ever really surprised us. There was, though, one occasion which was so completely at variance with the job in hand that for sheer incongruity it became fixed in my memory. British GHQ sent out to all units copies of a message received from the War Office. Mine was brought to me by a runner. The War Office letter said that there had been universal complaints that the pork and beans tinned rations did not contain any pork. It went on to say, 'M. And V. Ration: troops must not be misled by the name "pork and beans" and expect to find a ration of pork. As a matter of fact the pork is practically all absorbed in the beans.'

So then we knew!

An officer sits anxiously at the mine face excavated under the Hawthorn Redoubt at Beaumont Hamel. This mine would be blown at 7.20am on 1 July.

On 26 June we arrived at a village (Étinehem) 4 miles behind the line. Our artillery fire was a revelation to us. It seemed to us that nothing could stand up against it, yet there was a better display to come and still some Germans left to tell the tale.

 The delay was to our fellows like a red cloth to a bull. Everybody was eager to be 'over the top', our first big stunt. One felt proud to be with such fine fellows, men who, two years ago, were ignorant of the dangers of war. Now their only thought was to get at this nation that had set out to ruin all freedom and to endanger their homes, or to die a glorious death in the attempt. There were no white faces, no trembling limbs. In their hearts they were hoping to come through safely, not for their own sake but for the sake of those at home, but on the other hand they were quite prepared to die for the glorious cause of freedom and love.

Private Edward Higson, 16th Manchester Regiment

Very wet. Orders at last. Moved off 9.30 pm, as we neared the line met huge columns of infantry marching up. Just got to top of low ridge and can see the whole horseshoe-shaped line, lit up by shells of all description, a terrible though magnificent sight. Passed through Engelbelmer where we had to clamber over the ruins of our late billet,

Private Frank Williams, 88th Field Ambulance, Royal Army Medical Corps strewn across the road, open order now, for our position was already lit up from time to time by numberless star shells; nearing Mesnil a horseman rode up and warned us to put on our goggles, which I did quickly. For my eyes had already started to run and a strong smell as of mustard and cress filled the air (tear gas). The tears were running down my face so that I could hardly see at all and we practically felt our way along to Mesnil, where after a great deal of delay we got into dugouts, good deep ones I'm thankful to say, for my ears splitting almost from the continuous burst of shells and roar of our artillery; the sound was somewhat deadened down here.

Private Joe
Yarwood,
94th Field
Ambulance,
Royal Army
Medical Corps

I was sent up on 28 June to join the three squads who would deal with the wounded. I took the place of a man who had gone sick. He had been in the Boer War, and was old enough to be our father. He went sick and poor old Joe had to take his place, which I wasn't happy about, as I had to endure the bombardment.

The lads had blankets there in which to sew up the dead, and when I arrived they said, 'You, you long bugger, you'll need more than one blanket,' and they were actually measuring me up to see whether two blankets would be sufficient, as a joke of course, they were being funny, but it wasn't particularly funny to me.

Close to where we were, was a place called Euston Dump and nearby there was a battery of guns that were going night and day for the whole period, only stopping to let the guns cool. Every so often, I would pass through the guns just as they opened up again, woossh!, and my tin helmet would fall over my face with the shock. The only relief we had was the knowledge that the Germans were going through hell over there, and that made it easier for us.

Second
Lieutenant
Anthony
Nash, 16th
Manchester
Regiment

On the 29th Johnson and I went to evening service together and received Holy Communion. Morton Johnson and I had been very close friends since the day I joined the battalion. He was much older than myself but we got on exceedingly well together. Actually he was not fit to go into action as he had been a sick man for the previous fortnight, but he was determined to be with his company in our first big battle.

A British view overlooking the German trenches of the Schwaben Redoubt. Thiepval Wood is on the right. A ride can be seen through the wood, running in the direction of Thiepval Château.

The opposite view from the German-held Thiepval Château looking down the ride.

Private Edward Higson, 16th Manchester Regiment

At seven o'clock in the evening of 30 June, the battalion left the billets and started for the assembly trenches, the French villagers coming out to give us 'God Speed' and to wish us success. It was a glorious night and the boys, feeling the joy of the evening, were singing with heartfelt joy. It was a glorious thing to be on a journey like the Knights of Old, a journey of deliverance and of love. We were out to slay the dragon of hate and sin and felt honoured to have the privilege of being the slayer.

Private Sydney Fuller, 8th Suffolk Regiment

30 June: Smoke helmet inspection in the morning. We were given some very scanty instructions for the coming operations, and told that our battalion was to be 18th Division's Reserve, during the actual attack on the morrow. The CO had us on parade in the afternoon, when he gave us a short, serious address, the main thing he impressed on us being, 'Kill all you can, and don't take any prisoners.' He also said that 'The only good Germans were dead ones.' During the afternoon the enemy shelled the roads behind Bray, and also the village in which Grovetown camp was situated. There were thirteen kite balloons in the air, behind and to the right and left of us. Most of them flew coloured pennants from their mooring cables. We were issued with three days' rations, and two empty sandbags, per man. Our orders were to march off at 7.30 pm, but this was amended to 9.45 pm.

We were visited by a French soldier (who could speak English very well) in the evening. He had, he said, been at Verdun, and he described to us some of the things he had seen there. At 9.45 pm we marched off, loaded with our rations and various necessary instruments, etc. There was a very different feeling in most of us, when we marched off this time – we knew that at last we were to really fight the enemy, in a real battle, and not in the necessarily cautious and 'underground' way in which we had faced him until now. I could not help wondering where I should be by the next night at this time – dead, wounded and on the way to Blighty, or perhaps even a prisoner of war.

Second Lieutenant John Engall, 1/16th London Regiment

30 June: My dearest Mother and Dad,
I'm writing this letter the day before the most important moment in my life – a moment which I must admit I have never prayed for, like thousands of others have, but nevertheless a moment which, now it has come, I would

not back out of for all the money in the world. The day has almost dawned when I shall really do my little bit in the cause of civilization. Tomorrow morning I shall take my men – men whom I have got to love, and who, I think, have got to love me – over the top to do our bit in the first attack in which the London Territorials have taken part as a whole unit. I'm sure you will be very pleased to hear that I'm going over with the Westminsters. The old regiment has been given the most ticklish task in the whole of the division; and I'm very proud of my section, because it is the only section in the whole of the Machine Gun Company that is going over the top; and my two particular guns have been given the two most advanced, and therefore most important, positions of all – an honour that is coveted by many. So you can see that I have cause to be proud, inasmuch as at the moment that counts I am the officer who is entrusted with the most difficult task.

I took my Communion yesterday with dozens of others who are going over tomorrow; and never have I attended a more impressive service. I placed my soul and body in God's keeping, and I am going into battle with His name on my lips, full of confidence and trusting implicitly in Him. I have a strong feeling that I shall come through safely; but nevertheless, should it be God's holy will to call me away, I am quite prepared to go; and, like dear Mr Le Patourel, I could not wish for a finer death: and you, dear Mother and Dad, will know that I died doing my duty to my God, my Country, and my King. I ask that you should look upon it as an honour that you have given a son for the sake of King and Country. ...

I wish I had time to write more, but time presses. ...

I fear I must close now. Au revoir, dearest Mother and Dad. Fondest love to all those I love so dearly, especially yourselves.

Your devoted and happy son, Jack

It was the last day of June. The weather had been peculiarly piggish for more than a week – intensely hot and stuffy with no sun and frequent storms attracted maybe by the pseudo-thunder we had been having for so many days before. But on the morrow all would be different. Summer would begin properly. It must be summer in July. We would say 'rabbits' in the morning – if we remembered, and all would be well. We were inclined to hurry over dinner that night. The savoury which Miles had constructed

Second Lieutenant William Dyson, 1/16th London Regiment

as a Parthian shot was left almost untouched. Everybody was too occupied to bother about savoury, even a la Miles. It is the eve of 'the great offensive'. The warriors start putting on that curious medley of articles which compose 'battle order'.

The battalion is paraded in the streets of the little crowded village – 700 men who had been singing all afternoon eager to taste a new experience. Platoon by platoon it marches off. Those of us ordered to stand by in reserve have an appalling feeling of aloofness. Everyone but us seems to be moving into this strange new thing. For a moment the endless routine of trench warfare is broken. Now for the first time there is an 'eve of battle' feeling in the air. One began to wonder what Great Uncle Joseph felt before the Battle of Waterloo. The church clock strikes eight and still the traffic surges along in an endless stream. There is hardly 20 yards of road vacant for miles. Men, men and still more men, limbers without numbers, ammunition columns, GS wagons, horses and chariots 'a thousand three score and ten'. The reserve officers were to spend the

A German shell explodes in Thiepval Wood just prior to the assault.

In Thiepval Wood shortly before zero, a lance corporal in the 14th Royal Irish Rifles stands with a 2-inch 'Toffee Apple' trench mortar.

night in huts, but huts in French villages are like 'Jones' in Welsh. In the course of our search we passed a large white mansion with coloured lights outside. It is Divisional Headquarters and there in the gateway stands the General himself watching the troops go by.

Of the two officers and one other rank quoted here, 27-year-old Corporal James Parr and 20-year-old Second Lieutenant John Engall would be killed the next day, and 24-year-old Second Lieutenant Dyson would die of wounds two weeks later.

On the eve of battle a bloke came, I believe it was Lieutenant General Hunter-Weston. We were in this clearing in the wood and we all crowded round and he started talking to us. He looked like he'd just stepped out of a bandbox, all polished up with red tabs. He says, 'Now, you men, you will get on the top and you'll walk across with port arms and go straight into the German line.' There was a rumour that a bloke said to him, 'Where will tha be?'

Their wire was about four or five times as wide as ours. The quantity of wire they had, heavens, you couldn't have got through that in a month of Sundays. Our wire was narrow compared to theirs. When they were saying, 'Our guns will tear up the wire so that you can get through,' I thought, 'By God, I hope so,' but no. We knew all the time we were in for a bashing and we couldn't do anything about it. We weren't daft.

Private Frank Lindley, 14th York and Lancaster Regiment (2nd Barnsley Pals)

I returned to Corps Headquarters for regular briefings from time to time and was ordered to be available there for the early part of the night 30 June/1 July in case of any unexpected messages to VIIIth Corps from General Rawlinson's 4th Army GHQ at Querrieu. While I was in my own tiny office that night I was surprised and alarmed when there was a knock on the door and the officer in charge of No. 3 Post walked in. Clearly his presence there was a gross dereliction of duty as he should have been at his post of observation at least 10 miles away. He was in a pitiable condition and asked if he could have a talk with me urgently. He told me that he was certain he was going to be killed in the battle; that he was a wicked man and not fit to die yet. He then unfolded the story of his life in a flat toneless

Second Lieutenant Frederick Roe, 1/6th Gloucestershire Regiment

voice with his haunting pair of eyes fixed on mine. He said that although he was a married man he had for some years kept a mistress somewhere else. Every detail was forthcoming: how it was a most attractive little flat with lovely pink short window curtains in all the rooms. He was sure his wife knew nothing about this and how truly he loved his little mistress.

What really tortured him he said was what would happen to them both after his death which he declared was beyond question if he went into the line again. He begged me to let him sleep on the floor of my little bedroom so that he could gain some comfort by my presence and asked if he could be relieved of his work in the line. I talked to him for some time and tried to tell him that we were all secretly worried about what was likely to happen to us in the morning and that the worst thing that could happen would be, if we survived, the knowledge that we had failed to do what was expected of us and what we know we ought to do. I pointed out that if I relieved him of his duties I should have to put him under arrest. Eventually he quieted down a little and after promising to go back with him to his post as far as I could, we both went to sleep. We set off some time after midnight, after an hour or two of sleep. I was most uneasy at having to leave him when our ways divided because it was clear that he had not completely pulled himself together.

His corporal was a regular of the Royal Munster Fusiliers (Corporal William Cosgrove) who had been awarded the Victoria Cross during the Gallipoli campaign. In his posting order to me I had observed that after his rank and name were 'VC' but when I first met him he was not wearing the ribbon – the famous maroon is an unmistakable colour. When I asked him the reason he said that he had been so teased by his fellow soldiers in the regiment that he had never 'put it up'. I would much have liked to direct that he should do so, but in the circumstances it was clearly impossible to obtain any of the ribbon.

On our arrival I took this man aside and asked him if he would do all he could to help his officer; then I wished them both good luck and left them. I did not hear until some time afterwards that the officer had collapsed in some sort of convulsive fit and was immediately evacuated before the battle began. The result of course was that the corporal took over and ran the work of the post with no officer assistance.

There was to be no turning back, every man must advance at a steady pace. All officers had the authority to shoot anyone who stopped or tried to turn back. The wounded had to be left to be attended to by the stretcher-bearers and RAMC. The grimmest order to me was that no fighting soldier was to stop to help the wounded. The CO was very emphatic about this. It seemed such a heartless order to come from our CO who was a brigadier general of Church Lads Brigades and looked upon as a religious man. I thought bringing in the wounded was the way Victoria Crosses were won. But I realized that this would be an order to the CO as well as us from the General and that the whole of the attack could be held up if there were many wounded and we stopped to help them.

It was slow and hard work to get along that Railway Trench. We so often had to fling ourselves down in the trench, as the shriek of shells sounded as though they couldn't miss. When we got to the entrance to Southern Avenue, the area was so crowded with troops that it was some time before we got into it. It was marvellous how each section kept together in such a mix-up. We were all carrying so much it was like a free-fight to move at all. Over and above our ordinary equipment, rifle and bayonet, and ammunition in our pouches, I had a khaki bandolier full of .303, six loaded Lewis gun magazines – carried in a horse's nosebag – because we hadn't enough proper containers available, two Mills bombs, and a pick with the shaft stuck down my back behind my haversack, and we were called the Light Infantry! But most ironical of all was the dirty tricks our clumsy bad fitting 'tin-hats' played us. If the chin-strap wasn't trying to strangle us, the 'soup-basin' was falling over our eyes to blind us. Steel helmets always got more curses than blessings from us. After many stops and much struggling, falling down and getting caught in signallers' telephone wires, we reached our assembly trench at about 4.00 am Saturday, 1 July.

Sergeant Charles Moss, 18th Durham Light Infantry

Overleaf:
Deep inside the German trenches of the Schwaben Redoubt during intense fighting. Photograph taken by Colonel R.D. Perceval-Maxwell.

3 Awed and Shocked

'He told me that he had been shot through the middle of the back and that the bullet had emerged through his left ear. We were lying together, he wondering whether we would finish up in the same hospital. In this, I could not help feeling that he was being rather optimistic.'

Private Henry Russell, 1/5th London Regiment (London Rifle Brigade)

I left Marieux Chateau at about two o'clock in the morning of 1 July to return to my command post. I had got a lift as far as the area of the division behind the trench system. Then the trouble began. Every single yard of the communication trenches up to the front line was completely impassable and the confusion was indescribable. Reinforcement troops and working parties with materials and ammunition were trying to make their way forward against a stream of troops coming out of the line, including stretcher-bearers with casualties, walking wounded and exhausted troops. To make matters worse, many sections of these communication trenches had been destroyed by heavy artillery fire from the German lines, and this was unceasingly active. The noise was deafening and without intermission. I was therefore forced to make my way at ground level if I was to have any chance of getting into my observation post in time to see the attack go in. In the pitch dark and with only a small torch I found it impossible to move any faster than an infuriatingly slow pace, and the thick churned-up mud got halfway up my puttees. Somewhere during the journey I made a bad start to the day, for a German shell burst near enough to me to throw me to the ground and drive a jagged piece of shell casing into the palm of my right hand. I put on a first field dressing and later was too involved in the battle to do any more about it.

Second Lieutenant Frederick Roe, 1/6th Gloucestershire Regiment

Opposite: *German prisoners hurry from the Schwaben Redoubt and into British lines. This extraordinarily rare image was taken by Lance Corporal George Hackney.*

Private Edward
Higson, 16th
Manchester
Regiment

About midnight we entered the assembly or 'jumping-off' trench, situated between Maricourt and Carnoy; hot tea and rum awaited us, then bombs and extra ammunition were issued out. All these preparations were carried out without noise, no lights were shown, everybody knew his place and got to it quickly and quietly; every few yards along the trench were ladders, while on top across the trench there were bridges for the light artillery to follow us up. When all was ready we lay down waiting for the dawn.

It seemed years before the first ray of light appeared in the Heavens, but gradually the light grew stronger showing up the long line of khaki-clad boys. Their faces looked stern and strong and the way they gripped their rifles told how eager they were to be off. We were to be the third wave to go over; in the first wave were the Liverpool Pals, the second were the Bedfords.

At 6.00 am our artillery fire increased; hundreds of guns were firing as quickly as they could be loaded; the noise was so intense that one could not hear what the man next to you was saying. Suddenly a hedge, a very innocent looking hedge just behind the assembly trench, fell down and revealed to our gaze a long line of guns, wheel to wheel. These all opened fire at once and to this day I wonder why the drums of our ears were not burst open.

It had seemed impossible for the guns to fire any harder but now they opened up a final hurricane bombardment on the enemy trenches. Then, as a final precursor of the infantry assault, a number of mines were detonated under the German lines from Carnoy in the south to Beaumont Hamel in the north. Each was packed with tons of ammonal which when blown would take out significant enemy strongpoints to aid the British attack. At La Boisselle, two huge mines, 'Y Sap' and 'Lochnagar', were to be blown on either side of the Albert–Bapaume Road, under the enemy lines and the effect was expected to be devastating. The preparation had been meticulous.

Captain Stanley
Bullock, 179
Tunnelling
Company, Royal
Engineers

The ammonal was in tins, each weighing about 50 lbs., and fatigue parties were detailed off each night for about a week to carry this explosive from Bécourt Chateau up to the [Lochnagar] mine. Each man carried one tin, and I or one of the other Tunnelling Officers had always to meet these parties in order to see that the work was duly carried out and at the same time guide them through the trenches. As may be imagined, this was not a task particularly enjoyed by those concerned, as not only was it very heavy work as the trenches at the time were wet and greasy, but the job of carrying explosive about with the likelihood of shells dropping amongst you was not a particularly desirable one. By the time the infantry had been on this work for two or three nights the general impression amongst them was that they were getting up enough explosive to blow Fritz back to Berlin.

At 6.20 the guns opened, and I made my way to Observation Post with a telephonist. I passed through a ruined village on my way – not a soul to be seen – streets empty, billets cleared. At the OP I found H. of D/241 who was also observing for counter-attacks.

The bombardment roar was terrific. The ear-splitting bark of the 18-pounders, the cough of the howitzers, the boom of the heavy guns, swelled into a jerky roar that was flung from horizon to horizon, as thunder is tossed from mountain to mountain. It was wonderful music – the mightiest I have ever heard. It seemed to throb, throb into our very veins, beating up and down and yet never quite reaching a climax, but always keeping one's nerves on the thrill. And then at last, ten minutes before zero, the guns opened their lungs. The climax had been reached. One felt inclined to laugh with the fierce exhilaration of it. After all, it was our voice, the voice of a whole empire at war. At zero I looked out of the OP. The din had quietened a little. What I saw made me cry out, so that the others, telephonists and all, ran up to me. It was smoke and gas. For a mile stretching away from me, the trench was belching forth dense columns of white, greenish, and orange smoke. It rose curling and twisting, blotting everything from view, and then swept, a solid rampart, over the German lines. For more than an hour this continued, and I could see nothing. Sometimes the smoke was streaked with a scarlet star as a shell burst among it, and sometimes a smoke candle would be hurled high into the air, spluttering and making a cloud of its own far above the rest. It seemed impossible that men could withstand this awful onslaught – even if it were only smoke. And yet a machine gun played steadily all the time from the German front line. What fighters they are!

Second Lieutenant Adrian Stephen, D Battery, 1/4th South Midland Brigade, Royal Field Artillery

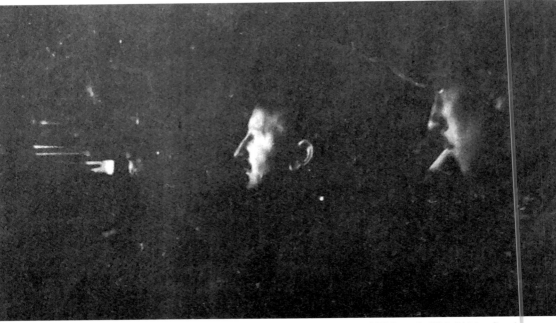

Captain Cowan and Lieutenant Geoffrey Huskisson, 153 Brigade, 36th Division, Royal Field Artillery, peer out of an observation post.

Second
Lieutenant
Frederick
Roe 1/6th
Gloucestershire
Regiment

The small telescope we had in our observation post enabled us to watch closely the German activities up the hill behind their front line as far as Serre, which stood out menacingly and very clearly on the skyline mot more than 1,200 yards away from our post. ... My field glasses enabled me to see very clearly indeed German activities a mile away. With telescope and glasses combined we found that we could see most clearly all the movements of the battle both on our front and on our northern front. ... My post was not more than a couple of hundred yards west and a little to the north of Matthew Copse, which meant that, as intended, I was as nearly as possible in the mid area of the whole of the 31st Division front. ...

After the attack had gone in, the artillery support was continuous ... the 18-pounders were brought up as close to the trench system as possible. The line of fire of one of these batteries was directly over the roof of my dugout which was in the support line only a few yards in front of the battery position. The guns were so close that on every occasion when a salvo went over, my carefully prepared safety roof on the dugout took off for a few inches. As it settled down again the corrugated iron sheets clattered back into place with the most infernal din imaginable, so that every word we spoke to each other had to be shouted as loudly as possible.

The birds were singing in the copses around. It was a beautiful day, beautiful. We had this morning chorus and then it all happened, just like a flash. We were stood there waiting, ready for the officer to blow his whistle, and our barrage lifted and then bang! a great big mine went up on the right-hand side. We saw it going sky-high, one huge mass of soil. It shouldn't have gone up till we were on the top because it alerted the Germans and they were up waiting for us and when we attacked they cut us to ribbons, totally ripped us to pieces.

Private Frank Lindley, 14th York and Lancaster Regiment (2nd Barnsley Pals)

I was in the first wave on the extreme left. We scrambled onto the fire step and then on the top, when I glanced over. They were all going on our right. There was nothing on our left. There was no cheering, we just ambled across, you hadn't a thought; you were so addled with the noise. Second Lieutenant Hirst was near to me, almost touching. He had just got wed before we came away, and was a grand chap, but it wasn't long before he got his head knocked off.

Out of the corner of your eye you could see the boys going down but there was no going back, they had what we called 'whippers-in' with revolvers and they could shoot you if anybody came back, so we moved forward as best we could, it was implanted in our heads. You could hear the bullets whistling past and our lads were going down, flop, flop, flop in their waves, just as though they'd all gone to sleep. As I laid flat out there in no-man's-land, up on top jumped one of our whippers-in with revolver ready, and we were all laid out in shell holes, and he said, 'Come on, come on.' He hadn't gone 2 yards before he went up in the air, riddled.

We had to dodge from shell hole to shell hole to try and get through. All their wire was piled up in great coils, tremendous, and there was just the odd gap. As soon as you made for that gap it was R-R-R-R-R, all you could do was dive in a shell hole, and the ground was pitted with shell

The explosion of the Hawthorn Redoubt mine, Beaumont Hamel, ten minutes before the men went over the top.

holes because our guns had tried to bust all their wire up. Bullets were like a swarm of bees round you, you could almost feel them plucking at your clothes. Them that made for the gaps in their wire were all piled up where the machine guns just laid them out. It was pure murder so we tried picking the Jerries off because they were on the trench top, some of them, cheering their mates on while our lads on the wire were hanging like rags. Some I recognized, 'That's so and so,' I thought, but one burst of their big machine guns and they were in bits. Arms and legs were flying all over.

I didn't know anybody in the shell holes I got in. We were all mixed up. There was no conversation, it was self-preservation, dive in and risk what you got. The final shell hole we got in was the finish, a whiz-bang came over us and split. I never heard it coming. Shrapnel went right through my thigh and took my trousers in with it. I looked down and there was blood running freely.

The road from Auchonvillers to Beaumont Hamel ran up a shallow trough, from which the ground rose on the south to Hawthorn Ridge on the crest of which the big mine was blown and on the north to another more distant crest, on which was situated the [ridge] redoubt. Halfway across no-man's-land (here about 400 yards wide) a sunken lane ran due north from the road, gradually flattening out to ground level on the northern ridge. Halfway again between this and the German line lay a small bank or linchet, giving some shelter from enemy fire. Apart from these features, no-man's-land was open and bare of cover.

Control of no-man's-land rested and had rested for some time with us and in the few days before the attack the REs had pierced a tunnel a few feet below ground from our front line to the sunken lane, opening up the exit on the last night. Unfortunately this exit came out a few yards too far north of a point where it was exposed to enemy fire in part, so that one had to use it on hands and knees. Its purpose was to serve as a sort of covered communication trench for the sunken lane. Through this tunnel our two front companies B and A were passed to the lane, which was to be the jumping-off line for the first wave.

The second wave (C & D) were to start from the old front line, the 10 per cent [reserve] under the second in command Major Utterson still holding the second line. The mood of all was astonishingly high and confidence universal.

A few minutes after the mine went up and we had seen the battalion on our right, the Royal Fusiliers, start off across no-man's-land, the first wave went forward. The east bank of the lane lay in a slight dip which concealed men getting out of it from the enemy view and fire, but two steps brought them into exposure and the bulk of the first wave got no further than the edge of this dip where they were swept away in swathes, and those who were still alive crawled or were dragged down into the lane which was now full of wounded. A party of about fifty men, with two officers, got as far as

Lieutenant Eric Sheppard, 1st Lancashire Fusiliers

the linchet, where they stayed till night gave them a chance to rejoin the unit in safety: from where they were they could not even see the enemy front, and would have been quite unable to defend themselves against a counter-attack. No men worth mentioning ever reached the enemy wire as far as I know. Meanwhile none of the second wave had got even as far as the lane, and when Colonel Maguire, the CO, sent me out to bring forward any I could find, I saw no one moving at all, and was hit in the head while still searching round.

Sergeant Charles Moss, 18th Durham Light Infantry

I wanted to see how our attack was going so I moved some of the chalk on the front of the trench in such a way that I would be protected from German sniper fire and took a good look at the German line in front of me. But all I could see was fountains of chalk and smoke sent up by our artillery barrage. It was like watching heavy seas rolling and roaring onto Hendon beaches I had seen the last time home during winter storms.

While I was watching I saw the barrage lift and storm further back over the third German line. As it got clear of one of the German trenches, out on top came scrambling a German machine gun team. They fixed their gun in front of their parapet and opened out a slow and deadly fire on our front. The gunners were without their tunics and worked their gun in their shirtsleeves in quite a different manner to their usual short and sharp bursts; their fire was so slow that every shot seemed to have a definite aim. Except for that gun team and the 'Mad Major', there wasn't another soldier in British Khaki or German Grey to be seen.

The 'Mad Major' was the name we have given to a British airman who flew low over the German trenches every morning, and there he was as mad as ever this morning.

Just as I spotted the German machine gunners come into action we got word to move to our 'jumping-off' trench to be ready to go over the top. We had to cross a communication trench to get there and as I got into this trench I nearly bumped into a soldier who seemed to be carrying a big piece of raw meat resting on his left arm, he was doing a sort of crying whimper and saying, 'Why have they done this to me? I never did them any harm.' Then I realized that it was the remains of his right forearm.

The 18th Durham Light infantry … initially made some progress but in spite of some claims that they succeeded in getting well on towards their brigade's Objective One, there is no established report that they did this. I certainly did not see any progress in that direction: if they did, no survivors ever got back to our lines to substantiate the rumours. … Only a very few men in small groups were even able to cross no-man's-land. I watched them shot down along a ragged line even before they got to our own barbed wire. I saw bodies lying entangled in its apron. Between me and the skyline of Serre the sun shining on the tin triangles fastened to the men's backs was a poignant and unforgettable witness of the failure of the attempt. …

I shall never forget the bewildering chaos around me. What was left of four battalions (93rd Brigade) was spread over no-man's-land, the mobile, the dying and the dead. They lay thickest of all on and behind our own wire and crowded impossible of extraction in what was left of completely flattened trenches. Stretcher-bearers were heroically bringing out as many badly wounded men as possible in what looked to me like a never-ending queue to the only regimental aid post I could see – that of the 18th Durhams.

Second Lieutenant Frederick Roe, 1/6th Gloucestershire Regiment

A couple of miles to the south, the men of the 36th Ulster Division were ready and keen to get going. They would attack the Schwaben Redoubt, a particularly strong position in the Germans' first defensive line. The Ulstermen were in Thiepval Wood, the trees helping to conceal their presence in the assembly trenches. In anticipation of a difficult task, leading battalions exited the wood just prior to 7.30, lying down in no-man's-land. These men would rush the enemy trenches, not waiting to form up in serried lines.

The air is rent with deafening thunder; never has such man-made noise been heard before! The hour has struck! 7.30 am has arrived. The first wave goes over. … We wait. Instantly the enemy replies, putting down a counter-barrage which misses us by inches. Thanks to the steep slope of Speyside we are immune. That half hour is the worst on record for thoughts and forebodings, so we sing, but it is difficult to keep in tune or rhythm

Lieutenant Colonel Frank Crozier, 9th Battalion Royal Irish Rifles

Artillery shells hammer the enemy's trenches on the Schwaben Redoubt.

on account of the noise. At last *our* minute, *our own* minute arrives. I get up from the ground and whistle. The others rise. We move off, with steady pace. As we pass Gordon Castle we pick up coils of wire and iron posts. I feel sure in my innermost thoughts these things will never be carried all the way to the final objective; however, even if they get halfway it will be a help. Then I glance to the right through a gap in the trees. I see the 10th Rifles plodding on and then my eyes are riveted on a sight I shall never see again … I see rows upon rows of British soldiers lying dead, dying or wounded, in no-man's-land. Here and there I see an officer urging on his followers. Occasionally I can see the hands thrown up and then a body flops to the ground.

Lieutenant Colonel Francis Bowen, commanding 14th Royal Irish Rifles

7.30 am: Zero. 14th R. Irish Rifles moved off to the attack in support of 10th R. Inni Fus at the same time our barrage lifts.

7.45 am: First Hun prisoners arrive, going like hell. Rec'd report from C Sergt Major R. that he had reached the sunken road afterwards known as the bloody lane.

8.10 am: Message from Willis. 'We are consolidating in front of "B" line, C and D are consolidating B line itself. Boys behaved splendidly. S Willis' (by runner). More Hun prisoners running through.

8.45 am: [German] Shoulder straps have Nos. 55, 8 & 135, these I sent
to Brigade. Battle Hd Qrs taking it in the neck & 5.9s. 107th
Brigade gone through to D Line.

The bursting shells and smoke make visibility poor, but I see enough to
convince me Thiepval village is still held, for it is now 8.00 am and by
7.45 it should have fallen to allow of our passage forward on its flank. My
upper lip is stiff, my jaws are set. We proceed. Again I look southward
from a different angle and perceive heaped-up masses of British corpses
suspended on the German wire in front of the Thiepval stronghold,
while live men rush forward in orderly procession to swell the weight of
numbers in the spider's web. ...

 My adjutant, close behind me, tells me I am 50 yards in front of the
head of the column. I slacken my pace and they close up behind me. 'Now
for it,' I say to Hine. My blood is up and I am literally seeing red. Still the
shells burst at the head of Elgin, plomp, plomp – it is 'good-bye', I think, as
there is no way round. 'This way to eternity,' shouts a wag behind. Thirty
yards ahead, still a shell – plomp – a splinter flies past my shoulder, and
embeds itself in the leg of a leading man behind. He falls and crawls out of
the way; nothing must stop the forward march of the column.

*Lieutenant
Colonel Frank
Crozier, 9th
Battalion Royal
Irish Rifles*

Crozier's men left the relative sanctuary of Thipeval Wood and made a dash across
no-man's-land to a sunken lane.

This spirited dash across no-man's-land, carried out as if on parade, has
cost us some fifty dead and seventy wounded. The dead no longer count.
War has no use for dead men. With luck they will be buried later; the
wounded try to crawl back to our lines. Some are hit again in doing so,
but the majority lie out all day, sun-baked, parched, uncared for, often
delirious and at any rate in great pain. My immediate duty is to look after
the situation and not bother about wounded men. ...

 All at once there is a shout. Someone seizes a Lewis gun. 'The Germans
are on us' goes round like wildfire. I see an advancing crowd of field grey.
Fire is opened at 600 yards' range. The enemy fall like grass before the

*Lieutenant
Colonel Frank
Crozier, 9th
Battalion Royal
Irish Rifles*

Germans surrendering in the background while in the foreground a member of the 36th (Ulster) Division lies wounded or dead.

scythe. 'Damned ____' shouts an officer, 'give them hell.' I look through my glasses. 'Good heavens,' I shout, 'those men are prisoners surrendering, and some of our own wounded men are escorting them! Cease fire, cease fire, for God's sake,' I command. The fire ripples on for a time. The target is too good to lose. 'After all, they are only Germans,' I hear a youngster say. But I get the upper hand at last – all is now quiet – for a few moments. The tedium of the battle continues.

Second Lieutenant Frederick Roe, 1/6th Gloucestershire Regiment

How do men conduct themselves at such a time, whether wounded or unwounded? I saw a great many who had become uncontrollable, shouting loudly and swearing violently. A few wept with the excitement. Others were desperately benumbed and quiet at the sight of such awful carnage. I saw quite a number of men with their lips moving soundlessly in some sort of prayer. … If I try to think back as to how I myself behaved, I can only remember an acute awareness of all that was going on, down to the smallest detail, and a feeling of overwhelming tiredness and brain-numbness which had to be fought against the whole time. Perhaps worst of all was the knowledge that I was entirely on my own: no appreciation of the general progress of the battle was at all possible and yet I was terribly concerned that I must do what I had been set to do in spite of all the adverse circumstances …

Two sights from this hour also cling to my memory. I saw through my glasses a shell explode close to a recumbent soldier. It shot him into the air like an arrow and apparently all in one piece. As the human missile slowed down at the top of its trajectory it turned very slowly into a horizontal position high up in the air and seemed to stay quite still for what seemed like an eternity of time. It then suddenly came hurtling down to the ground head first and did not move again. Sometime later in the afternoon I saw through my glasses a soldier sitting up in a shallow crater in no-man's-land and tearing up his shirt to make himself some bandaging. To my horror on the next morning, I saw that he was still sitting up in the shell crater.

9.30 am: Direct hit on Battn Hd Qrs, all the ruddy lights gone.
9.33 am: Lt C. reports that our shells are falling short on his sector (expect it is Hun enfilade fire [from] Beaucourt & Thiepval).
9.40 am: A message thru to say that the 12th Div is badly held up on our right.
9.40 am: Sent orders for more ammunition to be moved up.
10.30 am: Young Lack arrives back with twenty-five prisoners & a Hun helmet. He found a lot of Boches in a D[ug] O[ut] & as they came out he potted them as one would shoot ferreted rabbits. Hun got tired of this & survivors surrendered.
10.35 am: Asked Brigade for reinforcements.
10.35 am: Lt Wedgewood killed. Boche barrage still down on the edge of the wood.

Lieutenant Colonel Francis Bowen, 14th Royal Irish Rifles

Many battalions would lose more than three-quarters of their strength in the assault, but few would be as hard hit as the 8th King's Own Yorkshire Light Infantry. Attacking up a steep slope they were cut down, the wounded being picked off by snipers. The battalion suffered 539 casualties.

Sergeant Walter
Popple, 8th King's
Own Yorkshire
Light Infantry

1 July promised to be a beautiful day. The sun had risen high in the sky and we could hear the birds singing. I stood on the fire step and scanned the scene. Jerry had been pounded for a week and would be decimated. What few were left would not be able to offer any real resistance. I recall wondering if that was true as a shell burst in the trench 40 yards away, and an officer and three men were killed outright.

A loud blast on a whistle and the first wave began the attack, as the barrage moved forward. Then it was time for my platoon to go. A line had been cut in the barbed wire the night before, through which to advance, but as I did so I could scarcely believe my eyes. The first three lines were being mown down. I walked forward in a daze. Near the crest of the slope, I saw the reason for the carnage: Jerry had manned every single post. As I neared the enemy wire, I felt a sharp thud accompanied by a pain in my chest and I fell.

Running footsteps to my rear seemed to bring me back to reality. Then came the sound of a falling body, and with it the certain knowledge that a sniper was about. A German was firing from an advanced post, picking off anyone he saw, including the wounded. As I glanced upwards, he saw me. He fired, a bullet taking the heel off my boot. My rifle was somewhere around but my shoulder was so stiff that I couldn't handle it. Then there were the two grenades in my tunic pockets but I couldn't throw them that distance. All these thoughts flashed through my mind with the ugly realization that any pot shots might easily set off the grenades.

I came to the terrible decision that it was better to get it over with quickly and die, rather than be picked off piece by piece, so I raised my head and pushed myself upwards, almost kneeling to look straight down the muzzle of his rifle. A sharp crack, and my helmet flew off and my neck stiffened. I sank to the ground. Utter silence. At first there was a buzzing sensation in my head and then sharp piercing darts of pain. Had I been killed as I first thought? I dared not lift my head and there I remained through the heat of the day, wondering if in fact part of my head had been blown away.

Private Henry Russell had made his own preparations for going over the top. He had bought a large bottle of Worcester sauce from an advanced NAAFI, emptied the contents and filled the bottle to the brim with rum. A sip would help to stiffen his resolve or it could help deaden the pain should he be injured. That morning, 1 July, he waited with his comrades while a heavy final bombardment was laid on the German trenches, followed by a smokescreen to hide their advance. Going over the top, Russell saw comrades fall until few men appeared to be left.

I found myself in the company of an officer, Lieutenant Wallace. We dived into a flat shallow hole made by our guns, apparently both wanting to decide what we should now do. Lieutenant Wallace asked me whether I thought we should attempt to go on or remain there for the time being and, thinking the position over very rapidly, I came to the conclusion and told him that going on would, in my opinion, be suicidal, and that the best thing we could do would be to stay there and attempt to pick off any Germans who might expose themselves. We were not very clear as to how we were situated, but had a fairly shrewd idea that we were, in fact, surrounded. Lying on the ground, it was quite impossible to get any idea of our position. Lieutenant Wallace said, however, that we had been ordered to go on at all costs and that we must comply with this order. At this, he stood up and within a few seconds dropped down riddled with bullets. This left me with the same problem and, having observed his action, I felt that I must do the same. I, therefore, stood up and was immediately hit by two bullets and dropped down. Observing the wounds later, I realized that one had been made from behind and one from in front.

I had thought that a man who could stand up and knowingly face practically certain death in these circumstances must be very brave. I found out that bravery hardly came into it. Once the decision was made to stand up I had no further fear. I was not bothered at all even though I believed that I would be dead within seconds and would be rotting on the ground, food for the rats next day. I did not even feel appreciably the bullets going through and this was to me something extraordinary.

Private Henry Russell, 1/5th London Regiment (London Rifle Brigade)

Henry Russell crawled into a shell hole, where he met a wounded comrade.

Private Henry
Russell, 1/5th
London
Regiment
(London Rifle
Brigade)

He told me that he had been shot through the middle of the back and that the bullet had emerged through his left ear. We were lying together, he wondering whether we would finish up in the same hospital. In this, I could not help feeling that he was being rather optimistic. I did not expect that we could survive the day and when, a little later, after the failure of our attack, a heavy barrage of shellfire fell upon us, I was of the opinion that the situation was absolutely hopeless so far as we individuals were concerned. ...

We had not long to wait before a shell burst on the edge of our hole; it killed my colleague and injured me in such a way that I was virtually emasculated. The barrage continued for some time until I considered the situation was hopeless, and that even if a miracle happened and I did, in fact, get away, I would not be fit for anything in this world. I therefore decided to kill myself. To this end, I was under the impression that I had three choices. The first was to explode a Mills bomb which I was carrying in my pocket and kill myself in this way. This seemed to be a silly procedure because it would only be doing what the Germans were already attempting to do. The second was to take a very large dose of morphine tablets which I believed to be in my pocket. Some time before, I had buried a doctor killed in action and, on going through his belongings, I had found a tube containing a considerable number of morphine tablets. I intended to take all these but when I felt in my breast pocket, I found that they were no longer there and somehow or other I had lost them.

The third course was one which came to my mind as a result of a talk given to us by the Medical Officer before going into action. He said that, if wounded and bleeding, we should never take intoxicants, as the result would almost certainly be fatal. I, therefore, managed to get hold of the bottle of rum which I had put in my haversack, and I drank the lot hoping that it would result in my death. In fact, it did me no harm at all. It probably made me slightly merry and bright and rather stupefied. It also probably caused me to drop off to sleep, though I am not aware of this. However, I came to the conclusion, when I had recovered my senses, that, in spite of my condition (my left arm being torn and the bone shattered, my left thigh damaged, my right leg wounded and strips of flesh hanging down from my abdomen) it was still worthwhile making a serious effort to save myself.

Not every man in every battalion went over the top. A reserve was kept out of action to form the nucleus of a 'new' battalion should heavy casualties result from the opening attack. For those kept back from the first spasm of fighting, any private feelings of relief or disappointment were as nothing compared to the anxiety and nervous tension felt for mates in no-man's-land. Second Lieutenant William Dyson watched as he and his men mooched about, uncertain what to do.

The more energetic and restless arose and strolled aimlessly about, agitated for breakfast and played gramophones. Personally I lay in my valise and wondered at the strange incongruity of it all, sleeping at intervals. After a time I arose and shaved under difficulties. ... After a still longer time breakfast arrived. We made it last as long as we could – Army biscuits being the only substitute for bread, we did this fairly successfully – eggs also being plentiful. After breakfast rest awhile, walk about the orchards listening to the guns and the birds. Soon a stream of traffic begins to rumble down the road – ambulances. Rumours begin to fly about. We select the worst and believe them after the pig-headed manner of men.

We are then told we have been occupying the wrong huts and trundle along to some others 500 yards down the road. Opposite there is an iron crucifix and a little chapel which is temporarily converted into a signal station. From time to time an aeroplane buzzes over flying very low, wheels round, flies over again and drops a little coloured streamer into the blue. All eyes follow it to the ground. The signal orderlies run to fetch it and bring in the message. All through the morning – all the afternoon we watched anxiously for the messages to drop – odd disconnected messages they seemed, though on thinking the thing over afterwards one is rather struck with the amount of information we did get from the RFC. All the while ambulances streamed down the road and here and there we saw a face we knew. Some smoked their cigarettes cheerily enough, pleased at the thought of 'Blighty' before many hours were passed, – others were too low to think of anything but their wounds. Now and again long trains of ammunition limbers rumbled past towards the battle, and mule ambulances galloped back for another load.

Second Lieutenant William Dyson, 1/16th London Regiment

Second
Lieutenant
Adrian Stephen,
D Battery, 1/4th
South Midland
Brigade, Royal
Field Artillery

Somewhere to the right of that smoke the Infantry were advancing. I could see nothing. Reports and rumours came dancing down the wires.

'Our Infantry have taken the front line without resistance.'

'Prisoners are coming in.'

'Enemy giving themselves up in hundreds.'

'Infantry have crossed the Serre Ridge.'

'Beaumont Hamel is ours.'

'More prisoners reported.'

This continued until 11.30, when the smoke cleared, and I looked out upon the invisible battle! Far as I could see not a soldier could be seen, not a movement of any sort. Could it be that we held those trenches? Had we captured Serre? Once the village had been hidden by thick trees and hedges, now it stood bare and shattered, the trees leafless, as though a comb had been dragged through them.

The Germans were shelling their own trenches, that was all the sign of change I noticed. I tried to observe while F. ranged on hostile batteries, but the smoke was too confusing, and flying pieces and bullets made it a difficult matter. In the afternoon the Germans launched a counter-attack immediately opposite our OP, but unfortunately invisible to us. Their shelling was heavy and accurate. Our OP swayed perilously, our wires were cut in four places, within 100 yards of the OP; a linesman of D/241 mended them, and I have mentioned him for distinction. We sat in the dugout waiting and calculating. ...

I met an Infantry officer. He was grey in the face and had not shaved. 'Well,' he said, 'what do you think of it?'

'Seems all right.'

'Um, we got to their third line and were driven back; we are barely holding our own front line – we're – we're wiped out – General's a broken man.'

'But Gommecourt?'

'Lost.'

'Another Loos,' I said.

'Looks it.' He turned away.

I felt tired suddenly. The few yards home were miles. The world was full of stretchers and white faces, and fools who gibbered about the great advance.

But news from elsewhere was more cheery; down south we were doing well, and the French also, and our little battle here was only one pebble in the mosaic. What did it matter? We ourselves had been lucky; three men slightly [wounded] and one sergeant – a good fellow. Later on we would join in the great advance.

'Down south' or half-a-dozen miles as the crow flies, the troops were doing better, albeit not without heavy casualties. Near the village of Montauban, British troops were advancing successfully.

It was our job to capture the village of Montauban and at 7.25 am we got out of our trench and quickly formed up in sections, one man behind the other, each section 25 yards apart. Our rifles were slung on our shoulders, for the distance was 2,000 yards to our objective. At a given signal off we started, just as if we were doing a drill exhibition in England, each section keeping close together, the whole dressing by the centre, keeping just about 50 yards behind our creeping barrage. We scrambled over our old trenches, reached the German second, then the third line, wounded men of the other two waves shouting out to us 'Good luck, Manchesters'. Suddenly we began to notice the enemy artillery fire increasing; shells began to come over thick and fast. We were also being swept with

Private Edward Higson, 16th Manchester Regiment

About 3.30 pm: men of the 7th Queen's (Royal West Surrey Regiment) and 7th Buffs (East Kent Regiment) take cover along a road, on the way to their objective, Montauban Alley.

machine-gun fire from the left. Our fellows were falling right and left, the noise of our guns and the firing of the enemy's made it impossible to hear orders, but we looked to our captain. He was holding up his hand for a halt; our hearts were filled with anxious fears that we had failed. But no – we were only waiting until the unit on our left, which had been held up by barbed wire, got over the obstacle and cleared away the Germans who were hampering us on that side.

We waited twenty minutes and then started again, all the time our wounded comrades were calling out for help and begging for drinks. Much as our hearts inclined towards them we had to push on and leave the wounded to the RAMC, who were coming on later.

Lieutenant Anthony Nash, 16th Manchester Regiment

At 8.10 am came the news of French successes on our right and the Colonel told me to tell the troops. I went slowly up the line shouting at the top of my voice, 'The French have taken Hardecourt and Faviere Wood; Germans are surrendering along the line.' Only the two or three men nearest me in each spot could hear on account of the gunfire, but the news spread from man to man until such a cheer went up as drowned for the moment even the hideous row of the guns. …

At 8.20 am we got out of our assembly trenches and the troops lay down ready to move off sharply to time. By now we were being very heavily shelled and some of the men climbed out of the trench only to slide back at once – dead. I was standing by the Colonel, counting the minutes on my wristwatch: 8.27 – 8.28 – 8.29 – each minute an eternity of waiting – 8.30 and off we went.

We had to work most carefully to a timetable. We were to follow a creeping barrage put down by our own guns, and to press forward too fast would be just as fatal to our success. Our objective was Montauban and we had 3,000 yards to go before reaching it.

Private Edward Higson, 16th Manchester Regiment

When we reached to within 100 yards of the village, our artillery barrage lifted as we unslung our rifles and charged the waiting Germans. They fired at us until we got quite close up to them and then the row of steel got too much for them and scrambling out of their trenches they ran for it. Many of them did not run far, for the aim of our boys was splendid. Still

we had further to go to reach our objective, Montauban Alley, on the far side of the village. It was there that many of the running Germans had taken cover and we met with strong opposition, one team of machine gunners firing point-blank at us until we overpowered them. With one of these gunners I had my first real bit of bayonet exercise and his neck suffered somewhat in consequence. Eventually we got into Montauban Alley and my bombing section were detailed to go up the trench to the right for 200 yards, clearing the enemy out as we went.

About 6.00 pm and the objective achieved, the men of the 7th Queen's reached Montauban Alley, but only after heavy casualties.

There were only six of us so it was rather a thrilling job. We only got about 150 yards, for there we came up against a very strong party of Germans, who were successful in holding us up, but could not drive us back again. We held on there for an hour, when reinforcements came up and helped us to clear out the enemy.

A little later a sergeant and myself discovered a trench running underneath a road and being curious went to investigate. No sooner had we got within a few yards of the tunnel than we were fired upon. There were five Germans in the tunnel. The sergeant and I scrambled out on top, he going to one end of the tunnel and I to the other, then being of a kindly nature presented the inmates with a couple of bombs. There were two survivors, whom we shot as they came out, but before they were shot they accounted for the poor sergeant.

Through the fire we advanced in little columns in file, about a dozen men in each; no rubbing of shoulders for company and so presenting a good target for the enemy. We had to cross our front line trenches and those of the Germans, and their support lines and countless communication

Lieutenant Anthony Nash, 16th Manchester Regiment

trenches. These trenches were full of dead and wounded, ours and the Germans'. Small isolated parties of the enemy remained active and we had to clear a few machine-gun nests, German medical officers and our own were attending to the wounded. To cross the trenches each section carried a trench ladder which could be laid as a bridge from side to side.

Over these ladders the little columns would file, forming up again as they got across. There was no confusion, no hurry or bustle. On we went at a steady walking pace while the German barrage fire punished us severely. Occasionally a shell would drop right in the midst of one of our columns, totally obliterating it.

My own little party consisted of Pennington, Kelly, Stevens, Palmer, Thompson, Hibbert, Blears, Smith and Carroll. When any shell came uncomfortably close I shouted, 'Steady, men, steady,' as one would speak to children crossing the road, and steady they were. I felt quite curiously detached as if I were merely a spectator. My heart thumped a bit sometimes. … In sheer bravado I lit a cigarette, conscious of a hand that did not shake.

It was cruelly hard for men to see their best pals drop mortally wounded and not be able to stop and succour them, but our orders were of the strictest. No man was to check for any reason, save sheer inability to go on, so steadily onward we went, cries of comrades disturbing us more than the German messengers of death. …

As we approached Train Alley, I took a snapshot of our men approaching it and later I took a photograph of Montauban itself as we were advancing on it. I had carried for long a small VPK camera in my hip pocket. The snaps are not very good as I could not ask the troops to stand still and look pleasant!

We left poor Horley in Train Alley, his shoulder smashed by a bullet and cursing horribly because he could no longer go on. …

Now we swept up the last long slope into the village. We had arrived so far without undue exhaustion and into Montauban we poured, breaking down all resistance. Hardly one brick had been left upon another. … By 10.30 am our troops had reached Montauban Alley which was beyond the village and was our furthest objective.

Our orders were to consolidate and hold this trench with three companies, thereby defending the village against any counter-attack, whilst a fourth company remained in reserve along the northern perimeter of the village. Battalion Headquarters were established in Montauban and got into touch with Brigade HQ by means of visual signalling.

In Montauban were many dugouts containing equipment and stores. In one dugout we found forty Germans whilst in another we surprised a German artillery general having breakfast with his Staff!

We also captured a battery of field guns, and Aldous and Price chalked the name of the battalion on the barrels. I collected many very valuable maps and documents and orderly room papers and sent them back without delay. By 11.30 am my own job was done and I went along to Battalion Headquarters to report. By this time the reaction had set in, and I was feeling rather exhausted and sick. However, I had no time for reactions as Sotham told me that all A Company's officers had been knocked out during the advance and the Colonel wanted me to go up to Montauban Alley and take charge. I found there all that was left of A, B, and C companies, about 250 in all, and Johnson, commanding C Company, the only officer. Johnson decided to take the right of the line and I took the left. The men were terribly tired, and suffering from the same reaction that I had experienced momentarily, the inevitable reaction which follows mental exaltation, hard fighting and bodily fatigue. ...

It was vitally necessary to set to work at once and convert the old German communication trench into a fire trench for our own defence. In its present state, it was very deep; the men could not see over the top, and of course there was no parapet. For one short hour we should be free of shelling as the German artillery would not open fire on the village while there was any doubt as to their own people being still in occupation. ...

The men worked like Trojans and cut fire steps and platforms and reversed the parapet of the trench, until at last we had made it capable of defence. After their work they felt better and set to cleaning their rifles and ammunition. ...

The troops were tired out; they had not slept at all during the night and had fought hard in the morning. At noon the German guns started to shell us like blazes, and put down a barrage on the ground intervening between Montauban Alley, which we were holding, and the village itself. … All the telephone wires we had run out were destroyed by shellfire as quickly as we had put them out, and after eight wiresmen had been killed in succession trying to repair the line, I abandoned my attempt to communicate with Headquarters other than by dispatch runners. …

At 1.00 pm Johnson came along to say that he had found an old German dugout which he intended to use as Company Headquarters for himself. I preferred to establish my headquarters in the open trench, as being less likely to be known to the German artillery. His dugout was a long shelter with many compartments; one of these was full of wounded and another contained a carpenter's bench.

Private Sydney Fuller had watched the French attacking near Maricourt, their bayonets glistening in the sunlight. Then the Germans had begun shelling the British lines and the ground to the rear, just as the first German prisoners began to trickle in. Fuller noticed numbers of the enemy's shoulder straps denoting the regiments from which these men came: 190, 62 and 6. Later that morning, the Suffolks were ordered forward in case they were needed.

*Private Sydney
Fuller, 8th Suffolk
Regiment*

In the early afternoon the enemy's shelling gradually died down. Later, we moved to the left, taking up a position behind our own (53rd) Brigade's front. We passed along one of the 'Assembly' trenches. It had been heavily shelled by the enemy apparently during the morning. Several of our men were lying dead in it, killed by the enemy's shells. In one place a man was kneeling, as if in prayer, his hands covering his face. Lying in the trench behind him was another man, face downwards, half buried in the earth thrown into the trench by the shells. A short distance away another man was sitting on the fire step, buried to the knees, and looking as if he had been suddenly turned to stone. A little farther along the trench I slipped on something, and looking down I saw a piece of a man's backbone, and pieces of flesh strewn about the trench. Hanging down from the parapet, in the corner of the traverse, was a mass of entrails, already swarming with flies. And so on, here and there along the trench, wherever the enemy's shells had dropped in. We finally took up a position astride the Carnoy–Montauban road. The enemy's guns were by now quite quiet, and

A view from German-held Beaumont Hamel across no-man's-land to the sunken lane in the middle distance, from where the 1st Lancashire Fusiliers would launch their ill-fated attack.

The German front line trench at Beaumont Hamel, about 150 yards from the Hawthorn Redoubt mine explosion.

only a comparative few of ours were firing – Fritz was moving his guns back, we were moving ours forward. … Heard that our men had captured Montauban and Mametz.

Success was limited to the southern sector. Elsewhere, British troops barely secured any ground beyond their original front line, if at all. At Beaumont Hamel the ranks of the 1st Lancashire Fusiliers were shredded, while at the Schwaben Redoubt, the Ulstermen were being systematically driven out of the enemy's trenches, won at such cost that morning.

Lieutenant
Eric Sheppard,
1st Lancashire
Fusiliers

Sometime later, I should say about 10.30 am, the enemy apparently counter-attacked and drove out the Royal Fusilier elements still holding out in the crater, and at the sight of these coming back there was an incipient panic among the wounded and unwounded but badly shaken men in the lane. A number of them tried to escape through the tunnel and swarmed round the entrance, but the CO drew his revolver, threatened to use it, and the officers and NCOs managed to restore order and quieten the men, and organize the line for defence. The enemy counter-attack, a rumour of which had caused the alarm, apparently stopped after the recovery of their front line.

Soon afterwards, Major Utterson arrived in the lane, saying he had had orders from the brigade to renew the attack at 12.30 pm. Having only the '10 per cent' [reserve] and a few men of the second wave under his hand he had led them forward from the front line, but very few of them reached the line, and it was quite clear that a renewal of the attack was as far as we were concerned an impossibility. Soon after, I should say, about 1.00 pm, the wounded who could walk, of whom I was one, were ordered to make their way back through the tunnel.

Lieutenant
Colonel Francis
Bowen, 14th
Royal Irish Rifles

12.45 pm: Application for reinforcements from B line urgently asked for repeated to Brigade. Hun looks like counter-attacking. Heard that 11th Innis Fus lost heavily.

1.20 pm: Reported situation serious, mixed force of Brigade are holding C line but are enfiladed from Thiepval village.

2.05 pm: Received message from Lt Hogg that he was digging in between C & D companies with all available men. Why the devil don't they send reinforcements?

2.10 pm: Wright, the Bombing Officer, killed.

2.25 pm: The gallant Lack killed.

2.35 pm: Thiepval Wood has disappeared under the hail of shrapnel.

3.00 pm: A lot of men of the _____ have broken under Boche counter-attack from direction of Grandcourt. We had to stop them at once and turn them back, a desperate show, air stiff with shrapnel and terror-stricken men rushing blindly on!! These men did magnificently earlier in the day, but they had reached the limit of human endurance!

4.00 pm: Received message from Willis 14 RI that he was hanging on but hard-pressed; he was never heard of again.

6.00 pm: Two companies of 7th West Yorks wandering about the wood completely lost – I put them right. Young Gallagher of the 11th Innis Fus came and reported that the whole line had given way. I made him write it down and sent it to Brigade. This was corroborated later by a report from Monard, then later Peacock came along and we knew the worst – all the line had retired – indescribable scenes, men going in all directions, slightly wounded hobbling along, stretchers with badly wounded stuck fast in the trenches, and shells everywhere.

Two more photographs taken by Colonel R.D. Perceval-Maxwell, deep inside the Schwaben Redoubt. The right-hand image was taken in the wrecked fifth line of German defence, and the furthest point that the Ulstermen reached that day.

By early afternoon, Second Lieutenant Roe had seen enough upon which to make a report. He left his observation post to return to Corps Headquarters, taking with him, as he wrote, 'the undying memory of those north country soldiers still busily and steadily at work on their new defence line'.

Second
Lieutenant
Frederick
Roe, 1/6th
Gloucestershire
Regiment

I set off once more for Marieux Chateau over ground that was in even more unbelievable chaos than when I had traversed it in the dark in the early hours of the morning. I was dirty, muddy, dishevelled, and unshaven but worst of all I became aware that my puttees and my breeches were heavily stained with blood halfway up to my waist. The slight wound in my hand could not possibly account for this for I had bled very little. In moving about I must have come in contact with other seriously wounded or killed casualties.

I had only gone what seemed a very short distance when I passed what was left of one of our 18-pounder batteries. All the guns were out of action and lay grotesquely askew from their firing positions. Dead and wounded gun crews were lying around the guns and I went over in the mud to see if there was anything I could do. It was clear that the enemy counter-battery bombardment had been ranged on the site of the battery a very short time before I reached it. There was that all too frequent and quite unmistakable stamp of total disaster and a dreadful stillness. Then I came across the Battery Sergeant Major. He was a fine figure of a man and miraculously unwounded but quite clearly suffering from a complete breakdown. His eyes were wild and staring, he was dashing to and fro quite aimlessly and from time to time shouting loudly but unintelligibly. I succeeded in calming him a little and after a while he was able to tell me that the battery's guns had all been silenced and the men of the battery wiped out. He added that he was the only senior soldier left to take command. I had to leave him but promised that if I passed his artillery brigade commander's headquarters or could get a message through to him I would do so. There was also the possibility that if the battery's forward observation officer was still alive he might be able to come back to the battery to see why the guns were silent. In the familiar but indescribable chaos I completely failed to discover the Headquarters. On reflection I can see that I must have become obsessed with what I thought was a desperately urgent duty to succeed in getting back safely to Corps Headquarters and telling them what I knew.

I eventually arrived at Corps Headquarters sometime after 4.00 pm on that afternoon. I was thoroughly exhausted and still greatly shocked after talking to the Battery Sergeant Major. I must have looked even more disreputable than when I started my wearisome and hazardous trek back. If the plain truth is to be told, my report was received by the operations branch of the General Staff with complete incredulity. However, as at all times I had been accorded the privilege of personal access to the Corps Commander, General Hunter-Weston, I insisted at this point that I must myself tell him my own story. I was accordingly very reluctantly given immediate access to him. I had carefully condensed my meticulously kept official logbook and had written my report under four vital headings: the total failure of the assault on the enemy's positions on 31st Division's front; the excessively heavy casualties sustained; the complete destruction and resulting chaos of our front line system of trenches; and the elimination of all means of communication forward of Brigade Headquarters. The General listened to what I had to say courteously and most attentively without interruption. I had just come to the end of my report when a general staff officer grade 1 (GSO 1) came in and said that the 4th Army Commander, General Sir Henry Rawlinson, was arriving by car. Bidding me follow him, the Corps Commander hurried out to meet his Army Commander and as soon as we got fairly near I dropped behind and waited. Their meeting was characteristically brief but after the Army Commander had gone General Hunter-Weston told me that … he had given General Rawlinson the gist of my up-to-the-hour report on the situation in 31st Division. I heaved a deep sigh of relief and stole silently away.

The evening was quiet. For the first time in a week or more I heard the silence. It was fine, too, and warm. But our battle – our work – our hopes!

Bunches of brown figures, lines of brown figures, stretched out on the dried grass between the lines! Stray shrapnel burst among them, but they did not move; they lay still where they had fallen or dropped motionless

Lieutenant Adrian Stephen, D Battery, 1/4th South Midland Brigade, Royal Field Artillery across the wire, not far, poor fellows, on the road to Germany. That was all. Aeroplanes throbbed overhead; observation balloons hung quietly against the sunset. 'Z' day had ended.

I sat in my dugout and had a brandy. I think it was only the knowledge of what the Infantry had gone through that kept me from weeping. It was their ordeal – not ours; theirs the glory and the sorrow.

The collection of the wounded would prove extremely problematic, especially for those stuck out in no-man's-land. Elsewhere, in the front and support lines, terrible congestion and severe damage to trenches meant heroic efforts would be required to extract the casualties. Summer weather might keep the wounded warm but there would be no concealing darkness under which to work until late evening and even then only a few short hours would be available before daylight returned.

Lieutenant
Eric Sheppard,
1st Lancashire
Fusiliers

By evening when I got back to the lane, I found it held as a front line by practically every available officer and man in the battalion, and the collection of the wounded about to begin. This went on despite heavy sporadic enemy fire all that night. As far as we could make out, we had lost some 60 per cent of our men and rather more of our officers, but I never knew the final figures as I left Battalion Headquarters to command a company next morning.

The collection of wounded went on for the whole of this and the next, (I think) and part of the next night, and the Germans too helped by gathering those in the vicinity of their lines. No attempt was made to do anything by day, and we lost an officer and several men from aimless hostile fire during the collection work at night.

Private Joe
Yarwood,
94th Field
Ambulance,
Royal Army
Medical Corps

We were taking the wounded from a relay post at the end of the communication trench across Euston Dump to the main road where the dugouts were. Some of the injured had Blighty wounds and you could almost see the satisfaction on their faces. If a chap was able to walk, it was much better for him to walk than to occupy a stretcher, and where we could, we would carry his equipment and escort him down. I met one poor devil injured in the face. He had been a walking wounded case and he was an elderly man, too, and I felt very sorry for him. His face was bandaged but his wound was still bleeding, and the whole of his chest was covered with a thick mat of congealed blood. I thought he would go down any minute with loss of blood. I'd already got a case with me, but I got him carried out on a stretcher because, had he collapsed, he might well have died. And that's what I was doing, all day long, simply going backwards and forwards like an automaton; you didn't think much. If we'd been winning, that might have been some consolation, but we hadn't even got that.

There were so many more lying out in no-man's-land, but we couldn't reach them. We talked about it. One team tried to clamber out over the top, but one of the lads was shot straightaway, a bullet smashing his thigh, and the rest of the team scrambled back in.

It was with strange feelings that the little party of NCOs and men marched up to the firing line that night. Attempts at facetiousness fell flat. The continuous roar of guns and bursting of black and woolly shrapnel over the villages kept bringing us back to the situation before us. The last village we passed through was dimly illuminated by the lurid glare of burning houses in the main street. We reported to Brigade Headquarters and were straightway dispatched to our own.

An officer who had returned after fourteen hours in a shell hole asked if I would get two men and a stretcher and follow him into no-man's-land. One jumped at something to do and followed on through the old communication trenches we had learned to know so well. Then out over the parapet, over the endless maze of trenches straggling to and from the front line, stumbling about amongst the shell holes and barbed wire illuminated from time to time by the more brilliant of the German flares. At last we reached the front line, straggled over it with the stretcher and trundled on into no-man's-land. I was warned to have a revolver handy. Quite why, one didn't know, for the rifles of both sides were at rest. Only the artillerymen had the energy to carry on the noisy game, and the Germans, fearing another attack, kept putting up continuous flares.

Second Lieutenant William Dyson, 1/16th London Regiment

Lieutenant Arthur
Terry, 23rd
Northumberland
Fusiliers (4th
Tyneside Scottish)

I am writing with a heavy heart tonight. … The casualties have been very heavy so far as we can learn but the majority of the damage seems to have been done by machine guns so there is a good hope of a very large percentage making a good recovery and we are thankful to think it is so. The officers have caught it badly and the casualties include Campbell, wounded and missing. There seems to be little hope that he is living. Williams and Hall are killed and the CO, Adjutant, Major Bunge, Cubey, Bolton, Whitehead, Whittaker, Oliver and Luch have all been hit. Major Mackintosh is supposed to be wounded and lying out on the field still. They cannot get him in on account of snipers but are hoping to do so tonight. As for the men, I daren't think of the losses. For your sake I'm glad I'm not in it but such wild rumours come back to us that it makes one feel inclined to throw prudence to the winds and search round for some way of helping them in front. I believe that on the whole we have done very well but it doesn't seem to help much when one hears of the battalion being cut up. I have need of all my patience and the knowledge that my duty lies in being here. … It will be some time before the battalion is fit to go into action again and we will probably be relieved at the earliest possible moment. In that case I expect leave will be granted more freely – at least I hope so with all my heart.

Goodnight – I'm going out now to the refilling point. Routine goes on even though the battlefield is strewn with men.

For several nights, casualties were slowly gathered in, although in too many cases the wounded were never found and died slow, agonizing deaths. Sergeant Walter Popple had been brought down close to the enemy's wire, while Private Henry Russell lay seriously wounded in a shell hole. Both men would have to be the architects of their own salvation.

Sergeant Walter
Popple, 8th
King's Own
Yorkshire Light
Infantry

Night came, and I cautiously turned over and began to take stock. I gently lowered the bandolier full of ammunition from my shoulders, and the two hand grenades. Moving on my hands and knees, I crept to a large shell hole and despite the bodies around it, began to make myself comfortable. The bullet, I realized, had hit flush on the front of my helmet but instead of killing me outright it must have ricocheted upwards with such force that it ripped the straps from the flanges on my shrapnel helmet, sending it spinning into the air. The German, of course, would have assumed that I was dead.

All through the night, incessant calls were being made for stretcher-bearers, interspersed by rifle and machine-gun fire. The next day followed the same pattern, except that we were shelling Jerry's front line trenches with high explosive shrapnel that at times crossed the shell hole where I was sheltering, wounding me in the right leg and shoulders, some seven wounds in all.

I had to wait probably till about eleven o'clock that night before I dared to make any move to get away. When I did, I met a serious difficulty. I found that lying on the ground, it was quite impossible to decide in which direction to crawl and, in the end, decided on my direction solely because I could see a fire on a hill, and as I knew that we had come down a slope during our attack, I crawled in that direction. It turned out that this was the right way to go and I continued to crawl for some hours meeting with all sorts of obstacles such as barbed wire, shell holes and that sort of thing; all the while hearing the cries of wounded soldiers lying on the ground. I did not know what progress I was making and only hoped for the best.

After a long time, to my relief, I was challenged in English, having been spotted by one or two who had been sent out into an advanced post to give warning of any approach by the Germans. I crawled into this advanced post as well as I could and the occupants said they would do their best to get a stretcher to carry me away as, by that time, I was nearing exhaustion. I must have become unconscious at this stage because I remembered no more until dawn was breaking and I suddenly realized I was still lying in this old advanced trench. The occupants, by this time, were no longer there. Crawling along, I came to one or two of our troops lying in the bottom of the trench. They did not respond and, to my horror on feeling them, I found that they were stiff and dead. At this stage, I gave up and decided that if there was to be any hope I must call out and, doing my best, I shouted, probably not very loudly. I was heard by a private in the Middlesex Regiment who had been out in front with an officer and

Private Henry Russell, 1/5th London Regiment (London Rifle Brigade)

Two further images taken by Lieutenant Anthony Nash in Montauban Alley. The officer (right) is Second Lieutenant Harvey. On the left are the entrances to German dugouts.

who was going back to try to get assistance for the officer, who had been seriously wounded. He came over the top of the trench and helped me back to our front line trenches where there were many troops awaiting a possible counter-attack. They manhandled me along the communication trench for some distance, until they got me to a field dressing station where I was given some coffee and several injections, and left lying on the stretcher until an ambulance could carry me away. By this time, it was, of course, full daylight.

On the edge of the village of Montauban, Lieutenant Anthony Nash was holding on to his company's gains, although the situation was increasingly precarious as the Germans began to probe the defences thrown up by exhausted British troops. At 9.30 pm a small German counter-attack was beaten off but further attacks were expected and increasing in boldness and weight.

No word of relief had been received and the situation was far too precarious to admit of any man sleeping during the night. They were dead tired in spite of the rest I had given them earlier in the day, and I spent the entire night walking up and down the line watching and talking to the men to keep them awake. We were all very thirsty as we had no chance of refilling our water bottles since 5.00 pm on 30 June. One dear fellow gave me a spoonful of marmalade which was the nearest approach to a drink that I had for twenty-four hours. ...

I sent a note to Johnson asking him to come down himself or Elstob, as I felt further attack was imminent and I could get no satisfaction from Battalion Headquarters. He wrote back on a grubby slip of paper, 'I am sure you will do all possible. I am remaining on the right because I judge it to be the most dangerous. Good luck.'

All through the night the men stood at their firing positions with the remains of their ammunition laid out on the parapet.

We proceeded to straighten things up, attend to the wounded and count our losses. A dispatch runner reported that Morton Johnson had been killed while handing up ammunition to a machine gunner when the rest of the team had been knocked out. This was a bitter blow to me and I was just going along to his body when Corporal Waldron, one of my best scouts, came running down the trench in spite of a severe wound in his leg. He had been in charge of our extreme right post and reported that the redoubt of the 17th Manchesters had retired at the beginning of the fuss and had let the Germans in our right flank. These were then bombing their way down the trench with the intention of clearing Montauban Alley.

We had no bombs at all so I sent along to borrow some from the 55th Brigade on our left and then took a bombing party along the trench and sent another along the top to deal with the Huns. We drove them out of our own frontage and established a block where the 17th Battalion's post should have been.

I was the only officer left in the front line and I presented a curious sight; my tunic and puttees had gone long ago, the latter to put a tourniquet on Waldron's leg, and bareheaded and in my shirtsleeves, my face and arms covered with sweat and blood and grime, I looked anything but the conventional officer in command of a beleaguered garrison.

Lieutenant Anthony Nash, 16th Manchester Regiment

The 16th Manchester Regiment was finally relieved at 2.30 that afternoon.

Private Edward Higson, 16th Manchester Regiment

We started to retrace our steps to the assembly trench, back over the battlefield of yesterday, now strewn with thousands of our boys and the enemy. It was awful to see the boys who forty-eight hours ago were full of life, now lying upon the battlefield. We picked up as many wounded as we could and took them to the different dressing stations, then proceeded to the point of assembly to answer the roll. The Sergeant Major was there calling out the names – some were answered, others would never hear their names again on this earth but by this time would be answering the roll on the other side, for their entrance to that better land had been assured by the sacrifice they had made. 'They had lain down their lives for their brothers.' Greater love hath no man than this.

Lieutenant Anthony Nash, 16th Manchester Regiment

From my battalion 850 men and twenty-two officers went into action. Five hundred and sixty-five men were killed and wounded. Of the officers, Morton Johnson was killed, Allen was killed, Worthington was shot through the right lung and had his left hand shattered; Walker was blinded in both eyes, Horley had his shoulder smashed, Kerry had a severe scalp wound, Hook and Morris were knocked out with machine-gun wounds in the legs, Faux had his arm taken off by a shell splinter, Barr had his jaw smashed by a rifle bullet, Prestwich and Swaine were hit early in the advance, Slack was wounded by the same shell that killed his servant, Hanscombe was blown up by a trench mortar shell and had severe concussion, Megson got a machine-gun bullet through his leg and Elstob had a slight wound in the neck.

One week later, Nash was wounded by shrapnel in the arm and evacuated to England. As soon as he could, he went to see the mother of Morton Johnson at her home in Altrincham. 'She was very nice to me,' he recalled, 'and glad to have someone who could tell her about her boy. Johnson and I had been fast friends.'

Nash subsequently wrote to Agnes Johnson, sending her the photograph of her son taken just hours before he was killed.

2 July: Daylight. Got parties organized and put them cleaning up, cast away rifles, equipment, trenches full of debris, fallen trees, giants of the first mown down before the iron blast, along the trenches lay men in all positions of death, just as they had fallen, collected wounded and sent to 1st Aid Post which was like a butcher's shop. Only a few naked poles left of all that once was Thiepval Wood.

Lieutenant
Colonel Francis
Bowen, 14th
Royal Irish Rifles

It was Sunday morning really – the strangest I have ever spent. We had only two stretchers with us and were trying to find two men we knew to be particularly bad. It was impossible to find them in the dark and we just took the men who seemed to need us most and returned. It's no light task carrying a man over ground like that. We all took turns but it seemed appallingly slow. We had just reached the most difficult point in the journey where our wire had been most blown about by the bombardment when the Boche artillery decided to put what is known as a minor 'barrage' on that part of the line. Three times I tried to find a way through the wire and left bits of my breeches on it without success.

Second
Lieutenant
William Dyson,
1/16th London
Regiment

The only thing to do was to try and get him down into the trench, which was already full of wounded going down. After an unconscionable time we managed to get him down to the aid post. The men were absolutely done so we handed over the stretcher to proper stretcher-bearers and returned to the company. It seemed almost hopeless. All the stretchers were already in use. The men were too done to do any carrying. The day was fast approaching when no man can work and still crowds of men were out in front – had lain there all day and would have to lie there another twenty-four hours unless we could get them in before daybreak. Two sergeants and an officer volunteered and the four of us set out to see what could be done. We managed to get about half a dozen in some old how and then the daylight came in with a rush. The order was given to stand to and we had to come in. The doctor tells me everyone this side the German wire was got in before the second night was up. …

All this is simply between you and me, of course. It gives the darker side of the 'great push'.

Overleaf:
Signallers at
the bottom
of Lochnagar
mine crater at
La Boisselle.
The men are
signalling the
word 'Somme' in
semaphore.

4 Batter and Hold

'It is only by the grace of God that I am entering up the events of an extraordinary day. It would take reams to jot down everything that has happened, but it will always live in my mind as a day when I tasted death a thousand times.'

Second Lieutenant Charles Lloyd, Royal Field Artillery

———————

2 July: Just as dawn was breaking we moved up the road towards Montauban, past the now demolished barricade, across the old no-man's-land and enemy's erstwhile front line, relieving some of the Norfolks in trenches a short distance over. After daylight, as we were still a long way from the 'front', and were still in 'reserve', I had a look around the captured trenches. These had been literally smashed by our bombardment in most places, but few of the numerous dugouts were damaged – I only saw one which had an entrance blown in. German dead were everywhere, many being in the dugouts, as if they had died there after being wounded in the trenches.

Private Sydney Fuller, 8th Suffolk Regiment

In the case of those Germans who had been killed in the trenches, most of them appeared to have died fighting. Here and there along the parapets, or remains of parapets, were little piles of empty cartridge cases where they had lain and fired. In most cases they (the Germans) lay in the bottom of the trenches near the empty cartridge cases, many having a bullet hole in the head. I saw one pile of three dead Germans, the top one having on only trousers and socks, the lower two being in full equipment. Not much enemy shelling. Our guns were active about midday, and our OC said afterwards that the enemy had counter-attacked and had recaptured a small part of Montauban. …

Stretcher-bearers were searching the trenches and among the dead, for any who still had life in them. In the enemy front line, the enemy dead lay in threes in nearly every 'bay', some yellow in the face, some as black as negroes and in every conceivable attitude. In the evening the battalion moved to the left, relieving the Berks, in 'support'. We took over a trench called 'Montauban Alley', and other trenches (including Caterpillar Trench)

Opposite: An officer of 183 Tunnelling Company, Royal Engineers, looks warily over the top. His men had dug and detonated the large mine blown at Kasino Point, near Carnoy.

facing Caterpillar Wood. A and C Coys' Hdqrs were together, in Montauban Alley, using one telephone for both Coys. Montauban Alley was a wide, straight trench, and an enemy 4.2-inch howitzer battery was so situated that it could fire almost along it – enfilade fire, in fact. This battery continued to make things uncomfortable from time to time. There were no dugouts in the trench, and we had to dig small 'funk-holes' in the sides, for a little cover.

Lieutenant Arthur Terry, 23rd Northumberland Fusiliers (4th Tyneside Scottish)

It has been a curious Sunday. I got to bed about 5.00 am and had a few hours' sleep. Heron and one or two of the new officers under Capt Longhurst went up to the line at four this morning to take over the remnants of the battalion. It is rumoured that we are being relieved tonight and I hope that it is so. I went up to the Field Ambulance this morning but could get nothing definite there. Reports are very contradictory and the only thing one could be sure of was the condition of those who actually passed through the hands of the doctors. Major Mackintosh turned up this morning with his right arm shattered and a nasty wound on the chest but we are hoping it is not necessarily fatal. His physical strength and willpower enabled him to get to the ambulance on his own but it must have been absolute torture to him. One feels numb about the affair. It is most incredible that we will not see half the battalion again.

Private Joe Yarwood, 94th Field Ambulance, Royal Army Medical Corps

The next day the wounded were still waiting to be moved away, but we were lacking convoys. All these elephant dugouts had been turned into aid posts. There were piles of wounded lying on stretchers waiting for ambulances to move them.

I had just left the dressing station when we were shelled, but they landed with a pop and not an explosion, and then I got a whiff of it; it was tear gas. I rushed back to lend a hand getting as many under cover as I could. They couldn't get their gas masks on, so for an hour or so it was pandemonium trying to get these poor devils out of harm's way.

Our colonel, an Irishman by the name of Stewart, was a bit of a martinet and inclined to shout and bark and call you a bloody fool. He was very ambitious, a doctor in civilian life, and held the DSO and MC, and you don't get those for nothing. A brilliant officer, no doubt, but he was, to my mind, a little conceited, haughty even; you get it with some officers

who take a large size in hats. Anyway, when we were leaving the trenches, he sounded like a benevolent father, pleased and very pleasant for once because we'd broken all records with the number of wounded we'd shifted, although he couldn't quite show his gratitude.

We were told to clear out because our lot was decimated. I saw a battalion leaving and there was a band in front and then about three or four ranks of soldiers, and that was all that was left of a thousand: thirty or forty men.

Just around there I recall one poor devil who had been buried in the bottom of the trench, but not deep enough, with the result that the top of his skull was exposed just level with the top of the trench floor. There was a bald patch right down the centre of the poor fellow's skull where the troops had marched and worn the hair off his head. My God, what would his relatives at home think if they knew that had happened?

3 July: the wounded, arriving in overwhelming numbers, are receiving treatment at the 34th Casualty Clearing Station at Daours, 10 km east of Amiens. Both pictures were snapped by a medical officer. Ninety-two men died of wounds at Daours in the first week of the offensive.

On 2 July, small, consolidating attacks were made on the southern sector of the battlefield. After the capture of Montauban and Mametz on the first day, the pressure grew on Fricourt, which had withstood the assault, and the Germans abandoned the village the following day. On 3 July an attack was made on La Boisselle, which fell on 4 July just as the heavens opened and thunderstorms rolled through the region. The rain was a godsend to the men still awaiting collection from the battlefield.

In ever-decreasing numbers, the wounded from 1 July continued to come in, not just over the following hours or days, but even after a week. It was extraordinary how some wounded men had contrived to survive.

Sergeant Walter Popple, 8th King's Own Yorkshire Light Infantry

The third day I was exhausted, and it was on this day that a thunderstorm broke the terrific heat. By this time all the bodies around me had turned black. One of them had a waterproof sheet protruding at the back of his pack. I formed a ridge and the water trickled down into my mouth. The fourth day was relatively quiet but I realized that time was getting short and unless help arrived soon, I was finished. I made my mind up that, whatever happened, I must reach my lines by morning. Crawling throughout the night, I got to within a few yards of our trenches by daybreak. By a sustained effort, I rose to my feet and hopped the necessary distance. Machine guns opened out, but I held my course and was lucky to enter one of the lanes cut for the attack. A sentry shouted, 'Who's there?' I croaked, 'KOYLI'. To hear my own tongue being spoken was nectar. 'And yours?' 'Middlesex,' came the reply. 'Anyone else out there?' I told him no.

In a letter written to his wife two weeks after the assault, Lieutenant Colonel Johnson was astonished at the fortitude some men had shown.

Lieutenant Colonel Frederick Johnson, 88th Field Ambulance, Royal Army Medical Corps

We got some poor fellows in about eight or nine days after the first attack; they had been wounded and had crawled into shell holes. I had not been able to get at them for these eight or nine days, but when they came in they were as perky as one could wish. About four o'clock one morning I was called to come and see a case; he had been lying out in a hole for eight days. I went into the dressing station and here he was lying on his elbow on the stretcher smoking a cigarette. 'Good morning, Sir,' he said to me and grinned all over his face; I asked him how he felt, quite comfortable; his foot was gangrenous so I shipped him straight out of the trenches and the foot was taken off at the 88th HQ & then he was sent right on to the CCS.

The storm and rain had increased so much that we had to climb onto the
parados to save ourselves from the danger of drowning. We had put the
Lewis guns on the parapet in groundsheets; it was to the limit to see the
chalk bouncing up by the force of the rain. I was having to shake the guns
clear of the chalk to prevent them getting buried in it. To have fired them
would have been impossible if it had been necessary.

Sergeant
Charles Moss,
18th Battalion,
Durham Light
Infantry

We were wondering what we could do to get the flood out of our
trench when we saw two or three Jerries climb onto the parapet of their
trench and start digging – with those long-handled shovels of theirs –
they must have seen us because as the water came pouring out of their
trench, one of them lifted the blade of his shovel into the air and waved a
'wash-out'. I at once gave them the same signal with the butt of my rifle.
It seemed to me that this was an event that was apart from the ordeal and
enmity of battle. The forces of nature had restored the sense of common
humanity after all the carnage there had been since the battle started;
and not a shot was fired on either side while we stood in danger of being
drowned.

A wet and miserable day. ... I went up into the Hun trenches to look
for a dugout as a mess. We have mauled them about frightfully. In parts
they are quite flattened out. Numbers of 9.2 shells and 2″ mortar duds
lying about. If I had not other business to attend to I could have collected
innumerable souvenirs as helmets, rifles, haversacks and so on were lying
about in heaps. A lot of the dugouts had been blown in but others were in
excellent condition. Most of them were fitted with acetylene gas.

Second
Lieutenant
Charles Lloyd,
Royal Field
Artillery

In the afternoon while we were dozing in our respective bivouacs a
tremendous rainstorm came on. I was flooded out but felt so tired that
I just pulled my groundsheet over me and slept through it. Carver woke
me with ribald laughter at my plight. His own bivvy was watertight. Brind
was flooded out of the trench and took refuge in a dugout. When the rain
stopped Carver and I went to the Hun trenches to get material for the gun
pits etc. and select dugouts for the men.

Some of the dugouts are supposed to be still occupied by Fritz. There
certainly is a sniper somewhere in the valley as I have heard him several
times. He is somewhere near the crater. I went in front into each dugout

Found in Bosch Dug-Out,
Ovillers, July 1916

A souvenir retrieved by Lieutenant Patrick Koekkoek.

with the torch while Timothy carried the revolver. We did not encounter Fritz in hiding, however.

The dugouts are extraordinarily comfortable, even for the men and all of them are quite 40ft below the surface and have two entrances. We decided the trenches were too far away from the guns to make our mess in them, while the men, for some reason or other, would far rather bivouac in the open than use the dugouts.

Went over and saw the mine crater; it is appalling in its immensity. It must be quite 50ft deep and 80ft across. Got thoroughly soaked and caked in mud, while my puttees are torn to ribbons by the wire. My valise and everything are also soaked so there is nothing to change into.

The 60-pdr battery has annoyed Fritz tonight, but he is looking for it. Some of his stuff falling uncomfortably near us. We decided in consequence to sleep all together in the structure the servants have put up as a mess, to the right rear of the guns. Carter, Brind's servant, is a gallant old fellow. He has been standing on a bit of duckboard in the flooded trench he uses as a cookhouse, soaked to the skin, but still singing some ditty about *His Father's Pants*! Even the shelling did not disturb him though a couple of shells fell in the trench. His voice could be heard and his fire seen brightly burning well into the night.

One of our lesser heroes!

In a disused dugout I found a litter of pups; next day the mother deserted them, I suppose the noise was too much for her; so I took a pup and I am, with the aid of my servant, trying to rear it. At least I suppose I should say my servant is bringing it up with my assistance because he does all the work and I look on. I suppose it was about ten days old when I got it and it caused us no end of amusement in the trenches; he was not too steady on his legs at first as you would conclude and when he wandered round the floor and anything tickled his ears he would shake his head, promptly overbalance and roll on his back; he is growing fast and much more steady now and knows where to look for his breakfast, is cutting his teeth, but I am sorry to say that his manners in all respects are very unsatisfactory; but with a little judicious application of the hand I have no doubt that this can in time be remedied.

Some of the men took two of the others, but a sad fate befell the three remaining; one was trodden on and two days after the big 'stunt' we had a particularly severe thunderstorm which flooded the dugouts and the two leftovers were drowned. We had 'banked' up the door of my domicile when it started to rain but the barrier carried away and in came the water very fast; fortunately the pup was in a bucket hanging on the wall. I managed to rescue him, an electric torch and a pair of boots – when I went in again to see what could be done the water was up to my neck and all things that would float were practising naval manoeuvres with my torch for a searchlight.

Lieutenant Colonel Frederick Johnson, 88th Field Ambulance, Royal Army Medical Corps

The survivors, out on well-needed rest, had time to clean up and reflect on what had happened. Letters were written home to those desperate for news of loved ones. Battalions redced in size by half or more awaited new arrivals who were assimilated into the ranks as they arrived.

Rifleman William Lynas, 15th Royal Irish Rifles

Left: *German dead in the front line at La Boisselle.*

Right: *Debris belonging to German soldiers lay everywhere.*

Dear Wife,

I am sure you are wondering why I have not written to you before this. Well, Mira, we have been on the move the most of the time since we came out of the trenches [and] we are away down country now to get made up to strength. It may be three or four weeks before we are back to the firing line. I need hardly begin to tell you about the gallantry of our boys for I am sure you have read more in the papers than I am fit to tell you. There is one thing, Mira, they did not disgrace the name of Ulster or their forefathers. Little did you think as you sat writing that letter on the first day of July that our boys had mounted the top and made a name for Ulster that will never die in the annals of history.

No doubt Belfast today and the rest of Ulster is in deep mourning for the dear ones that have given their life so manly, may the Lord comfort

all of those who have lost a beloved husband, a brother, a son and lastly may the Lord watch over those dear orphans, as the Rev Cochrane used to repeat from the pulpit, Some are sick and some are sad, Some have lost the love they had. There is one great comfort to know that they fell doing their duty for King and Country. May the Lord comfort all our dear lads who are wounded and in hospital, may they have a speedy recovery. Well, Mira, in regards to my uncle I have tried to find out if anyone knew anything about him but no one seems to know anything … last seen of him was going over no-man's-land that is between the German lines and ours but I am still living in hopes of hearing something about him yet.

With love to you and kindest regards to all at home and may God comfort you and strengthen you is the earnest prayer of your loving Husband,
Willie xxxxxxxxxxxxxxxxxxxxxxxxxxxxxx

We are right back in a place behind Amiens, bathed in the deepest summer peace. No sounds of the guns reach us. Behind this farm, among its big trees, is a charming garden; Madonna lilies and roses mix with onions and peas; rosemary and potatoes, pinks and turnips, currants, strawberries, peonies all jostle each other. This afternoon all was basking in the sunshine, a fresh breeze stirred the trees, and there was a pleasant accompaniment of birds' songs and farmyard sounds. On one side of the garden was an orchard, where some red cows, ready for milking, were grazing eagerly on the old pasture, across which long shadows fell. Rich fields of corn and other things lay round the farm, and in the near valley, and between the woods on high ground opposite, where a little church stood up. Far away across the Somme, miles of unbroken fields sloped up to the horizon, with here and there a dark clump of trees or a wood that served to mark the distances. Utter and most refreshing peace and beauty brooded over the whole.

Captain Harold Bidder, 1st South Staffordshire Regiment

The battalions of the Tyneside Scottish and Tyneside Irish had suffered grievously in the opening assault. In early July, Lance Corporal George Brown arrived in France with a draft and, after an interminably long journey, was sent to the village of Divion to join the 21st Battalion, Northumberland Fusiliers, known as 2nd Tyneside Scottish. The reception Brown and his friends received was sobering.

Lance Corporal
George
Brown, 21st
Northumberland
Fusiliers (2nd
Tyneside
Scottish)

We were marched from the train to the billets situated in a not over clean farm building and on the way subjected to the scrutiny of the fellows whose comrades we were now to be. We were very uncomfortable under this staring scrutiny and for some reason a fierce antipathy came into being – they were obviously miners and we were obviously black coat [office] workers. Halting before the billets we stood, very ill at ease, and silently cursing our luck at finding our new pals so hostile – they stood round in small groups gazing at us with a stony stare unblinking and expressionless. We whispered hoarse comments on the whole business and fell to wondering moodily as to the row which seemed to be brewing.

After some minutes of this, waiting to be herded into pens like sheep – no one seemed to know who we were and where we had to go – we began to notice that the unfriendly attitude of the Tynesiders was not directed against us in particular but was the general attitude. They were only partially dressed and what uniform they did wear was in very bad condition. No belts, very few hats, no puttees, dirty boots. Most of them had cigarettes hanging from their lower lips and their conversation consisted of a series of grunts. These fellows are not unfriendly, I thought. They are down and out. No spirit, no cheerfulness. That fellow's eyes over there. Look at them. He seems half dazed. Those men there. Look how they walk, dragging their feet. These fellows have suffered and their memories are too vivid to be brushed aside, too near to be laughed away. What ghost is it that seems to be haunting them?

At nightfall we were paraded for our first experience of the trenches. Silently we moved off and we new recruits were excited as could be. Here at last we had come to the goal, at last we were to show our mettle. Whispered questions – 'Where abouts is the Line?' Grunted replies from men who had lost all illusion as to glory and had no illusion at all about the horror and filth, gave us no indication of what we would have to experience.

'Break step.'

'We must be near the Line now, Corporal,' said my neighbour gloomily.

I tried a whispered conversation with my fellow Tynesider, a man named Johnson, who was burdened with a cough more appropriate to a sanatorium patient, than for a supposedly fit footslogger. He was a miner from Ashington, had a wife and three kids and was a bitter opponent of wars and officers. His bitterness was unlimited in spite of his inability to express his feelings in any other than two or three vile and blasphemous sentences. These he used in turn with unvarying emphasis and I suppose it gave him some satisfaction to blow off steam in this fashion. He had been in La Boisselle which, he told me, had been hellish in its dreadful slaughter. In my ignorance I tried to pacify him by pointing out that nothing could be worse than the 1st July and he had managed to come through unhurt.

'Not hurt? Good God, you don't know, but you will soon.'

'Know what?' I asked.

'Oh! for God's sake shut up or talk of something else.'

More men were making their way south to the Somme, men who had seen action in the Ypres Salient or around Loos. They were charmed by the pleasant rural sights of Picardy and the small, quaint, untouched villages well behind the line. And then they began to approach the battle zone.

On every hand were signs of The Curse. Roads cut up and rendered impassable for all ordinary traffic: derelict farms: fertile fields churned into a wilderness of mud by the multitudinous feet of armies: villages half-depopulated, sudden, unplanned gaps in the rows of houses, craters in the village street, littered with a debris of crumbled stones and mortar that had but lately been houses, shattered roofs and walls, and gaping window sockets. And everywhere in possession, that hydra-headed, care-defying blade, Private Thomas Atkins.

Private Thomas Lyon, 1/9th Highland Light Infantry

For two nights we bivouacked in a field only a few kilometres distant from the fighting line. Our knapsacks containing greatcoats and all our belongings save cleaning kit, i.e., towel, soap, razor, etc., had been left in one of the villages through which we had passed, and now our sole protection from rain and cold was the waterproof groundsheet that each man carried. By fastening two or three of these together, and with the aid of some boughs to serve as supports, little tents were fashioned just big enough to hold two or three men in a lying posture and huddled closely together for warmth. Line after line of these low tents sprang into being, until the field presented somewhat of the appearance of a settled camp.

Although so near to the scene of hostilities we were really fairly safe, for between our place of encampment and the German lines rose several sharply defined ridges which effectually prevented enemy observation, especially as, by reason of the vigilance and alertness and daring of our own aircraft, the enemy was unable to use his aeroplanes or balloons for that purpose. He was a very short-sighted enemy indeed.

The last evening being cold, innumerable small fires of brushwood and twigs were lit all over the field, and around these the men sprawled in attitudes of ease. And while some sang and were merry, others gave themselves to talk of the yesterdays and tomorrows, or were silent in presence of the surge of memories or hoped-for things that they saw limned in the red heart of the fire.

The spectacle of that gloomy field with its twinkling fires, the figures of the men moving about in dark silhouette against the soft and varied radiances lives in the memory. For many so sadly many of those good fellows were destined not to outlive the morrow.

During the first week of the offensive, small-scale operations continued to advance or straighten the line on the southern flank, where there appeared some promise of successes despite German counter-attacks. On 7 July a major attack was made on Mametz Wood, a large and forbidding wood bristling with machine guns. The attack, spearheaded by the Welsh Division, was broken up. Elsewhere attacks on Contalmaison also met with stiff resistance. Once again, heavy rain began to fall.

Sergeant Arthur Perriman, 11th South Wales Borderers

On 5 July we halted behind Mametz. Here we were to learn our task, with our sister battalion 10th South Wales Borderers, was to attack Mametz Wood.

Part of the time was spent searching for Germans who may have been left behind in the course of [the] German retreat, or identifying and burying our own dead. On the afternoon of 6 July we were told the battalion would move forward at 8.00 pm to take up position in Happy Valley from which attack would be made on Mametz Wood. There were, however, plenty of odd jobs to be done in the meantime – the drawing and issuing of bomb buckets and jacket Mills bombs, and small arms ammunition. Punctually at 8.00 pm following roll call the battalion moved off laden like pack mules. The bombardment by both sides continued unabated. Our ammunition, sandbags, barbed wire, and spiral steel stakes were added to our already overburdened state and restricted progress. It was dark when we reached the German communication which would lead us to Happy Valley. Immediately there was trouble. The trench had not been constructed to provide easy access for troops laden as we were, and to add to the difficulties, telephone wires erected by signallers to forward positions became entangled with rifle and other impedimenta.

Fed up and worn out, we reached Happy Valley at 2.30 am. Our journey was not made any easier when the Germans sent over tear gas shells. There was nothing to do but to stand around or doze off until dawn. With the coming of daylight it was possible to take stock of our position. The communication trench cut through Caterpillar Wood which passed the background of the valley. Some 300 yards or so ahead lay Mametz Wood – our objective.

7 July: Two Observation officers from the artillery in Pommiers Redoubt as troops assault Mametz Wood close by.

Private William
Thomas, 14th
Royal Welsh
Fusiliers

We marched through the old front line and pushed uphill to Mametz. Coming out of the eastern end of Mametz we entered the newly captured long German communication trench a mile or so long leading from the village to Happy Valley or Death Valley and the Quadrangle immediately in front of Mametz Wood. Unlike our communication trenches, this Danzig Alley had no duckboards like our own had. So one slopped away in about a foot deep of red muddy slosh. By nightfall we had moved up to occupy a position SW corner of the wood somewhere in the vicinity of Step Trench, an old German trench system leading into Mametz Wood at this point.

By the time we got to this point it was dark. … While waiting for others to move, a German soldier loomed up out of the night and surrendered to us. By what I could see of him in the dark he was a chap about 5′7″ or 5′8″ of a Bavarian regt, and had apparently had enough of the war and just walked across from the wood and gave himself up. After this episode we retreated in single file across the open towards the Quadrangle Trench, nobody firing a shot at us, but as soon as the head of the column reached down into Happy Valley the German artillery opened up on us and we all had to run the gauntlet of the valley before reaching the 'Quad'. It was morning by the time we reached the comparative safety of the Quadrangle Trench facing the South End or narrow end of the Wood (Mametz) but we lost several killed and/or wounded here in the valley before morning. I had a look at the road at this point leading from Mametz Wood and there were several of our men who were killed by shellfire during the night lying thereon. I remember one in particular, Sgt Davies from Llandudno, whose torso only, appeared on this metalled road. He had a brother in our company and of course he did not know until morning that his brother had been killed during the night.

From now on we did nothing else but consolidate by interminable carrying parties up and down Danzig Alley, from the morning of 5 July until eve of the final assault on Mametz Wood 7 July.

Opposite: *One
of the walking
wounded from
the fighting at
Mametz Wood
walks through
Pommier Redoubt.
The redoubt had
been captured on
1 July.*

Major Geoffrey
Hardwick,
59th Field
Ambulance,
Royal Army
Medical Corps

7 July: We were rudely awakened this morning at 7.00 am by the arrival of urgent orders to send all available bearers and MOs [Medical Officers] to 57th FA [Field Ambulance] at once as a big attack was going to take place this morning. There has been a terrific bombardment last night and we were talking about it here and I little thought that we were going to pass through about the liveliest forty-eight hours I have ever experienced. …

Boyle and I and the men were equipped with steel helmets and a tin of bully and biscuits and we marched off to Bapaume Post. There was a big steel dugout situated 1½ miles up the road to Albert – that same road on the slope of the hill just beyond Tara Valley. It was an appalling day – continuous heavy rain. It is beyond me to describe decently the extraordinary picture of that area, not only the road, but the country around – one could see for miles as we were fairly high up. Away to the north and south one could pick out easily the various line of trenches as the earth thrown up was white chalk – straight ahead were the remains of what had once been <u>La Boisselle</u> – and to the right about one mile away was Bécourt Wood where Grieg and the ADS [Advanced Dressing Station] were. The road was full of people – supporting troops lying about in the open on either side. Steam cookers, ambulance cars, pioneers, water carriers, ammunition, etc. and coming down in squads of thirty and forty were Hun prisoners guarded by about six men with bayonets fixed – beastly looking men, tall and short, and many wearing large convex glasses for short sight. The noise was the limit as our batteries were firing like hell, big heavies and field [guns] and also a couple of batteries of Trench 75s – all this going on as far as one could see, both N. and S. apparently the Boche has not been firing on this hill, as the air was stiff with troops. It seemed especially extraordinary after Flanders where a mile further back one would not have liked to expose oneself so much.

Sergeant Arthur Perriman, 11th South Wales Borderers

The Germans had done themselves well. Well constructed timber-lined dugouts had been constructed in Caterpillar Wood. Those of the officers had excellent bunks, tables and chairs. There were allotments where seasonable vegetables were growing. The attack had been arranged for Zero hour – 7.00 am but was changed to 8.00 pm. Rations for the day were issued. For fifty-two of us I was allocated 1½ loaves of bread, a piece of boiled bacon weighting about 16 ozs after the Somme mud had been removed, a small quantity of biscuits, some currants and sultanas, and a petrol tin of tea. As I displayed the rations which would not be the 'last supper' but the 'last breakfast' for some of us I reminded my lads of the parable of the 'loaves and fishes', adding that as I had not the miraculous powers of Our Lord Jesus Christ, section commanders should toss up, winner taking the lot. At this, one of the lads said, 'Say, Sarge, the buggers do not intend us to die on a full stomach, do they?' There followed an issue of rum to those who wanted it. Bombardment from both sides was terrific. The Germans sent over a quantity of tear gas shells necessitating putting on goggles to protect the eyes. We were now awaiting orders to advance.

An artillery barrage was provided to cover the advance and the Borderers set off. The ground was undulating and gave decent cover until 150 yards from the wood, where the terrain dropped away affording the enemy an open field of fire. There was little resistance until the men got within 50 yards of the wood.

Without warning, not that we expected any, the whole front we were holding was subjected to murderous machine-gun fire. What had happened was the Germans had provided a rear-guard protection with three machine guns dug deeply into the ground. Our advance was watched by means of periscopes and fire was held until we provided an ideal target. Our advance was immediately checked. Casualties were becoming heavy. About 11.30 am – I was without an officer incidentally – an order reached me from the Company Commander to retire my platoon to a jumping-off point in Happy Valley, I was met by my company commander, who, on instructions from 'higher up' to collect a platoon for the purpose of attacking and capturing the three machine-gun posts which were inflicting so many casualties. He chose my platoon, in which he had supreme confidence emanating from previous escapades. I would have to mention and pay tribute to my platoon, for the wonderful co-operation they gave me, and refer to the fact, that on this day, there were six who had not yet reached the age of 18 years.

After briefing, we knew our expedition was a hazardous one to put it mildly. The German shelling on our position had intensified as to become a living hell. What our individual feelings were as we moved off remained inexpressible. Proceeding up Caterpillar Wood, which route would lead us to a rough farmyard road, our first objective: shrapnel and machine-gun fire spelled instant death. The Company Commander was the first to go. I was about a yard behind him when he was hit. He fell without

Sergeant Arthur Perriman, 11th South Wales Borderers

uttering a sound. I examined him and found he was dead. Moving on, I became the second casualty. Hits in the abdomen, leg and hand by shrapnel made it impossible for me to participate in any further action. I handed over charge to my supernumerary sergeant. There were no means of communicating casualties to the regimental casualty post so I had to make my way back to Happy Valley the best way I could.

Taking Mametz Wood would require days of battering and sacrifice. Time and again the Welsh Division were called upon to break into the wood. Three days after the first abortive attack, and after five days of fatigues during which hundreds of rolls of barbed wire, iron pickets, sandbags, picks and shovels had been carried up the line, it would be the turn of Private Thomas and his comrades.

Private William
Thomas, 14th
Royal Welsh
Fusiliers

On the afternoon of 9 July we marched back through and beyond Mametz and here we piled arms in a corn field, had a double ration of a sort of afternoon breakfast, lashings of tea. We were briefed for the attack that was going to take place the following morning but we were that tired with fatigue work and marching in our fighting order for 4/5 days without much rest that we slept soundly until the small hours of the morning of 10 July.

On waking, the men collected Mills bombs as well as other impedimenta such as telephone wire and an extra 250 rounds of small arms ammunition.

Private William
Thomas, 14th
Royal Welsh
Fusiliers

Our packs would be collected and placed in storage with the QM at Transport lines. A piece of red flannelette was placed under the flap of the haversack so that any of our troops in the rear could identify us. ... We marched back up the line in dead of night through that old familiar place, Mametz village again, which by now of course was the target for big crumping by German Artillery. Then down into Danzig Alley communication trench and eventually into our assembly trench, the old familiar Quadrangle right in front of the wood. We arrived there about two hours before zero hour which in our case being first wave over would be

the unearthly hour of 0400. As soon as we were in position our barrage of artillery commenced pounding onto the wood making such a continuous swish of shellfire that we could hardly hear ourselves without shouting to one another. …

Right on the dot of zero hour (0400 hours) we were away in extended order but no sooner had we left the safety of our trench when the Germans started to shell us with big stuff. We suffered a few casualties right away and were soon down into 'Happy Valley' and here met a withering German machine-gun and rifle fire from our immediate front as well as being enfiladed from our right flank. This is the spot where we lost most of our comrades, many being killed outright with either MG or rifle fire as above the staccato or MG fire we could distinguish the crackle of rifle fire.

We were now close up to the Germans in the wood so their artillery were not in a position to fire at us. I and two or three that survived in the valley went up towards the derelict battery position of German 17-pdrs which had been dug into the overhang of the grassy bank. I had a look in as I passed this gun position and the German gunners were sat on their gun seats with their arms on the breech blocks as if they were still active but on a closer look one could see they had been dead maybe three or four days as their faces and hands had turned into a greyish green colour. By this time there were only four of us left out of our platoon. I had lost my

Unloading ammunition at a battery position. The guns needed resupply almost around the clock.

mate Sammy Soar from Nottingham somewhere down in the valley as I never saw him again. It transpired after that he had been killed early on in the assault. I, with what was left of a Lewis gun team, only two of them standing, one holding the gun on his shoulder and his mate carrying some of the panniers and firing at the same time, pushed on through the barb wire in front of the German trench and our objective, and it was here that we came up against further German resistance in the shape of a counter-attack from a party of bombing German infantry.

We had managed to get into their trench and they were probably some reserves that had to come to the rescue of their comrades in the trench. They were somewhere way back in the wood itself. I caught a glimpse of some of them but not able to fire rifle shots at them and they were not able to aim rifles at us. At the point of entry into the trench I recall vividly that it was full of dead and/or dying German infantry, casualties apparently inflicted by our artillery barrage of a few moments ago.

I remember well the ashen pallor on the faces of those who had faces left. Quite a lot of them were just hunks of bodies, some torsos, some just limbs. Death to them would be instantaneous, mercifully. There must have been a platoon strength of German infantry defending this part of the wood, but they were all killed. After a pause we attempted to move forward but were pinned down by strong counter-attacks with the rattle of MG fire and hand grenades thrown by German troops coming forward from the rear. A few seconds later I was wounded by a German hand grenade of the stick bomb Percussion type which wounded me in the right foot (a broken bone in the instep), splintered part of the fibula below the right knee and a bit of it in my left elbow. The flash of the hand grenade flew up the right-hand side of my whole body into my face and temporarily blinded me in the right eye.

Hobbling out of the wood and taking cover in a freshly blown shell hole, as there were several about; now looking towards the furthest north-west corner of the wood some ¾ mile away I could see several hundreds of fully accounted German reserves silhouetted on the skyline pouring into the wood from the north, coming in across our front from the direction of Contalmaison. When I say fully accounted I could discern clearly from out of my left eye that they were wearing their full packs on their backs so that they must have been waiting in reserve for our main attack to materialize.

There was nothing more for me to do but as I came out of the wood I noticed our second wave, men of the 13th Battn, were moving forward into the wood and leap-frogging the position that I and my two Lewis gun comrades were occupying. I attended to myself with my own field dressing which I had on me and managed with this to stem the flow of blood coming out of my right knee. I couldn't move at all as there was too much fire of one sort or another going on. A German Spandau was 'phat phatting' away somewhere to my right and shells were swishing overhead and dropping immediately behind. After a while things quietened down a bit and I decided to leave the safety of my shell hole and hobbled away back towards the spot whence I came.

Thomas hobbled out of the fighting until he came across some stretcher-bearers who carried him to a first aid post in a deep German dugout before he was sent down to a casualty clearing station. During the fighting, he had thrown one of the two detonated Mills hand grenades that he was carrying, but forgot about the second one in his left-hand trouser pocket. This was only discovered when he was being undressed in a ward, causing no little consternation amongst the staff.

As the fighting raged in Mametz Wood, Rifleman Giles Eyre and his battalion approached the Somme battlefields reinvigorated by the sights of Picardy. Entering the fray too was Private Thomas Lyon, 1/9th Highland Light Infantry. The men, both experienced campaigners, appeared to be touched once more by the idealism and sense of adventure that brought them into the army in 1914 and simultaneously awed by the monumental British and Empire effort being made in France.

For hours our feet beat in rhythmical unison, and we moved up that interminable highway, dusty, thirsty and sweaty, but full of vim and vigour, for the varied busy sights around us, the traffic, the troops, the guns, all proclaimed in unmistakable terms that the British Army, after two weary years of position warfare, undermined and outgunned, was at long last leaping forward at the enemy, fresh and dauntless, its ranks filled with the best material that a soldier can wish for – enthusiastic, high-mettled

Rifleman Giles Eyre, 2nd Kings Royal Rifle Corps

young men, whom love of country had summoned from the four corners of the world.

This highway was a veritable processional route of the British race. The ceaseless stream of Yorkshiremen, Welshmen, Scots, Irish, South Africans, men from Cornwall and the Fen Country, battalions of short, sturdy fellows from the great industrial centres, ploughboys, miners, clerks, students, labourers, pioneers from rough Colonial backwoods and the products of public school and Varsity, marching cheek by jowl in a comradeship cemented by a common purpose and a mutual respect welded these representatives of the various rungs of our social ladder into a vital, harmonious whole such as the wild, fantastic theories of political tub-thumpers, social reformers and scatterbrained and unbalanced dreamers and theoreticians will never achieve. For this mass of Britain's

German prisoners carry a wounded Tommy out of the firing line. This picture was taken by an officer in the 1/4th Yorkshire Regiment.

splendid youth, marching onward into battle with a song on its lips and a steadfast courage, represented reality and all that was best in our race, and hallmarked the age-old truth that the way to the stars lies through selfless sacrifice.

This vision of radiant manhood tramping undaunted towards the life-searing heat of the flame of conflict, impressed itself deeply on my receptive mind, and has ever remained a symbol to strive after. ... Unity born of understanding, achievement through mutual striving! This the pregnant message that those about to die flung to the legions that would follow them. Will it ever be understood, I wonder?

'Show a leg there, boys! It's after 6.30, and breakfast is up.'

The voice of the Orderly Officer was cheerful [even] if his raps on the walls of our little tents were peremptory and commanding.

In the manner of worms we slid and wriggled out of our bivvies and, having scrambled to our feet, stood blinking in the bright morning sunshine. A little later the battalion, in column of route, was moving towards the firing line. The roar of the guns, from being dull and distance-muffled, became sharp and distinct. A squat, fat, green-painted monster, standing in the middle of a farmyard, barked as we passed by.

'We're getting' into it now!' said Corporal Popple, in tones of immense satisfaction, then sang with gusto, 'Come on along with me an' have a jubilee, In ma old Picardy home.'

An excited ejaculation passed rapidly along the ranks: 'German prisoners!'

The rear of the long column swung inwards with a serpent-like motion: men were sidestepping and craning their necks to see ahead on the white, dusty roadway.

The prisoners trailed past us, perhaps 300 of them, dust-grimed, dejected, and surly of aspect, and escorted by a score or so of Tommies whose smiles out-beamed the sun. A little farther on we passed another band of prisoners, then, beside a tent that served as a casualty clearing station, we saw a crowd of Germans, bandaged of head or limb, awaiting their turn for medical treatment. Our fellows hailed all these parties with good-humoured chaff and badinage, but few acknowledged the greetings

Private Thomas Lyon, 1/9th Highland Light Infantry

by so much as a smile. They preserved a stubborn silence and feigned a total lack of interest in us.

The effect of these successive encounters on the spirits of our men was remarkable. The very air seemed stimulant with a sense of victory. A strange exultation possessed everyone, an irrepressible and irresponsible gaiety and light-heartedness, an eagerness to be up and doing in the thick of the fight. ...

We strode forward with a step as buoyant and chatter as merry as though we had been going home on leave. And now the land immediately ahead and on either side was ripped and scarred by a series of white chalky lines that zig-zagged and criss-crossed like the lines of a puzzle. We were into the world of trenches again, yet lo! we walked upon the surface of the earth without fear. The wonder of it acted like wine in our veins.

'By hokey! it's been some Push right enough,' said one: and there was something of awe in his tones.

'Look over there! That's the front line now,' said another and pointed towards the farther distance, where in the upper air tiny shrapnel clouds were seen to form like toy balloons and, expanding and drifting, grow fainter and fainter until they faded into nothingness. And the sudden spurts of debris that shot up high and dark, like infernal fountains, against the horizon, we knew for the bursting of heavy shells. We came upon a squad of French soldiers at work on the road, repairing the damage done to it by shells. Others were filling up an old communication trench that ran by the roadside and might constitute a danger to traffic if allowed to remain open. ...

When we had reached the crumbled white ditch that had formerly been the British first line of defence we moved off the roadway and, having halted, piled arms and 'fell out'. All day long, under the blue tent of the summer sky, we lay on a barren strip of ground, rumpled and uneven, hashed and torn by the shells that had deluged it, the debris of which, jagged splinters of steel and iron and empty shell cases, still littered it. Such grass as still remained in isolated patches was yellow in death: even the rich blood that had freely flowed there had failed to revive it.

For, until a fortnight before, this had been no-man's-land, the narrow barrier interposed between the warring nations. For nearly two years a curse had lain upon this land: nor man nor beast walked there by day or night. The peril of death was upon it. Yet now we idled away the long hours in peace and security on that once unhallowed spot: we ate our dinner with the relish of hungry men; we made merry, impelled by our sense of victory; individually we mused and marvelled over the story of this place. We were thrilled by the wonder of the thing.

Before us and on either side, crowning ridges and traversing the hollows, stretched the interminable white streaks that showed where the former enemy fortifications had been fortifications deemed by their holders to be impregnable, but now blown and battered out of all semblance to even the crudest trench. At regular intervals in the upper air, and extending in a curving line along the whole front were British observation balloons. From our point of vantage we could count sixteen of them. ...

On the summit of a ridge, some 200 or 300 yards distant, was a system of trenches that had suffered less from the bombardment of our guns than others in the vicinity. A few of us made a tour of exploration there. It was a strange sensation one had in walking about these desolate trenches, so dilapidated and containing so many relics of the men who had been their tenants for so long a time. A sensation as of walking the streets of a city of the dead.

At the crossways, German signboards still stood to direct the wayfarer, and above the entrances to the dugouts were other boards of designation. On the doorjambs and other woodwork were pencilled drawings and inscriptions, just such expressions of whimsy as we had often recorded in an idle moment in our own trenches. A muddied German greatcoat lay on the firing step, with a half-dozen broken and crumpled cigarettes in a pocket: stuffed between two sandbags in the parapet was a Bavarian newspaper, a small local print, dated 24 June; in a niche in the parados was a soot-blackened mess tin supported on two bricks above a handful of grey ashes; and there was a profusion of scraps of equipment and clothing and empty beer bottles.

In trench warfare one comes to regard one's foes as impersonal – forgets that they are men very much like ourselves, having pretty much the same sensations and feelings, living amid conditions similar to our

The remains of the village of Contalmaison, just to the west of Mametz Wood, after its capture.

own, suffering the same discomforts and hardships, alternately cheered and disheartened by the same sort of happenings. One has the feeling of being opposed to a colossal machine rather than men of flesh and blood, which is not surprising when one considers that sometimes for months on end one may be in and out the trenches with monotonous regularity and yet never see a German. But walking thus through their old trenches one was brought into a closer human sympathy with the Germans than ever before: by that I mean that one realized them as men like ourselves, living or having lived in the trenches a life like unto that we knew.

As Rifleman Eyre approached the trenches fought over on the first day, the true extent of the carnage became apparent as he looked through the flotsam and jetsam of war. It was hard to not to feel a certain sympathy for the fallen of both sides.

The day is blazing hot. Over the tangle of trees and broken houses by Albert a couple of observation balloons hang in the sky like monstrous swollen sausages. Away on our right a flicker of dazzling white high up, surrounded by the spreading cloudlets of Archie bursts, denotes one of our planes on observation bent.

Rifleman Giles Eyre, 2nd Kings Royal Rifle Corps

We are now scrambling over what must have been the British front line trenches, a maze of humps and hillocks, half-filled-in ditches, mounds of faded and burst sandbags, barbed wire clumps sticking out here and there, shell holes, smashed trench boards and a litter of rusty tins, pieces of equipment, broken rifles and goodness knows what else. We strike out into what was once no-man's-land, a welter of confused destruction and shell holes. … Here all the casualties have not been gathered in yet, and horrible-looking bundles of khaki, once men, still lie in shell holes. We pass one close in a shell hole by the cart track. Lying on his back, his steel helmet half concealing his blackened features. Clothing all awry, legs drawn up. Must have been hit somewhere in the stomach. A storm of fat buzzing flies hovers over this poor wreckage of humanity. We hurry by, averting our faces.

'Time they took all these poor blighters in,' mutters Oldham. …

We scrambled on past all the pitiful litter and on to that gash of chalky hummocks and dirty bags running across our front that had been the German front trench. Here the havoc was unimaginable and stood revealed in all its ghastly details under the rays of the bright sun. A strange, mephitic, indescribable smell hung about here like a tangible pall. Bodies were numerous, twisted in all the attitudes of death. Quite a lot of ours – Lincolns, Scots, Yorks, mostly in shell holes before the trench. This itself was practically flattened, bags all down and destroyed, but here and there the openings of dugouts stood unharmed.

Bloated, grey-clad figures littered the whole place. Some crouching against the sides, some lying stark and still, sightless eyes staring up at the blue vault of heaven. One dead German on a stretcher with bandages all over him, by a dugout entrance. And all around a littler of uniforms, torn overcoats, accoutrements, tangles of barbed wire, letters and packs of cards scattered all over.

A wrecked and overturned machine gun with two or three dead Huns by it at one angle of the bay. A crazy direction board with big Gothic letters, '*Graben II*'. Helmets, caps, bayonets, all the flotsam of an army.

'Good Lord! It must have been a hell of a hot show judging by all this!' muttered Rodwell, staring at this scene of wanton destruction with bulging eyes. 'Let's have a look in the dugouts!'

We moved along the wrecked trench. ... We descended a few dark steps into a dugout, but we quickly sought the open air again. It was a shambles of dead humanity!

Across towards the patches of woodland, that I later learned was Shelter Wood, the trail of the battle tide was much the same. It looked as if a hard fight had been waged here all right.

The dead, swollen bodies of the Germans bore mostly the same shoulder numeral – 111th Regiment. We foraged around for a while picking up a few of the usual mementoes. Most of the letters were still

In deep contemplation: two officers belonging to the 1/4th Yorkshire Regiment in Shelter Wood.

damp; the rain had smudged the ink and the letters were running over all the page. Still some were faintly decipherable. What misery, what heart searchings were contained perhaps in some of them. And their owners? Mostly littering this stricken field. We picked up a few scraps here and there and attempted to decipher a few words. Both O'Donnell and I had a nodding acquaintance with German. '*Liebchen*,' read one, 'I am writing under the roar of guns which never ceases. For one week now the British have been bombarding constantly. We expect their attack at any time. We have been ordered to hold our trenches at all costs, so pray the good God …' and there the fragment ended. Many others were in a similar strain, and we quite visualized what a hell it must have been for them.

I am trying to send home certain Boche souvenirs – with which this country is littered. I enclose here the epaulette from the shoulder of some defunct German, with the number of his regiment on it. I am trying to send the bolt of a German rifle, a German soft forage cap and the outer case of a German bomb: I hope they reach you. I have collected one or two other good souvenirs: two bits of nose cap that I found sticking in the parados of the trench over my head, two days after the first strafe; a French bullet found in these trenches; and a bit of shell that fell from the skies, off an 'Archie' – one of ours. I am going to make a valiant attempt to send home some Boche souvenirs: bombs, cartridges, mess tin and the autograph of a Boche soldier who I hope is now extinct: one Tas Kraus. The bombs are in pieces, after explosion, therefore perfectly safe.

Second Lieutenant John Godfrey, 103 Field Company, Royal Engineers

I have a German rifle in my tent which I thought of bringing home, in spite of the regulations to the contrary, but I abandoned the idea on account of its bulkiness. Upon telling my servant this today, he offered to take the rifle home for me, when he goes on leave. I asked him how he proposed to do it, adding that he would certainly be stopped.

'I should carry it instead of my own rifle, Sir,' he said.

'And how would you account for not having a rifle on landing in France again, after your leave?' I asked.

'Oh,' said he, with a grin, 'you've got to risk something in this world if you are going to have any success. You should just see me play nap, Sir!'

Lieutenant Colonel Rowland Feilding, 1st Coldstream Guards

Souvenirs recovered in early July: two officers of 183 Tunnelling Company are delighted with their pickelhaubers, two of the more sought-after items of German property.

A water tank with a picture of the Commander-in-Chief painted on the side.

Catapillar Driver's Handy work! SERGT G. SECTION.
Painting of Haig. on Water Tank.

It was very clear to everyone that there would be no decisive breakthrough and that the Germans would contest every wood, valley and lane. This was industrial warfare – modern warfare – on an epic scale, with on every side the evidence of its power to destruct and crush. In the south, the offensive had breached the second line of German defences and now new objectives hove into view.

Through dust and heat and a myriad flies, the sweating division wound its way through Fricourt. Hugging the side of the road to let pass the endless traffic of ambulances, horses, lorries, prisoners of war, water carts, walking wounded, limbers, dispatch riders, food and fodder wagons which poured ceaselessly from the forward area, the column wriggled forward, stumbling and jostling while it exchanged familiar obscenities and blasphemies in jest or in execration, with those who passed down the valley towards Corbie and Amiens. ...

Up through the ruins of Montauban, where the enemy still grinned in his ghastly sleep, the division wound its way along the pitted road. My eyes swept the bitter landscape, from a corner of which the shattered wooden crosses, in ragged disorder, beckoned to my disciplined and orderly spirit. The squat stump of an old fruit tree on the edge of a cemetery stripped of its leaves, curiously reminded me of a friendly veteran in the garden at Pinner.

My company was tried, had been refined. Sure. Sure as God made little apples ... and here and everywhere death stalked. There would be no ripened fruit in the autumn. How many of the men who bravely stepped behind me would return? How many in the presence of physical death were ready to put off this mortal body, as part of a wholesale massacre, limbs hurled hideously to the four winds, or crushed in the shambles of a dugout? How many realized the fullness of spiritual life?

I think I could read the thoughts of these untutored lads. The full tragedy of modern warfare was laid bare to the eyes of many for the first time. The ribaldry tossed from mouth to mouth was the camouflage for fresh horrors, which nearly every step revealed. The bloated carcasses of animals with distended stomachs lay in every ditch; and each bend of the road multiplied the bodies mutilated beyond recognition, distorted from almost any semblance of human form lying everywhere unburied.

Lieutenant Colonel Graham Hutchinson, 33rd Battalion, Machine Gun Corps

Poor little apples: fear was in many hearts, fear of the unknown. The air reverberated with the thunder of bombardment. Great shells hurled themselves through the trees shorn of their summer splendour, torn and jagged, and buried themselves beneath the undergrowth of Mametz Wood, hard by the bitter road. ...

My company passed up the gentle slope to Bazentin, lying bleak, its shattered walls, gaunt, pink-dusted ruins echoing with the unceasing chatter of machine-gun fire, and wound its way through woods in which wild strawberries still held their sweet greeting for the passer-by; while a fitful bombardment plunged indiscriminate shellfire among the clattering bricks, from the midst of which a splintered crucifix reared itself as the symbol of sacrifice.

It was noon. The company spread itself in a ditch from which, across the valley through the dust and haze of the British bombardment, could be seen the leafy trees of High Wood, to the left flank the village of Martinpuich with its halo of pink brick dust, and to the south, Delville Wood, sprawling upon the hillside. And beside the wood, Waterlot Farm, the name familiar in all Flanders. A runner, great beads of sweat on his brow, fear in his eyes, brought a message for me to report at Brigade Headquarters installed in a deep dugout, cut from the chalk of the hillside.

The valley had been filled with tear gas. Men, presenting the appearance of hideous pantomime figures from a Tibetan passion play, groped with monstrous nose and eyepieces. I, dragging my feet through rifles, coils of wire, boxes of bombs, and those mechanical contraptions which are the panoply of war, with smarting blood-scared eyes, joined the group of battalion commanders behind the blanket curtain. My brigadier, Walter Baird of the Gordons, explained briefly that the battalion deploying in the valley east of Bazentin, with the whole division, was to attack at 9.30 the following morning. The objective was firstly High Wood and Martinpuich, and thence an unlimited field of advance through the city of Bapaume. The deployment ground was to be reconnoitred during the evening.

I returned to the company, little better informed, but with a map, well marked with arrows pointing to the east. An unfortunate shell, during my absence, had killed one and wounded three men, one of whom I met

upon the pathway, happy with men from other units with their 'Blighty ones'. Late in the afternoon, with my section commanders, I passed along the narrow road leading down to the valley, at the higher end of which, now wreathed in smoke, stood High Wood. For a few minutes I conversed with a major of Indian Horse and learned that the cavalry were concentrating in Caterpillar Valley and would break through, so soon as High Wood was captured, and this, the last line of German defence, had been pierced. The British artillery still continued its hurricane fire upon the wood, while observation officers directed it from vantage points in Bazentin. On my return, having viewed the ground for deployment, I questioned a gunner as to the enemy's disposition and strength. 'It's a cakewalk,' replied the gunner. 'Nothing can live there, my dear fellow, nothing can live there!'

An observation balloon rises from the ground behind Carnoy. These balloons allowed observers to see much further than ground-based observers, helping the artillery engage targets miles behind enemy lines.

Private Thomas
Lyon, 1/9th
Highland Light
Infantry

In the early evening the battalion was again formed up, and the order was given to march. Our way led through the complex maze of the former German trenches, and we took in every detail with absorbed and wondering eyes. For us the place seemed peopled with the ghosts of our foes: so vividly could we picture them in their life behind the lines. There was a piquancy, droll and delightful, in the sensation of being where they had so little expected us ever to be.

As we went further, evidences of the ferocity of the struggle became more remarkable. In the newspapers we had read a few days previously that 'The village of Fricourt is now in our hands.' When we came to Fricourt we remembered and laughed over the naiveté of the phrase, for Fricourt was but a name and a rubbish dump, an extensive litter of smashed bricks and crumbled mortar: not one stone had been left standing on another.

All the surrounding country was pitted as with a gigantic species of smallpox: or like a sea that has been churned into a mass of seething whirlpools and then suddenly petrified. Of grass or other living growth there was none: the shattered earth stretched bare and bleached under the august eye of the sun: there seemed no inch of it that had been left untouched by the devastating artillery fire. Such trees as still stood were white and gleaming skeletons clean stripped of leaf and twig and bark. In one place a few dozens of these gaunt spectres of trees were thinly clustered together, the pitiable monument of a dead and vanished wood.

At the ruins of Mametz village, motor ambulances were gathered in great numbers, and in front of improvised dressing stations were groups of wounded men. Now that they were out of danger and setting out on the primrose path that leads to Blighty, a marked cheerfulness was in their demeanour, and they shouted to us that it had been another great day: the cavalry had been in action, we had cleared the Germans from High Wood, and we had taken many hundreds of prisoners.

Thereafter we passed numerous batches of these prisoners being herded down from the line by small parties of British soldiers, and there was a constant stream of our own wounded, some painfully walking alone or assisted by a comrade, others on stretchers whose bearers were often Germans under the armed surveillance of a Tommy. The road ran at the foot of a long ridge which rose immediately on our right, and to the left was a level space stretching across to the dark bulk, white-scarred, of Mametz Wood. Over this space guns were scattered in prodigal profusion, battery upon battery standing unscreened in the open, in the positions they had but newly taken up. And all vomiting forth flame and noise without cessation.

The air shivered with the tumult of cannon. From the other side of the ridge came the muffled drum roll of several batteries of French 75s. Overhead great shells shrieked on their passage from the guns in the rear. ...

A halt was called, the last prior to our going into action. We established ourselves in a series of newly dug man holes (like shallow graves) that stretched in a line between the road and the wood. Darkness fell. But in every direction it was riven by yellow flashes of light: and the air was thunderous with the incessant roaring of guns and bursting of shells. The forward horizon was aflare as far as eye could see: at points innumerable and ever changing there were volcanic bursts of savage flame in ceaseless succession: all up and down the long battlefront the glare in the sky flickered and danced, was here vivid and there faint, but was unbroken. And in this warmly luminous upper air a myriad star shells winked in and out, soared and drifted and fell, like so many green rushlights.

The spectacle was as magnificent as, to the imaginative eye, it was full of terror. Fascinated, we lay in the strangely troubled dark and watched this fantastic demoniac revel of light, the roar of the guns still surging through the air in a shattering devil's tattoo. Then the order was given to fall in, and we went forward into action.

The last portion of Mametz Wood had been taken on the afternoon of 11 July and the line pushed forward. Then, on 14 July, a large assault was made at dawn, pushing the Germans back to the next ridge and their next line of defence, which included the formidable looking High and Delville woods, which would host the next phase of fighting over several weeks. As a prelude to that next stage, the 33rd Division was pressed into action on the morning of 15 July, including the 1/9th Highland Light Infantry, which took up positions the night before.

Lieutenant
Colonel
Graham
Hutchinson,
33rd Battalion,
Machine Gun
Corps

During the night, patrols went out to make contact with the enemy. They were fired upon from the wood's edge and by riflemen lying out in scoops and in narrow trenches west and south of the village. They discovered that the Germans had laid out several strands of wire, uncut by the artillery, and, hidden by the long grass, forming a considerable and dangerous obstacle. The Brigadier was wrathful: repeatedly he requested a further bombardment, but such requests were made in vain or were not practicable. He fumed with anger, cursed the higher command through the bristles of a red moustache. As a sound tactician he was not unfamiliar with the results to infantry of a frontal attack against uncut wire, enfiladed by well-posted machine guns. 'PBI' [Poor Bloody Infantry], I reflected, a sobriquet, so truthful: an infantry so soused in blood.

In the early morning, under cover of a thick mist, the 100th Brigade was deployed in the valley some 800 yards west of High Wood. A heavy dew was on the ground and hung like pearls upon each blade of grass. After the turmoil of the preceding night an eerie stillness pervaded the atmosphere. No shot was heard, except a faint echo from the flank. Men spoke in whispers. Their faces were pallid, dirty, and unshaven, many with eyes ringed with fatigue after the night, hot and fetid, gaseous and disturbed by shellfire, in Bazentin. Few there were whose demeanour expressed eagerness for the assault. They were moving into position with good discipline, yet listless, as if facing the inevitable. Their identity as individuals seemed to be swallowed up in the immensity of war: devitalized electrons. I, with my company, was deployed behind the Glasgow Highlanders, which with the 16th Battalion King's Royal Rifles was to lead the assault upon the wood. By 8.30 am the brigade had deployed into position and lay down in the long grass awaiting the signal to assault, timed for an hour later.

I passed the time with dried blades of grass, chivvying the red ants and preventing them from crossing a narrow trench which I had scratched with a fingernail. And I pencilled a sketch or two. It was restful and pleasant lying in the warm humid atmosphere, belly to the ground, in the quiet of the early morning. I looked up suddenly. The mist was clearing, rising rapidly. The sun peered through, orange and round, topping the trees of High Wood. Then its rays burst through the disappearing mists, and all the landscape, hitherto opaque and flat, assumed its stereoscopic vivid form. The wood seemed quite near, just above us up the hillside; a little to the left behind a broken hedge was an abandoned German battery, dead gunners and horses around it. The village of Martinpuich, jagged ruins and rafters all askew, broken walls and shattered fruit trees, looked down. Both trees and village appeared gargantuan, and the men awaiting to attack like midgets from Lilliput. From my cover, I scanned the landscape. Not a shot was fired. The men crouching in the grass must be visible to watchful observers in the wood, but all remained quiet. I glanced down at my watch. Ten minutes to go: the attack was timed for 9.30.

High Wood was in our hands! The Germans had been cleared from it that day! So we had been informed. And now the leading platoon was marching in single file along the outskirts of the wood, the others following at discreet intervals. Ever and anon an enemy shell came screeching into the wood, and the roar of its explosion was accompanied by the sharp sounds of the rending and splitting of trees, and of the crashing of their fall.

Private Thomas Lyon, 1/9th Highland Light Infantry

In silence for the most part the men trudged along in the darkness that was disturbed by the flicker of light from the distant bursting shells, but every little while came a questioning whisper, 'I wonder where old Fritz is? Where's the front line? No sign of it here.' Then suddenly without warning the darkness of the wood was broken by a score of tongues of flame: and the noise of the artillery and shell bursts was drowned in the splitting roar of rifles and machine guns fired at close range. And the air was full of flying, hissing bullets.

For an instant our fellows stood paralyzed. One fell and lay moaning: another dropped to his knees, then pitched forward and lay dumb and still. A voice, hoarse with some kind of passion, rang out, 'Get down, men, get down!' And all threw themselves on the ground, crouching low as they might, and waited in blind wonderment for what seemed an endless time, while they sought by a sort of instinctive prayer to gain mastery over the fear that was in their hearts. And ever the streaming bullets swished over and about them with the sound of a scythe swung fiercely among hay: and ever a moan came from out the darkness at some new point or a mad, stabbing cry or a sobbing gasp that told a life was finished.

'Dig yourself in and don't expose yourself!' The order passed from lip to lip, and entrenching tools were got out. With feverish quickness the men began to dig, though daring hardly to raise their bodies from the ground. A few carried proper spades and, on their knees and crouching low, threw up the earth with a passionate energy. Each man knew that he was digging for dear life, and breathed more freely when he had scraped away enough of the earth's surface to afford him some protection from the perpetually menacing bullets.

The battalion stretched now across and through the narrow wood, some platoons being in the open on the left of it, others in the wood itself, and others on the right. All were digging themselves in with that tireless impetuosity occasioned only by pressing danger. It was, however, the company on the right of the wood, that which had first advanced, which sustained the heaviest casualties during the night: at other parts of our line there was almost complete freedom from enemy annoyance, and the men there had no idea that their pals, only a short distance off, were paying so heavy a toll. ...

The infinite weariness of that night! Time seemed to have been suspended: the moments dropped slowly and fitfully: the minutes dragged out into interminable hours. ... The officers moved about, encouraging and cheering the men with brave words, and themselves exhibiting a marvellous calmness of demeanour and contempt of danger. And ever and again the Commanding Officer would appear at each part of the line, walking upright and fearless, and in his voice was always that note of confidence and of comradely sympathy that never failed to put fresh heart into our fellows when they were in a tight corner. Everything was all right if only the Colonel were with them: he'd never let them down, he knew the game of soldiering through and through, and he knew and understood his men; he made them feel that he was one of themselves and always he did his utmost and best for them. A rare chap, the Colonel! So the boys thought and reasoned. Once the CO started to move forward from our line towards the hidden Germans. Our men called to him not to go farther, as the danger was great. He paused for a moment. 'It's all right, boys,' he said kindly. 'I've got to go forward a little way, it's to help you. I'll come back.' Then he strode on, two other officers and his faithful batman following close on his heels. And yet again he stood sadly regarding two still forms that lay at his feet. 'Poor boys!' he said in a tone of infinite pity: 'poor boys!' and turned away. …

The Glasgows crouched low in their shallow ditch and wondered what was to happen now. A feeling was abroad that they would have to go 'up and over' and clear the wood at the point of the bayonet, and all hoped that it might be so. Action was what they wanted, the chance to do something. At one part of our line our fellows saw Germans moving about in the farther recesses of the wood, and for an hour or two our snipers who naturally comprised every man who could see a target put in some really successful work: as did also the Lewis guns.

And then soon after nine o'clock in the morning, and when somehow they were not expecting it, for their thoughts were on a breakfast of bully and biscuit, the order came to go 'up and over'. They were to clear the wood and go on to a certain point beyond it. For a quarter of an hour our artillery rained shells on the corner of the wood that held the Germans, and on the enemy's supports. And our men jested among themselves. The tension was over: they were going to get their own back now: they had stormed a Boche stronghold before, and had come out 'laughing': this might be a sterner job, but the Glasgows could do it if anyone could. … There was discussion arising from surmise as to the disposal of the remainder of the brigade and division, as to which battalions would be acting in concert, and then 'Up! over you go, men!'

And they were on the surface of the ground and running forward. A withering blast of machine-gun fire met them almost at once, and many stumbled and fell ere they had gone more than a few yards. But the others trotted on throwing themselves down full length at intervals to regain breath and secure cover, and by a vigorous rapid fire to cover the advance of another section of the line.

I could see the broad kilted buttocks and bronzed thighs and knees of the 9th HLI lining the slope ahead of me. They were lying in regular lines. A wind seemed to stir the tall grass. My heart thumped in my throat, I raised my head as the Highlanders rose to their feet, bayonets gleaming in the morning sun. My eyes swept the valley – long lines of men, officers at their head in the

Lieutenant Colonel Graham Hutchinson, 33rd Battalion, Machine Gun Corps half-crouching attitude which modern tactics dictate, resembling suppliants rather than the vanguard of a great offensive, were moving forward over 3 miles of front. As the attackers rose, white bursts of shrapnel appeared among the trees and thinly across the ridge towards Martinpuich.

For a moment the scene remained as if an Aldershot [training] manoeuvre. Two, three, possibly four seconds later an inferno of rifle and machine-gun fire broke from the edge of High Wood, from high up in its trees, and from all along the ridge to the village. The line staggered. Men fell forward limply and quietly. The hiss and crack of bullets filled the air and skimmed the long grasses. The Highlanders and riflemen increased their pace to a jogtrot. Those in reserve clove to the ground more closely. I, looking across the valley to my left flank, could see the men of the 1st Queen's passing up the slope to Martinpuich. Suddenly they wavered and a few of the foremost attempted to cross some obstacles in the grass. They were awkwardly lifting their legs over a low wire entanglement. Some 200 men, Major Palmer at their head, had been brought to a standstill at this point. A scythe seemed to cut their feet from under them, and the line crumpled and fell, stricken by machine-gun fire. Those in support wavered, then turned to fly. There was no shred of cover and they fell in their tracks as rabbits fall at a shooting battue.

Up the slope before me, the line of the attack had been thinned now to a few men, who from time to time raised themselves and bounded forward with leaps and rushes. I could see men in the trees taking deliberate aim down upon those who still continued to fight, or who in their scores lay dead and wounded on the hillside. My orders were to move forward in close support of the advancing waves of infantry. I called to my company, and section by section in rushes, we were prepared to move forward. As we rose to our feet a hail of machine-gun bullets picked here an individual man, there two or three, and swept past us. I raised a rifle to the trees and took deliberate aim, observing my target crash through the foliage into the undergrowth beneath. On my right, Huxley, commanding a section, had perished and all his men, with the exception of one who came running towards me, the whole of the front of his face shot away. On my left two other sections had been killed almost to a man, and I could see the tripods of the guns with legs waving in the air, and ammunition boxes scattered among the dead.

The difficulties of those within the wood were tremendous: the undergrowth was so thick that progress was almost an impossibility. A terrific fire of shrapnel was now playing as well upon the advancing line: in ones and twos and threes the men were falling. On the left flank a subaltern, the only officer left of his company, rallied his men and urged them on: then he too suddenly pitched forward and lay still. Immediately a young sergeant jumped forward and took his place at the head of the line, such a thin, scattered line and shouted, 'Come on, you fellows: keep in line close up go easy in front. … Down!' They lay panting for a few moments, thankful if they had the protection of a clump of grass or a cluster of nettles. 'Forward!' shouted the little sergeant and jumped to his feet. He took two paces forward, then spun sharply round on his heels and fell headlong as a bullet crashed through his brain. And a Lance-Jack leapt forward and put himself at the head of the company.

Private Thomas Lyon, 1/9th Highland Light Infantry

The farthest advanced had gone barely 200 yards, and only a few were left, widely scattered. Many were isolated and were crawling on hands and knees and dodging from shell hole to shell hole for essential cover: yet always advancing. But now they saw their effort was vain: their fighting strength was spent, they were a mere handful and leaderless: the one duty that remained was to retire whence they had come.

A German gun captured by the Black Watch near Contalmaison.

Lieutenant
Colonel
Graham
Hutchinson,
33rd Battalion,
Machine Gun
Corps

The attack of the Rifles and Highlanders had failed; and of my own company but a few remained. My watch showed that by now it was scarcely ten o'clock. I hurriedly wrote a message reporting the position and that of the attack for the colonel of the 2nd Worcesters, Pardoe, gallant soldier and good friend, who was in a sunken road with his battalion in reserve 300 yards to the rear. I gave this to my runner. 'Keep low,' I said, 'and go like blazes,' for the waving grass was being whipped by bullets, and it scarcely seemed possible that life could remain for more than a few minutes. A new horror was added to the scene of carnage. From the valley between Pozieres and Martinpuich a German field battery had been brought into action, enfilading the position. I could see the gunners distinctly. At almost point-blank range they had commenced to direct shellfire among the wounded. The shells bit through the turf, scattering the white chalk, and throwing aloft limbs, clothing, and fragments of flesh. Anger and the intensity of the fire consumed my spirit, and not caring for the consequences, I rose and turned my machine gun upon the battery, laughing loudly as I saw the loaders fall.

I crept forward among the Highlanders and riflemen, spurring them to action, giving bullet for bullet, directing fire upon the machine-gun nests, whose red flashes and wisps of steam made them conspicuous targets. The shellfire increased from both flanks, and the smooth sward became pitted and hideous, but as each shell engraved itself upon the soil, a new scoop of cover was made for the safety of a rifleman. A Highlander, terror in his eyes, lay on his back spewing blood, the chest of his tunic stained red. I tore open the buttons and shirt. It was a clean bullet wound, and I gave words of encouragement to the man, dragging him to a shell cavity, so that in a more upright position he could regain strength after the swamping of his lungs, and then creep back to safety. The dismal action was continued throughout the morning, German fire being directed upon any movement on the hillside. Towards noon, as my eyes searched the valley for reinforcements or for some other sign of action by those directing the battle, I descried a squadron of Indian cavalry, dark faces under glistening helmets, galloping across the valley towards the slope. No troops could have presented a more inspiring sight than these natives of India with lance and sword, tearing in mad cavalcade onto the skyline. A few disappeared over it: they never came back. ...

I realized the utter futility of any further attempt to advance, and bent my energies to extricating such men as remained alive and unwounded from the battleground, now the point of concentration of guns and machine-gun fire, upon which it was suicide to remain.

The remnant of the battalion, on reaching their former trenches, and being reinforced by the men of another unit, again took up the task of 'holding the line'. As the long hours of the day wore on, stragglers, those who had been cut off, continued to arrive, and each brought a tale of other pals lying wounded and dead 'out yonder'. It was impossible to reach them and bring them back then, although many volunteered to make the attempt. When night fell, a party was sent out to bring back such of the wounded as were at all accessible: and lives were saved thus and others were lost in the work of salvation.

Private Thomas Lyon, 1/9th Highland Light Infantry

Bodies just brought down from the line await burial. The dead men are still lying on stretchers and covered with blankets.

The battalion was relieved on the morning of 16 July. Their Commanding Officer, Lieutenant Colonel John Collier Stormouth-Darling, surveyed the survivors of the battalion of which he had been so proud. Only arbout 200 answered the first roll call out of perhaps 800 who had gone forward.

Private Thomas
Lyon, 1/9th
Highland Light
Infantry

Talking to a brigade officer, he was heard to say in reference to those who
had fallen, 'Six hundred of the best soldiers that ever wore the King's
uniform': then, with a sudden note of bitterness, 'I wish to God the honour
had been mine to go West with them!'

Lieut Col John Collier Stormouth-Darling, DSO, was killed in action
about three months later. It was almost impossible to convey the measure
of the sense of loss experienced by the Glasgows at his death. No battalion
commander was ever more beloved of his men: their admiration for him
as a gallant soldier and courteous gentleman amounted to veneration. His
first thought was ever for the welfare and comfort of his troops, and in his
endeavours to ensure those he spared himself not at all. His manner of life
was Spartan in its simplicity, and when the battalion was in circumstances
particularly dangerous or nerve-racking or arduous, he was ever at hand,
sharing the lot of his troops.

Private
Sydney Fuller,
8th Suffolk
Regiment

20 July: It was impossible to get any rations or water up to the line during
the day – too much enemy shelling. Our valley was not shelled so much
as on the previous day. Aeroplanes were very active, and one of 'ours' was
brought down by a Fritz in the morning. In the afternoon there was a bigger
scrap in the air, over Longueval – about half a dozen planes of either side.
One of the enemy planes was a Fokker monoplane – rather larger than
our Morane monoplane, but of similar shape. It was very dark in colour,
almost black, and was very fast. It tackled one of our Bristol Scouts, but the
Scout got away after some acrobatic flying. Fritz then went for one of our
de Havillands, which, after scrapping for about two minutes, dived as if hit.
Fritz hung on to his tail and followed him down, and another of our DHs
followed Fritz. The three planes came down in a straight line without firing
a shot as if all were on one string, until near the ground in the direction of
High Wood. Then the first plane suddenly turned to the left, and the one
behind Fritz opened fire, driving him down quite near the ground, when
there was suddenly a tremendous burst of rifle and machine-gun fire from
the ground, and Fritz turned on his side and went down out of our sight as
if out of control. The most peculiar thing about this scrap was that it stopped
all shelling for a time. When it began, the guns on both sides were at it
hammer and tongs, but no sooner did the planes get really busy with one

another, than the men serving the batteries round us ceased their work and stood watching the fight. In about half a minute the German shells ceased coming over and everything seemed to be strangely quiet, the only sounds being the rattle of the planes' machine guns and the roar of the engines overhead, and the excited comments of the men, spectators on the ground. When the scrap finished, away went the guns again – 'the mixture as before'. I remember thinking at the time that the 'Germans were human, after all' – from what we had been told up to then, planes crash during the scrap, and only one German, so it was not a 'decided' battle.

23 July: Mametz Wood. This spot was lately made famous for all time when it was captured by the Welch Division in which by some stroke of a pen we are not included. Yet we may claim a share as here we are, holding in and in close support ready to move up to any new line there may be; the latest advance was reduced to 50 yards; the enemy has regained his balance and hit back with many a jab and counter-thrust; we still retain the initiative in this one-time pleasant wood now largely splintered to fragments with whole trunks fallen at all angles and the ground cratered out of semblance, we dig for dear life. Twenty yards from my shell hole where I crouch, a heavy shell made a hole 15 feet deep, mud and earth spattered us but no one was hurt. …

Lieutenant Martin Evans, 9th Welch Regiment

Time passed laggardly. The next evening – times and days are disjointed as I try to recall and piece this together – they ordered me to take a party of fifty men back a mile or so to an Engineer's dump. In the din and racket all around it was remarkable that we ever found this. Daylight was fading; we began loading trucks with coils of barbed wire. A ticklish job and a scratchy one, ruinous to clothes and temper. To get the trucks along this recently captured tram line, we hitched some poor patient and wondering horses. What do these poor creatures think of man's madness? We had to wait until dark before venturing up, the men were given hot tea by the REs and the sapper asked me in to share his in his flimsy funk hole.

Luck so far was on our side; we got the cargo into Mametz, just. And then hell was let loose by both sides. We got the horses unlimbered and they went back, I think without harm. I trust so. Our journey up had been delayed owing to the track lines being broken at many points. Imagine our feelings at every stop while trucks were lifted, hitched and hauled back onto the rails. We dumped the stuff at the prearranged spot not a moment too soon. Flashes from the guns, ours and theirs, lit up the night, the air was rent with hurtling iron, explosions crashing on all sides, MG bullets screaming and whistling past, trees leapt up and toppled over, fountains of earth rose and fell. ... The book of rules says spread out, don't all get hit at once. In practice this happens. The men turn to their officers for protection as though their saviours, endowed with power from above. Mutual and moral support is gained by close proximity. The men bunch and hunch in the merest apology for a trench; if we go, let's all go together. We are dazed and bewildered and dazzled by the noise and near misses. Try as I will to get my fifty spaced out, they must creep back for the comforting assurance weaned from close companionship. ...

At 3.00 am the hate had subsided enough to warrant running the gauntlet of this wicked wood; we pushed the trucks out of this farcical shelter, joy rode them back, sitting on them and propelling with our feet. Within an hour we reached that rear dump, understanding that another journey would be required of us later in the day. ... The Colonel, who is usually coldly aloof, almost hugged and almost wept over me when he saw we had come through unscathed and I recounted haltingly our nocturnal Via Dolorosa.

On Monday, 24th, at stand-to, we had a nerve-wracking time, an overdose of concentrated hate lasting three solid hours; every shell they had seemed to be hurled at this trench, they were bent on destruction. I thought Mametz bad enough and that there we had reached the zenith, here it was several degrees worse in unadulterated, wholehearted fury defying description; we experienced the torments of hell; this is perhaps hell itself purging us if we deserve it for the hereafter. During this excruciating avalanche we crouched or lay flat on the floor of our ditch, shrapnel burst above our heads and rattled on our helmets, we got our faces and clothes covered with powder, earth and fine dust churned up. Missiles of all calibres fell on all sides, hardly one direct hit, they were missing us by feet, firing blind as we were just behind their skyline. Between two vanished villages they doubtless guessed we had dug a line of sorts.

It was no smiling matter then when I prayed with more fervour than I thought myself capable of. Death was not even around the corner, it was staring us in the face; any moment would be the last, one almost wished to be spared further anxiety on this score, let's be done with it. I suppose I feared the last plunge into the Unknown. I commended my dear ones and ourselves and tried with little result to remember a few hymn lines, my functioning brain had atrophied. And then I felt wonderfully calm or was it mental inertia? Or simply helplessness; there was nothing to be done except wait for the next half minute.

My batman, Smith, crouching by my side, had a neat triangular slice ripped from the brim of his helmet, he sticks to me like a leech night and day. Does he think I exude safety – some protective influence of which I am unaware?

The large mass of wounded was taken back at night from Contalmaison to Fricourt, and I got chiefly odds and ends; men who could walk and had lost their way. One afternoon we had a lot of shelling all round and a good many casualties were brought in to be dressed. One was a German infantryman, a miserable, scared man of about fifty. He was not severely wounded, but had a superficial slash across one shoulder from a piece of shell case.

Captain Philip Gosse, Royal Army Medical Corps attd, 10th Northumberland Fusiliers

There was still some shelling going on outside while I was bandaging him, when suddenly we heard the awful scream of a huge shell approaching. The German's nerves were all to pieces, and no wonder; while mine, I am ashamed to confess, for I had not his excuse, were not as steady as they should have been. There was a terrific crash and explosion, the dugout shook, and the daylight which came down a shaft was blotted out. When the light returned, I found myself lying on the floor closely embracing and as closely embraced by my German prisoner. There is no concealing the fact that it was an undignified position for a British officer to find himself in. It would have been difficult, indeed useless, to try to look stern, brave or dignified as I disengaged myself from the enfolding arms of my patient. Perhaps it was the reaction from acute terror to the absurdity of the situation which made us both laugh and laugh again. Fear makes strange bedfellows; and it is a great leveller, sweeping aside all distinction of rank, birth and race.

Overleaf:
Australian soldiers march a batch of German prisoners down a main road and into captivity.

5 Toil and Strife

'I went into action that afternoon, not with any hope of glory, but with the absolute certainty of death. ... You read no end of twaddle in the papers at home about the spirit in which men go into action. You might almost think they revelled in the horror and the agony of it all.'

Second Lieutenant Arthur Young, 7th Royal Irish Fusiliers

———————

Beneath the pallid light of the moon, the earthen walls, sandbags, and sleeping men seemed to be fashioned from a single substance: a mass of monotone.

Splashed in as if by a scene painter's brush, dark shadows lay beside the traverses and dugout doors. Numbers of bayonets, fixed on rifles that leant against the parapet, appeared like scratches on a photographic negative, and, in contrast with these, inky spectres moved slowly in the moonlight, their helmets seemingly covered with snow, their faces obscured by shadow. Rembrandt himself might have been pleased with such a scene.

As the myriads of flies had gone to rest, abandoning for the time being the human wreckage in the vicinity, the night was now still. From the fire step of this front line trench one could see many a grisly tenant of no-man's-land. Yonder, the body of a corporal had lost its feet, eaten away by rats, and beside an upturned pack the moon shone luridly on a skull. Within a restricted range of vision, appalling relics lay strewn among the grass and wire entanglements, huddled and stretched in a score of different attitudes. Smitten down side by side, two fellows lay stark and rigid, the one wearing upon his face a frozen grimace of agony, the other a placid calm.

Here [Serre], only a few short weeks before, a grim tragedy had been staged. The occasion was the memorable 1st of July; the scene, the left flank of the British attack. Down on the Somme the tide had surged forward triumphantly, but here it had been otherwise. Broken and mangled, dauntless men of the New Army had vainly crossed this

Second Lieutenant Geoffrey Fildes, 2nd Coldstream Guards

Opposite: *Lieutenant Richard Hawkins in a trench and a bad mood, as he later recalled.*

intervening stretch of no-man's-land, and also the ground beyond. Rifles, bombs, helmets, and packs were still scattered in wild confusion among the dark silent bodies. A close scrutiny revealed something of the order of their formation, for here and there we could make out eloquent details of individual equipment. Traces yet survived to bear testimony of those frenzied moments. Clutched in a mortifying hand was a canvas bucket containing Lewis gun magazines: the carrier had been shot in the act of clearing the parapet and lay sprawling in a heap where he had fallen. Among the equipment cast aside were rusting rifles, their magazines charged full, their bayonets still sheathed. These bodies had evidently belonged to the supports. Thus shrouded by the gloom, these relics still awaited burial. The place was a Golgotha, a charnel house, amidst which, even at this moment, one could hear the sounds of trench rats as they revelled at their ghastly work.

Then a step in the trench behind diverted attention. It was Sergeant Gill, of the Lewis guns.

'Good evening, Sir. I'm thinking things look pretty quiet tonight.'

'Let's hope they will continue so, Sergeant.'

The vast swarthy figure stepped up beside me on the fire step and sniffed the air.

'Streuth!' The involuntary remark was cut short by the sound of a hearty expectoration. 'Them stiffs are horrible, Sir!'

A silence fell between us, broken at last by his hoarse whisper. 'There's a deal of harm comes from them pore chaps, Sir; one can 'ardly figure the amount. It's a wonder to me we don't all catch a fever. These trenches must be swarming with microbes and bacilluses. A bullet's all right – I've no objection, scientifically speaking, to that sort of thing – but swallowing dead men's germs is 'orrid. Lice are all right, too; but microbes are different.'

'Where have you found out all this, Sergeant?'

'Oh, I'm a reading man, Sir, in a way of speaking. I'd done my time with the Colours and was a Reservist before the war.'

'What was your job?'

'Engineer's foreman at Birmingham.'

'And that's why you took to the Lewis guns, I suppose?'

'You're right, Sir. Machinery is my job.'

'I've noticed your South African ribbons,' I observed. 'What service did you see out there?'

'Modder River, Bloemfontein, and various places. That was a cushy show, Sir, and no mistake; though we had our share of casualties.'

'It's a strange thing how some chaps pull through,' he continued by and by.

'Some don't seem to have any luck at all, others don't seem to be ever without it. Look at me: there's hardly a man left in the battalion what I came out with in '14. Landreecis, Marne, Ypriss, they all took it in turn. An' then there's the general wear and tear, chaps like Sergeant Buck killed in a stray dugout. It all reckons up to a considerable total when you think of it. I've seen fellers come out here, and a month later they were shouting 'Carry on' in hospital – nice clean Blighty ones, you know, Sir. That sort gets home before they've wore out a pair of boots – a-swanking, they are, with gold stripes before they've ever seen an Alleman – others get done in almost before they've seen a sandbag. There's a deal of difference in luck. Some's bad, some's good, and some's middling: that's my class. Twenty-four months I've been on this job, and never a scratch, Sir. They offered me a rest a while ago, but I didn't fancy the idea. They puts you into the police

Trônes Wood after weeks of attention by the artillery from both sides.

somewhere, but that isn't what you'd call a popular job. Some chaps enjoy themselves watching estaminays [estaminets]; I don't.'

I nodded in sympathy. However, the sergeant's flow of philosophy, entertaining though it was, showed no sign of abatement.

'Well, let's hope the war will be over before very long, Sergeant. Keep an eye on that emplacement of yours. I must have a look at the mine shaft, and if you should want me I shall be there.'

'Very good, Sir,' came the inevitable reply.

The offensive continued to exploit the ground to the south. Into August, the fighting for Delville Wood and High Wood continued, the ownership of both disputed until September. And then there was fierce fighting around the villages of Pozières, Longueval and Guillemont. This was attritional warfare in which tenacious defence slowly but surely weakened against dogged, irresistible force. German counter-attacks might retake surrendered ground, but it was never consolidated for long before the Allies launched their next assault. To the casual eye, August would not look very different from July. The place names changed but not the campaign.

Major Neil
Fraser-Tytler,
D Batt, 149th
Brigade, Royal
Field Artillery

1 August was a stifling, almost tropical day, and I spent the morning handing over to my successor. I am afraid it is a terrible legacy: there is nothing good to show him. The gun position was literally smothered with bluebottles; there was a forward gun in a very dangerous spot and two distant observation posts with lines which needed ceaseless effort to maintain. We had a long and desperately tiring walk, first to Hardecourt, then to Trônes Wood and eventually back by way of the forward howitzer.

On the eve of departure one realizes more the foulness of the spots in which we spent so many happy hours fighting. Now all the jump and life seemed to have gone out of things, and there was nothing left but the appalling stench, the torn up ground, and the eternal cloud of flies rising in front and giving a friendly hint to prepare to meet some fresh horror.

By the afternoon, as I had only one gun to get away … it was like waiting to leave school, and we were all as nervous as cats lest some disaster should happen before we escaped. Our gun team and horses came up at 10.00 pm, and the relieving gun arrived soon after. Poor people, their troubles had already begun, as their cook's cart, following behind their gun, had been scuppered on the way up. …

Even as I went I saw our red SOS rockets rise behind Trônes Wood and heard the roar of gunfire reopening. In the streets of Maricourt there was the usual hopeless congestion. French traffic was moving every way at once and under no sort of control, but we eventually burst our way through and reached our wagon line near Billion Wood at midnight. It was wonderful to see and smell once again fresh grass and trees with leaves on them, after a month in that dusty wilderness of a modern battlefield.

As Fraser-Tytler's battery was preparing to leave the line for some well-deserved rest, Lieutenant Andrew Buxton and Second Lieutenant Robert Vernède were marching the other way with their battalion, 3rd Rifle Brigade. The march was hot and it was exhausting. At least their cookers arrived.

Yesterday we had a march in marching order; first 5 miles, then a halt which extended to three hours, during which time packs were not allowed to be taken off owing to something being expected to arrive at any time, then

Lieutenant Andrew Buxton, 3rd Rifle Brigade

Three officers of the 1/4th Yorkshire Regiment relax out of the line. The contemporary caption notes that all three were killed on the Somme.

about 7 miles when more men dropped out than I have ever seen do so before. It was very hot, but it was largely due to the men finishing their water bottles too soon and also either having left behind their rations or eaten them overnight and so being probably faint from want of food. We had paraded at 9.00 am and got in at 8.15 pm. Fortunately the cookers by leaving overnight had got here first and had tea ready. Half the men on getting here at once departed to look for water, with canteens in their hands, but found none; a quart of tea though was ready for each, which they got all right. A good many would have approached drinking a gallon if they had had the chance, I think! I do feel so intensely for fellows feeling seedy like that, and especially through no fault of their own. I did not have my horse and was carrying a good deal, though not so much as the men, but kept cooler than any one I think and felt no worry. It is a blessing to be so fit. One or two men were even sweating through the backs of their jackets, poor dears! A wash would have been a joy, as you can imagine, but we had to 'turn in' without. I had, though, a good 'bath' in a little water this morning.

Second
Lieutenant
Robert Vernède,
3rd Rifle Brigade

10 August: You would be amused by the place in which I write this – a small scoop in the side of a trench, like a rabbit burrow, to which I've retired after a somewhat disturbed night in the bottom of a trench – disturbed only by rain at 4.00 am after which I wandered about till breakfast time, getting damp and fearing greatly that the fine weather has gone for good. The night before I was in yet another place – resembling a hare's form more than anything else. I made it myself out of an old shell hole with a hurdle on the top, covered with wild mustard and old sandbags to keep out the dew. Bitterly cold it was, too, as nowadays I carry all my goods on my back in my haversack – plus the Aquascutum strapped to it. Not even a pack. I think I am about as Red Injun in colour as I ever have been, including the knees.

No. 12 Platoon is not in luck at the moment. I told you about Sgt: next day a corporal recently appointed was taken ill and sent down; and yesterday, while I was instructing the platoon in the bayonet, a fat shell pitched about 30 yards away, and knocked out Sgt D., breaking his leg below the knee. It was luck having only one man hit – a little nearer and the whole platoon might have been; but, of course, he is a great loss – the only really good

NCO I had left. The doctor thinks he won't lose it. He shed his gore all over my only pair of bags as I was helping to carry him in, and there's no water to wash them in. Such is life at the moment. Later in the day I had an endless walk with C. through a trench – three hours we took – eating dust all the way, through awful smells and every form of abandonment, from rifles and tin hats to dead men. Oh dear, I don't like war.

The flies are disgusting and the mosquito netting is very useful. I'm afraid I envied Sgt D.

I think it must be Friday, the 11th of August, and I am lying in my scoop again at 3.30 pm, whence I move very shortly. My schedule for this afternoon was lunch at 1; write to you 1.45–2.15; bath at 2.15; sleep 2.30–4; tea at 4, start at not much later. As usual, things cropped up and have done me in. The postman arrived and departed about 1.45! Buxton has gone up; Brown has gone sick; and messengers have been arriving with messages, effectually preventing me from sleeping at all, and it's now nearly teatime. On the other hand, it's a fine day again: I have had a magnificent hot bath in half a small tin of water; and your letter has arrived. …

I had a most tiresome working party last night: was given a guide and a map reference; didn't trust the guide going up, and took my own way to the map reference. On arriving found that though I'd got to the right place, sure enough, the reference had been given me wrong! Meant another two hours' work for everybody. Got into a shelling and had three men hit (all very slight, I'm glad to say) and one with a sprained ankle, from dodging shells. Allowed the guide to guide me back, with the inevitable result that he lost himself and us; then struck across country and very lucidly exactly hit our trench. But not enough sleep quite. Still, it's a beautiful day.

12 August: Must send this off – no time to write more. We are working desperately hard – very little sleep. I'm afraid letters are likely to be very irregular at present. Don't be worried by that.

14 August: We are having a fairly peaceful two days after two fairly hot ones. I got about three hours' sleep in forty-eight – constant shelling – fearful smells and working like navvies. Did about double the ordinary infantryman allowance myself. The flies are disgusting now. I think

the platoon is getting rather friendly at last – had about half a dozen of them chatting to me during the shells, when they most want a little consolation. … I can't distinguish sunburn from dirt on my face now. If I rub too hard the skin comes off; and if I don't, the dirt remains on! I am in my rabbit scoop again. My last bed was a ledge of chalk about 1 foot wide and 4 long, at an angle sideways – not very comfortable! Oh dear, there comes the QMS for the letters. I must finish.

16 August: No letters for two, three days, so a little flatness. But I hope soon I shall get three or four to make up. The weather has turned misty moisty, which is rather a nuisance when one sleeps without any bedclothes. I tie things like a sock or a towel round my knees and get my legs into a damp sandbag to keep warm; and really was quite warm last night.

Quite a slack day yesterday and might have for some days. … Did I tell you of a rather nice boy in my platoon who writes a family letter daily always beginning – 'Dear Mum and Dad, and dear loving sisters Rosie, Letty, and our Gladys, – I am very pleased to write you another welcome letter as this leaves me. Dear Mum and Dad and loving sisters, I hope you keeps the home fires burning. Not arf. The boys are in the pink. Not arf. Dear loving sisters Rosie, Letty, and our Gladys, keep merry and bright. Not arf.'

It goes on like that for three pages – absolutely fixed; and if he has to say something definite, like acknowledging a parcel, he has to put in a separate letter – not to interfere with the sacred order of things. He is quite young and very nice, quiet, never grouses or gives any trouble – one of those very gentle creatures that the war has caught up and tried to turn into a frightful soldier, I should think in vain. I can't imagine him sticking anybody, but I'm sure he would do anything he felt to be his duty. _____'s servant is also another of the gallant lambs. He is a squat little elderly man of about 45 – was a comedian of sorts, and looks it – has a wife and five children – was rejected six times by the doctors and got in as a bandsman; then shoved out here into the front line. He sings comic songs and cheers the others and waddles about manfully, but is no more a fighting ruffian than a child of six. Yet he too takes part in the bloodiest of battles of the world.

Three images of the ground near Delville Wood, August 1916. These were taken by an officer of the 9th Rifle Brigade.

Three converted German trenches, shewing DELVILLE WOOD in centre. 18/8/16

A 9.2-inch
howitzer of 121
Siege Battery,
Royal Garrison
Artillery, in the
act of firing near
Ginchy.

18 August: I forgot to answer your question about the small dog in the photograph. It doesn't belong – was only a farm creature of one of the mixed French types, introduced as a mascot. The troops like a mascot – in fact, I believe that is why the very young officer is better than the older ones. They like some young frolicsome creature like – barking at their heels and playing about in their midst. There are two or three lurcher creatures kept at the transport, but they don't go into the front line as much. One big puppy doesn't seem to mind shells a bit.

I am afraid I am in for a Lewis gun course. I suppose other people would like it, so pig-headedly, I don't. The thing is a machine, and, anyway, like Howard, I don't like leaving the platoon in these strenuous times. The course is, I believe, a week, far from the firing line. At present I am at the transport on my way, as it were: might be recalled, but don't think it's likely. I asked to be left with the platoon and can't do more.

Second Lieutenant Vernède had been permitted to go on a course when the division was scheduled to take part that afternoon in a large-scale attack in the direction of Guillemont and Ginchy. It was hardly surprising that the trip was summarily cancelled and he was told to immediately return to his unit. As Vernède made his way back, his friend and fellow officer, Andrew Buxton, made final preparations. He had already gone forward with his commanding officer to reconnoitre the ground over which the 3rd Battalion would attack and to get a view of Guillemont, the objective.

Lieutenant
Andrew Buxton,
3rd Rifle Brigade

Got attack orders from Pigot. Zero time 2.45 pm. A Coy were on left, B in centre, D on right, C behind D in 'Sherwood' trench, and D half in 'Mike' [trench] and half in 'New' [trench]. Cut steps to get out by. Shelling tremendous. When D advanced we advanced into 'New', where we stayed three or four minutes, then advanced into 'Mike', where we were intended to stay until 4.45 pm, when advance again to the Boche line presumed taken. Reported to Pigot at HQ and ordered by him to reinforce E[ast] of

Station. … Went back and gave my orders; very difficult to make myself heard. Heard Brown was killed. Saw Boche being shot like rabbits, ghastly. When first advanced saw four partridges get up in front of 'Mike' and fly straight over Guillemont; thought our barrage must kill one, but didn't! The ten minutes' hurricane bombardment was terrific. When Pigot told me reinforce he said, 'I congratulate you.' Got over pretty easily. … Found B in a deep 30 ft dugout where I made my HQ; entrance just like rabbit hole under large mass of concrete. Place an awful sight of dead and wounded. A fine Boche doctor walking about doing good work; three or four Boche wounded by dugout. … C Coy dug in well, railway station taken without opposition. I had orders to hold the station and not have less than fifty men in it. There were three machine guns and a Lewis gun of B Coy there too. In the Boche dugout we found field glasses, revolvers, endless equipment, iron rations, rifles, Very lights, a bottle of brandy and of Hock, cigars, cigarettes, aerated water, two bugles, flutes and medicine cases.

19 August: Men were digging all night. In case of counter-attack did not allow anyone to sleep till well after dawn, though men quite done up. They were completing the station trenches all night.

The programme was to get to halfway through Guillemont by a further attack at 5.00 am, but this had to be cancelled as the 73rd Brigade got hung up on our right yesterday afternoon. (It was an ever-memorable sight to see them advance yesterday.) Continued working and clearing dead from dugouts, etc. Used telephone wire, but frightfully difficult to get bodies out. Buffs got in yesterday on our right quite easily. … Venner was killed after we got to Boche trench; only saw him just before he died. My Sergt Major, also Page, my orderly, killed today by same shell. Buried them, and Jock Henderson and Venner, after dark; also others of our men and lots of Boche.

20 August: A little dozing, but practically no sleep. Dugout full of debris, signallers, orderlies, etc. Boche shelling very nasty but ours far heavier. Guillemont appears like a ploughed field. Our dugout has two entrances, both very dangerous. Cleared out the dugout by a chain of men. In evening put on a working party to dig trench along lines of Boche front line towards D Coy. Men very done, but had to be done by dawn. Five men

wounded by digging onto a Boche bomb. Had a Coy of Fusiliers to help. Pigot sent in afternoon congratulations on work and also saying, 'Now get some rest.' Did not pass on latter part of message as too important to continue work. Men very rattled. Cpl Hogben killed today, also Wedlock of A Coy. Arthur turned up in afternoon; so ripping to see him. He asked where Guillemont was!

Reverend Arthur Buxton was Andrew's brother and a priest attached to the division that included the 3rd Rifle Brigade. He searched for and found his brother, quickly penning a letter home to their parents to let them know both sons were alive and sound. His letter also underscored how badly the battalion had suffered.

Reverend Arthur Buxton, Army Chaplains' Department, attd 24th Division

22 August: I know you will have been anxiously waiting for a letter, but I simply could not write till our time in the trenches was over. … The fact that we both are well and (Andrew especially) have come through without a scratch is simply providential and due to prayer. He has been through an inferno! I have only just seen him once since Thursday, so can't say much from him, but about (I mustn't give numbers) of wounded men of our battalion have been through our dressing station, so I've heard a good deal of what it was like. I simply can't give a connected account, but just a few facts will show. Out of our mess of seven officers, Brown and Venner have been killed and Catchside wounded; Andrew, Vernède, myself and Chamberlain are all right. A Company's sergeant major and his runner are dead. Last week I went for a walk with three charming young officers, Henderson, Daly, and Barnard – today I am the only one left, all the three killed. Out of four company commanders only Andrew and Boscawen are left, the other two wounded badly; it's too awful for words. It's marvellous that our dressing station is still standing; two other regimental ones are knocked out and a dispatching station, and only this morning we had a terrific shelling and of course a direct hit from the big stuff they were sending over would have done for the place and all in it. Two men on Friday were standing in the doorway; both were blown in – one died in five minutes, the other badly wounded. Oh! the loss of precious lives is awful, so are the sufferings of the wounded. The constant danger, the noise, the smells are past words. But if I

feel it bad, it's ten times worse for Andrew, and even if he doesn't get some decoration you can believe me he has more than deserved it.

I trust we will get out all right tonight. I long to leave it all behind and I suppose some unfortunate fresh troops will come in and carry on. I only trust they'll take us right away from these sights and sounds.

The battalion was relieved. Andrew noted that 294 officers and other ranks were casualties, including eight officers killed and eight wounded. Robert Vernède wrote to his wife.

23 August: I am very fit and well, but I'm afraid you've been left without a letter for five days and I only hope you haven't been worried by it. I might have sent you a Field postcard, but the fact is that I thought that might make you worry rather more, and I hoped that, as my last letter told you I was going on a course, you would at all events think I was in some safe spot instead of the very unsafe one where I was.

Directly after I finished that letter to you I was wired for to reinforce the battalion in an attack ... I knew something was going to happen shortly. I had proposed to [Andrew] Buxton that I should go up with the platoon instead of [Second Lieutenant Ernest] V[enner], and that had been arranged; but at the last moment the CO insisted that V[enner] should go, as an old and regular soldier. C[hamberlain] was necessary as Lewis gun officer, and the choice lay between [Lieutenant Anthony] Brown and me. Brown was taken because owing to the bayonet course I had missed some attack practices he had had. V[enner] and Brown are both dead now, shot through the heart. You will see the account of the Push in *Times* of 21st. I went to the transport with four others when the battalion went up, stayed a night there, and wrote to you on the 18th. The attack came off at 2.30 pm, and at 3.30 the five of us were sent for to Brigade HQ. No time to pack anything, a blazing hot day, and I had to borrow the Quartermaster's revolver as I'd lent mine to V[enner]. An hour and a half's walk to Brigade HQ, where we heard that things were going very well, but more officers were needed. ...

From there we had a three-hour walk to the front line. Shells most of the way, and the wounded streaming down an open road. We passed A.D.,

Second
Lieutenant
Robert Vernède,
3rd Rifle Brigade

hit through the leg, but filled with delight because he was going back to
Blighty alive and kicking: then, rather badly hit in the shoulder – heaps of
bandaged men, including two of my platoon. The men of all regiments, and
wounded in every variety of way. To read in the papers you might suppose
the wounded were whisked from the battlefield in a motor ambulance. I get
rather tired of all that false and breezy representation of a battle.

I've never been so hot in my life as when we came to Batt HQ, just
behind our jumping-off trench. There we heard of Brown and V[enner] and
many others, and from there we went on to join our Coys, in the various bits
of Boche trench they had taken. No guide, a hail of shells and a sort of blind
stumble through shell holes to where we fancied the new line was. I found
C Coy at last. HQ in a 30 ft deep Boche dugout, choked with dead Germans
and bluebottles, and there we had our meals till we started back at 4.00 am
this morning (five days). In between that time I certainly spent some of
the most unpleasant hours of my life. It seems that the battalion had done
extraordinarily well and gained the first of two objectives. The second was
to be won that night, and next day we were to be relieved.

Unfortunately a battalion on our right had been held up and we had
to wait for them in a trench choked with our dead and Boche wounded
and dying for two days and then [D Company] do another attack. The
men had been in high spirits over the first part, but naturally the reaction
was great when they found that instead of being relieved they were to dig
in, and I had never seen them so glum. Here again the breezy reporter
is revolting. The Push itself is done in hot blood: but the rest is horrible,
digging in when you are tired to death, short rations, no water to speak of,
hardly any sleep, and men being killed by shellfire most of the time.

I was given the C line in front of HQ to hold with two and a half
platoons, and luckily the Boches never really found it, and I had fewer
casualties than anybody. I slept in the bottom of the trench, sometimes
in rain (in shorts), without any cover and really never felt very cold. Also,
though I don't suppose I got more than an hour at a time, I never felt done
for want of sleep. C[hamberlain] and Buxton were the only officers left.

The second attack was made yesterday, and only our D Coy was sent
off at the start. C Company was to support it if it needed reinforcement. My
dear, you never saw anything more dramatically murderous than the modern

attack – a sheet of fire from both sides in which it seems impossible for anyone to live. I saw it from my observer's post about 100 yds away. My observer was shot through the head in the first minute. The OC of D Coy had been badly wounded, and Butler led them on most gallantly. The last I saw of him was after a huge shell had burst just over him (laying out several men) waving on the rest. None of the D officers came back, and very few of the men.

Again the right batt failed, and this time the Rifle Brigade was inevitably involved in it, as far as D Coy went. We gained a certain amount of France back by digging a trench in front of my bit of line about 100 yds from the Boches in the dark, lit by terrific flares from the German lines. After that we hunted for our wounded till 4.00 am. I found [Lieutenant] S[haw] S[Stewart] about 50 yds from the Boche trench, shot through the heart. R. got back wounded in several places. Butler was last heard of in a shell hole about 10 yds from the Boches. He was an awfully gallant fellow. The whole thing was almost too bloody for words, and this, mind you, was victory of a sort for us. We fancy the Boches lost far more heavily, as our guns got on them when they were reinforcing.

I'm too sleepy to tell you any more. The battalion did magnificently: captured many prisoners and advanced several hundred yards; but the cost is very great.

27 August: I'm still without leisure. Buxton has gone sick for two days at least. The troops after their push are bivouacked in an open field with no cover but their waterproof sheets – constant showers – not very comfortable for men who have hardly slept and never ceased working under shellfire for a week. Some old noodle's fault, I suppose.

My dear, some of the men are too quaint. One lad, whose brother was killed the last night in the Boche trench, came to me to ask how to write to his sister-in-law about it. He had got as far as 'My dear Lil, I now have great pleasure in telling you that Tom …' and there he had stuck. I had to draft a more sympathetic letter for him. The same on being asked if he would like to help bury his brother said, 'I will, if you like, sergeant.' Yet he was quite upset.

The GOC congratulated the brigade today in the rain; it somehow seemed unnecessary.

Pure chance: Sergeant Hugh Bourn Godfrey (known as Huborn) serving with 121 Siege Battery, meets his brother Jim (right) on the Somme battlefield. Jim had emigrated to Australia before the war. This would be the first and last time they met. Both brothers survived the war.

Reverend
Arthur Buxton,
Army Chaplains'
Department,
attd 24th
Division

29 August: I saw Andrew today 'resting' at a field ambulance. I fear nothing will persuade him to stay there if the battalion moves again. He is not sleeping well, and his mind is going over the horrible time he went through. I don't think he could stand another winter here.

Andrew Buxton was just one of thousands of men whose endurance was tested to the point of collapse in August. Rest and recuperation were urgently needed, but infrequently received. The sounds of battle were clearly audible in the villages where men were billeted and where, even there, safety was not guaranteed.

Major Rowland
Feilding, 1st
Coldstream
Guards

This morning at ten o'clock, I went to Mass. As I was leaving the church I met Cecil Trafford, who asked me to his mess (Headquarters, 1st Scots Guards).

The latter is a house with a sort of garden or small yard in front of it. As we were crossing this there was a sudden loud explosion, and bits flew through the air about us. We looked round and saw [Second Lieutenant] Leach, the bombing officer of the battalion (who had just come from visiting my own mess), on the ground, 4 or 5 yards away. He lay on his back, in a pool of blood, his arms outstretched and both his hands blown off. His brother officers soon began to collect around him, so I left, but I do not think he then had more than a short time to live.

Later. I have learnt some particulars about poor Leach's accident. He was detonating a bomb in the orderly room, which is a shed opening onto the yard, when the safety pin slipped. Seeing that it was going to explode, and some of his men being in the shed, after ordering them to lie down, he picked up the bomb and dashed outside to get rid of it. He then had less than four seconds in which to decide what to do. I can only suppose that seeing Cecil and myself in the middle of the yard he came to the conclusion that his one chance of throwing it safely away was gone.

So he turned his back to us, faced the wall, and hugging the bomb in his hands, allowed it to explode between his body and the wall.

It is impossible to speak much of such courage and self-sacrifice. He is since dead. He was only twenty-two.

The British public at home was fed a remorseless diet of newspaper reports extolling the virtues and fortitude of the Allied soldiers. Now, civilians were able to witness the offensive for themselves in a full-length film capturing in astonishing detail the initial July assault. The film had premiered in London on 10 August to huge public adulation – around half the British population saw it – and three weeks later it was being shown in France and Flanders and, on 5 September, in Morlancourt village.

Tonight I have been with others to see an exhibition of the 'Somme film', which was shown upon a screen, erected in a muddy field under the open sky. Presumably by way of contrast Charlie Chaplin was also to have appeared, and I confess it was chiefly him I went to see. However, I came too late, and saw only the more harrowing part of the entertainment.

This battle film is really a wonderful and most realistic production, but must of necessity be wanting in that the battle is fought in silence, and,

Major Rowland Feilding, 1st Coldstream Guards

moreover, that the most unpleasant part – the machine-gun and rifle fire – is entirely eliminated. Of the actual 'frightfulness' of war, all that one sees is the bursting shells; and perhaps it is as well. I have said that the battle is fought in silence; but no, on this occasion the roar of real battle was loudly audible in the distance.

I must say that at first the wisdom of showing such a film to soldiers on the brink of a battle in which they are to play the part of attackers struck me as questionable. However, on my way home, my mind was set to rest upon this point by a conversation I overheard between two recruits who were walking behind me.

Said one, 'As to reality, now you knows what you've got to face. If it was left to the imagination you might think all sorts of silly b____ things.'

I wonder where his imagination would have led him had he not seen the cinema. Would it, do you think, have gone beyond the reality? Hell itself could hardly do so. I think sometimes that people who have not seen must find it difficult to comprehend how undisturbed life in the trenches can be on occasion: equally, how terrible can be the battle.

Terrible, but also how impressive it was, too. The men who fought on the Somme could not help but be awestruck by the vast scale of the effort.

Second
Lieutenant
Geoffrey Fildes,
2nd Coldstream
Guards

Lying in bed at night, we grew accustomed to the ceaseless rattle of the window casements, and no longer heeded the noisy vibration of the few remaining panes.

Curtains of split sandbags, screening the open apertures, palpitated backwards and forwards with the aerial disturbance of the guns. Shaken by the discharges of the howitzers over by Albert, even the walls quivered convulsively, while the whitewashed ceiling by the window flickered in response to the storm outside. So, assailed by the hundred-fold notes of the British artillery, ears became deadened, and sleep stole over us at last. Gliding by degrees into a peaceful world, one grew unconscious of the echoes of the night.

Although darkness rendered the drama more impressive, nevertheless a wonderful sight was to be seen by day. To accomplish the short walk

from Méaulte to Albert was truly to witness a national pageant. There, a concentration of fighting energy was displayed sufficient almost to win the Boer War; all within the bounds of one man's vision. It was not so much by the number of troops, though these attained many thousands, but rather by the latent capacity of the material burdening the landscape that the spectator was impressed.

Yonder, where additional railway tracks had been lately completed, stood long platform cars of iron supported on multiple bogie carriages; but it was not upon these great chassis that the eye dwelled, for all their imposing bulk, but upon the vast forms that snuggled on them like beasts in their lairs. Stretching into the air from their long mouthing snouts arose ponderous forms of 15-in guns, mammoths among ordnance. These, grouped at intervals along the curved railway track, comprised the great bassoons of Britain's orchestra; here lay the produce of toiling Woolwich and the lusty men of Armstrong's. Theirs were the prodigious missiles that, speeding over the clouds at a height of 15,000 feet, filled our ears with the shriek of a hundred Valkyries.

Beyond, aligned in ordered rows, battery by battery, stood a park of pigmy brethren. These were the 18 lb field-guns – of no great account, one might be tempted to think – but ask the army of von Arnhim! These were they whose flaming sleet thrashed down the massed counter-attacks of Germany; these were the barrage-makers! At a short distance, rising in tier above tier of wooden boxes, lay pyramids of munitions: food for the 15-pounders, the 4.5-inch howitzers, and the 6-inch field guns. Long and short, lean and squat, field gun, howitzer, naval gun, and giants of the RGA [Royal Garrison Artillery], all might draw their daily rations without fear of the morrow, for behind these mounds of supplies, flowing ever forward to the front, now rolled the death torrents of industrial Britain. To turn in whatever direction you chose was to encounter further amazement. There, where the railroad skirted a row of silvered poplars, engines of half a dozen great railway companies at home snorted to and fro, each thinly disguised beneath a service coat of paint. Behind them, laden with hundreds of duckboards and miles of barbed wire coils, trucks were being shunted amid a continuous clink of couplings. Down the Albert road, ceaselessly engaged on the upkeep of the highway, worked a familiar friend of other days: an English steamroller, complete even to the prancing horse that adorned the front of its boiler. Even these had been mobilized and put into uniform.

But these sights belonged to no particular roadside; they covered the landscape, they mingled into the picture of encampments and bivouacs. This memorable scene was composed of something more than several divisions of troops, something more than a scattered mass of artillery and engineers' dumps. Here lay a tangible proof of England's will, a token of what the folk at home had undertaken on our behalf.

This concentration of artillery would be used in the next phase of the offensive backed up by a new and secret weapon, the tank. The Commander-in-Chief would use this weapon of terror as the spearhead to a large-scale assault of the enemy line between the Albert–Bapaume road to the village of Combles. Some forty-eight tanks would be deployed with their specially trained crews, although mechanical problems would knock out about a third of these tanks before the troops attacked. Nevertheless, the tanks offered something new, a weapon that would crush enemy barbed wire with ease, cross trenches with impunity and knock out enemy machine-gun nests with alacrity. Their sight alone would put the fear of God into the enemy and renewed confidence into wilting Allied troops. The Allied punch would be such that the newly constructed German third line would be breached and five divisions of cavalry would be on hand to push through any gap created. One of those who would take part in the attack was Raymond Asquith, son of the Prime Minister, Hubert Asquith.

Yesterday we had a Brigade Field Day under John Ponsonby illustrating all the newest and most elaborate methods of capturing German trenches with the minimum of casualties. The 'creeping barrage', i.e. the curtain of shellfire which moved on about 50 yards in front of the advancing infantry, was represented by drummers. The spectacle of the whole four battalions moving in lines across the cornfields at a funeral pace headed by a line of rolling drums, produced the effect of some absurd religious ceremony, conducted by a tribe of Maoris rather than a brigade of Guards in the attack. After it had gone on for an hour or two I was called up

Lieutenant Raymond Asquith, 3rd Grenadier Guards

by the Brigadier and thought at first that I must have committed some ghastly blunder but was relieved to find that it was only a telegram from the corps saying 'Lieut Asquith will meet his father at crossroads K.6d at 10.45 am.' So I vaulted into the saddle and bumped off to Fricourt where I arrived exactly at the appointed time. I waited for an hour on a very muddy road congested with troops and lorries and surrounded by barking guns. Then two handsome motors from GHQ arrived, the PM in one of them with two staff officers, and in the other Bongie, Hankey, and one or two of those moth-eaten nondescripts who hang about the corridors of Downing Street in the twilight region between the civil and domestic service.

We went up to see some of the captured German dugouts and just as we were arriving at our first objective the Boches began putting over a few 4.2 shells from their field howitzer. The PM was not discomposed by this, but the GHQ chauffeur to whom I had handed over my horse to hold, flung the reins into the air and himself flat on his belly in the mud. It was funny enough.

The shells fell about 200 yards behind us I should think. Luckily the dugout we were approaching was one of the best and deepest I have ever seen – as safe as the bottom of the sea, wood-lined, three storeys and electric light, and perfect ventilation. We were shown round by several generals who kept us there for half an hour or so to let the shelling die down, and then the PM drove off to luncheon with the GOC 4th Army and I rode back to my billets. In the morning I went to an improvised exhibition of the Somme films – really quite excellent. If you haven't seen them in London I advise you to take the earliest opportunity. They don't give you much idea of a bombardment, but casual scenes in and on the way to the trenches are well chosen and amazingly like what happens.

8 September, 1916: We move either tomorrow or the day after. Probably tomorrow. We are only allowed 50 lbs of kit, which is a bore. It would be awful to arrive in Berlin looking a perfect scarecrow. The noise of the bombardment made me feel quite sick. I am so sorry for the wretched Hun.

A new offensive might be just days away, but there would be no halt to the constant pressure exerted upon the enemy, who were numerically and materially outnumbered and outgunned. Guillemont, one of the best-defended villages in the German line, fell on 3 September and now Ginchy, a second strongly held mass of bricks, was about to fall also. The attitude of those who assembled to attack was no longer born of anything resembling enthusiasm but rather of a dulled and stubborn sense of determination and duty.

Ginchy Wood: even as shells burst just over the ridge, this man is off on a search for souvenirs.

Second
Lieutenant
Arthur Young,
7th Royal Irish
Fusiliers

9 September: It was about four o'clock in the afternoon when we first learned that we should have to take part in the attack on Ginchy. Now, Auntie, you expect me to say at this point in my narrative that my heart leapt with joy at the news and that the men gave three rousing cheers, for that's the sort of thing you read in the papers. Well, even at the risk of making you feel ashamed of me, I will tell you the whole truth and confess that my heart sank within me when I heard the news. I had been over the top once already that week, and knew what it was to see men dropping dead all round me, to see men blown to bits, to see men writhing in pain, to see men running round and round gibbering, raving mad. Can you wonder therefore that I felt a sort of sickening dread of the horrors which I knew we should all have to go through? Frankly, I was dismayed. But, Auntie, I know you will think the more of me when I tell you, on my conscience, that I went into action that afternoon, not with any hope of glory, but with the absolute certainty of death. How the others felt I don't exactly know, but I don't think I am far wrong when I say that their emotions were not far different from mine. You read no end of twaddle in the papers at home about the spirit in which men go into action. You might almost think they revelled in the horror and the agony of it all. I saw one account of the battle of Ginchy, in which the correspondent spoke of the men of a certain regiment in reserve as almost crying with rage because they couldn't take part in the show. All I can say is that I should like to see such super-human beings. It is rubbish like this which makes thousands of people in England think that war is great sport. …

The bombardment was now intense. Our shells bursting in the village of Ginchy made it belch forth smoke like a volcano. The Hun shells were bursting on the slope in front of us. The noise was deafening. I turned to my servant O'Brien, who has always been a cheery, optimistic soul, and said, 'Well, O'Brien, how do you think we'll fare?' and his answer was for once not encouraging. 'We'll never come out alive, Sir!' was his answer. Happily we both came out alive, but I never thought we should at the time.

It was at this moment, just as we were debouching onto the scragged front line of trench, that we beheld a scene which stirred and thrilled us to the bottommost depths of our souls. The great charge of the Irish Division had begun, and we had come up in the nick of time. … Between the outer fringe of Ginchy and the front line of our own trenches is no-man's-land – a wilderness of pits, so close together that you could ride astraddle the partitions between any two of them. As you look half-right, obliquely along no-man's-land, you behold a great host of yellow-coated men rise out of the earth and surge forward and upward in a torrent – not in extended order, as you might expect, but in one mass, – I almost said a compact mass. The only way I can describe the scene is to ask you to picture five or six columns of men marching uphill in fours, with about a hundred yards between each column. Now conceive those columns being gradually disorganized, some men going off to the right, and others to the left to avoid shell holes. There seems to be no end to them. Just when you think the flood is subsiding, another wave comes surging up the beach towards Ginchy. We joined in on the left. There was no time for us any more than the others to get into extended order. We formed another stream, converging on the others at the summit. By this time we were all wildly excited. Our shouts and yells alone must have struck terror into the Huns, who were firing their machine guns down the slope.

That numbing dread had now left me completely. Like the others, I was intoxicated with the glory of it all. I can remember shouting and bawling to the men of my platoon, who were only too eager to go on. The Hun barrage had now been opened in earnest, and shells were falling here, there, and everywhere in no-man's-land. They were mostly dropping on our right, but they were coming nearer and nearer, as if a screen were being drawn across our front. I knew that it was a case of 'now or never' and stumbled on feverishly. We managed to get through the barrage in the nick of time, for it closed behind us, and after that we had no shells to fear in front of us. I mention, merely as an interesting fact in psychology, how in a crisis of this sort one's mental faculties are sharpened.

Instinct told us, when the shells were coming gradually closer, to crouch down in the holes until they had passed. Acquired knowledge on the other hand – the knowledge instilled into one by lectures and books (of which I have only read one, namely Haking's *Company Training*) – told us that it was safer in the long run to push ahead before the enemy got our range, and it was acquired knowledge that won. And here's another observation I should like to make by the way. … The din must have been deafening (I learned afterwards that it could be heard miles away) yet I have only a confused remembrance of it. Shells which at any other time would have scared me out of my wits, I never so much as heard and not even when they were bursting quite close to me. One landed in the midst of a bunch of men about 70 yards away on my right: I have a most vivid recollection of seeing a tremendous burst of clay and earth go shooting up into the air – yes, and even parts of human bodies – and that when the smoke cleared away there was nothing left. I shall never forget that horrifying spectacle as long as I live, but I shall remember it as a sight only, for I can associate no sound with it. …

We were now well up to the Boche. We had to clamber over all manner of obstacles – fallen trees, beams, great mounds of brick and rubble – in fact, over the ruins of Ginchy. It seems like a nightmare to me now. I remember seeing comrades falling round me. My sense of hearing returned to me for I became conscious of a new sound; namely the continuous crackling of rifle fire. I remember men lying in shell holes holding out their arms and beseeching water. I remember men crawling about and coughing up blood, as they searched round for some place in which they could shelter until help could reach them. By this time all units were mixed up: but they were all Irishmen. They were cheering and cheering and cheering like mad. It was Hell let loose. There was a machine gun playing on us nearby, and we all made for it. At this moment we caught our first sight of the Huns. They were in a trench of sorts, which ran in and out among the ruins. Some of them had their hands up. Others were kneeling and holding their arms out to us. Still others were running up and down the trench distractedly as if they didn't know which way to go, but as we got closer they went down on their knees too. To the everlasting good name of the Irish soldiery, I did not see a single instance of a prisoner being shot or bayoneted. …

There was no other officer about at the moment so I had to find an escort to take the prisoners down. Among the prisoners was a tall, distinguished looking man, and I asked him in my broken German whether he was an officer '*Ja! Mein Herr!*' was the answer I got. '*Sprechen Sie English?*' '*Ja!*' 'Good,' I said, thankful that I didn't have to rack my brains for any more German words. 'Please tell your men that no harm will come to them if they follow you quietly.' He turned round and addressed his men, who seemed to be very gratified that we were not going to kill them. I must say the officer behaved with real soldierly dignity, and not to be outdone in politeness by a Hun I treated him with the same respect that he showed me. I gave him an escort for himself and told off three or four men for the remainder. I could not but rather admire his bearing, for he did not show anything like the terror that his men did. I heard afterwards that when Captain O'Donnell's company rushed a trench more to our right, round the corner of the wood, a German officer surrendered in great style. He stood to attention, gave a clinking salute, and said in perfect English, 'Sir, myself, this other officer, and ten men are your prisoners.' Captain O'Donnell said', 'Right you are, old chap!' and they shook hands, the prisoners being led away immediately.

Final preparations were under way for the next phase of the Somme battle, with a heavy, softening-up barrage during which the tanks were brought forward to the fascination of everyone who was privileged to see them.

A tank photographed by Sergeant Huborn Godfrey. According to the original caption, this tank has just returned from action on 15 September.

Gunner William Dawson, C Company, Heavy Branch, Machine Gun Corps

When unloaded, they [the tanks] were placed on special rail trucks and each accompanied by its crew on the train to the siding. When they were unloaded we moved across country to some fields, officers and men being billeted in the farmhouses and buildings. The camouflage that had been so carefully and studiously carried out was immediately covered over by Royal Engineer camouflage experts with irregular patches of dark red, black, brown and dark green. There was also feverish activity filling ammunition belts, taking on board 6-pdr quick-firing shells, overhauling the tanks which by now had done a considerable mileage. We also gave demonstrations before General Joffre and other French officers, Sir Douglas Haig and a number of GHQ staff officers. It seemed as though we were being looked upon as a sort of circus which continued when we moved to a point close behind the line near Bray-sur-Somme known to us as 'Happy Valley'. Crowds of officers and men from all around came to see 'the show', including my two brothers who were sergeants in the Coldstream Guards. They had been told by another sergeant who had been to Albert with the GS wagon, he had just seen the most amazing and weird machines that one could possibly imagine, and they concluded they must be the secret 'thing' with which I was connected. These demonstrations were rather hard on us close before our first battle and meant a lot of work, in fact one tank somehow caught fire, but with so many men and extinguishers available it was soon out without serious damage.

Gunner Archie Richard, D7, Heavy Branch, Machine Gun Corps

It took two or three days to get up to the line, where we put the noses of our tanks under a steep embankment for shelter from the shells. It was while we were waiting to go into action that Jerry started to shell the ground behind the embankment where the artillery was. The gunners had come up for the attack and they had to wait for orders to move up. The shells were going over the top of us and dropping amongst the tethered horses, killing and wounding any number. We all carried revolvers, and an officer came to me and said, 'Richard, let's go out and see what we can do about these horses.' It was a terrible sight, horses with their legs off, squirming and screaming, so we had to put them out of their misery. I remember that vividly. It was my first taste of carnage.

Two nights before the attack, we started to move up from Happy Valley and the next night we proceeded to our starting points. The way was lined with troops watching these strange and fearsome machines pass by. Our starting point was a little beyond Trônes Wood and a short distance from Angle Wood after which we were to attack the enemy lines along by Leuze Wood and beyond. The ground over which we had passed was in a terrible state – villages completely blown away, roads obliterated and unrecognizable, woods blown to pieces, only stumps of tree remaining, trenches practically obliterated with shell holes, and other parts consisting of shell holes in shell holes, and hardly a square yard of level ground. Hundreds and hundreds of dead, both German and British, with tangled barbed wire all over the place. What made it even worse was rains had made the blown-up earth more difficult owing to the spongy softness. The condition of the ground could not possibly be worse.

Gunner William Dawson, C Company, Heavy Branch, Machine Gun Corps

My Dear Mother,

You will probably be rather anxious about me so I will send you a line to tell you that up to the present time 4.00 pm I am quite fit and well and my body is still whole!! – except where some skin is removed as a result of a football match some days ago!

Well, we are now just about ready for the biggest fight in the history of the world.

You will see that the French are attacking with us on our right on a whole front of 45 miles and we are attacking on the front we left some six weeks ago.

The 15th Sept '16 will truly be great for the Allies. It is hoped that this push will make the Germans retire some miles and shorten his line or better still – if we can get cavalry through and capture his guns – surrender or rather sue for peace.

We are in support of the attack and will soon be in it and will get most of the shelling.

By the time you are starting breakfast we will have captured three objectives.

A new invention is being used for the first time and old Fritz won't like it either. You will read about it afterwards for certain. The preparations

Lieutenant Alex Thompson, 1/6th Northumberland Fusiliers

have been tremendous and everyone has had to work night and day to get things ready and without giving old Fritz the tip what is happening. If he knew I bet half his army would surrender tonight. Our batteries are nearly on the front line trenches and the shells are stacked thick in every shell hole and trench. Same with all the other various stores which are everywhere.

There will be no question of failure as nothing will be able to live under the artillery fire we are going to bring to bear on his trenches. High Wood will get something tonight and tomorrow morning. He is holding the east corner very strongly so that he will have tremendous casualties. No one knows what will happen after tomorrow. …

I can assure you that we are winning and winning rapidly.

Your Loving Son

Alex Thompson

Lieutenant
Edward Tennant,
4th Grenadier
Guards

We came here at 1.30 am yesterday morning, and after a heavy meal I slept till 11.00 am. I feel none the worse for the unpleasant three days and feel more than ready to go in again tonight, which we shall do. … I will write to you whenever I get the chance, but no one knows what may happen in the next day or two. I pray I may be all right, but in any case, 'Where is Death's sting?'

Guardsman
Norman Cliff,
1st Grenadier
Guards

Deafened by the continuous bombardment which seemed liable to burst our eardrums we crouched in our trenches, each man wrapped in his own thoughts whilst presenting a clam exterior to his mates, and cracking the occasional grim sally to evoke nervous grins in response. As to living up to our reputation, our most fervent hope was simply to live, though that seemed to be the unlikeliest possibility. Something approaching a massacre was inevitable and mention on the casualty list was the probable fate awaiting all but the few whom luck would preserve – until another day. …

The tension had varying effects according to a man's temperament. There was Knox, for instance, nicknamed Knocker. Tall, stringy, wild-looking, he was the heaviest drinker in the battalion, out of pocket within hours on pay day, and perpetually borrowing sums he could never repay. For all his antics he was freely forgiven because they aroused more hilarity than censure. He was the one man who exulted in action, was impatient to get at the Hun, rehearsed the murderous things he hoped to do, in bare feet lunged about with his bayonet, and had to be restrained before an attack was due to begin. He usually emerged, bloody but unsubdued.

The non-stop noise of gunfire had reached an unbelievable and indescribable pitch of intensity carrying every gradation of sound that the ear was capable of assimilating and the nervous system of the body absorbing. The vomit of the earth cast skywards by bursting shells, the spawn of gas and cordite, the stench of rotting bodies of men and horses were continuously present. There was nothing here to make a pleasant and entertaining story of the heroics of War. No, all that it amounted to in that non-stop swamping of the senses was a frantic desire to get away from it all, even momentarily, for a little peace and quiet, to be able to eat a meal in comfort, to go to the latrine without expecting to be blown up with your breeches down. There was a heartfelt wish by all to get out of this Hell of sound and sudden death for just a brief respite. We were crazed with the intensity of it all and performed our duties automatically whether with guns or horses, such is inbuilt discipline.

Driver Ernest Reader, Royal Field Artillery

While tapes had been laid down to Hop Alley, at one period one of our crew got out and guided our driver with red and green light showing from a belt he had round him. The going was very bad, we arrived at our starting point, Sergeant Davies was in charge. Davies was the gunner on the starboard side, Hobson [as] loader. I was gunner on the port side with Day [as] loader. Doodson and Leat were on the machine guns and Wateredge driver. At zero we moved off to the roar of artillery and machine-gun fire, I think we all had the wind up but we were a good crew and collected. We were getting along very nicely, all guns manned when there was a crash and we stopped dead, a shell had hit us on the starboard side and Davies was shell-shocked. We put out the flags to show we had broken down, the infantry were then passing and we could not help them. We got Davies out and the RAMC took him away.

Gunner Albert Smith, D1, Heavy Branch, Machine Gun Corps

Guardsman
Norman Cliff,
1st Grenadier
Guards

Two Guards brigades were poised to lead the assault and, ready to follow them, we of the 3rd Brigade huddled in whatever shelter we could devise in Trônes Wood. ... The night was bitterly cold and we shivered in shell holes with sleep out of the question, whilst a collection of magpies chattered, no doubt disgustedly, over the revolting scene. As dawn broke we hurried to our assembly position south-west of Ginchy, and, dodging shell hole and rifle fire, lugged boxes of ammunition to the chaps waiting for the 'Go' signal in the front trenches. Braving terrific fire, they sprang into action and amongst the first of those from high and humble homes to die side by side was the Prime Minister's gifted son, Lieutenant Raymond Asquith. Those who had survived thus far seized the first two objectives, and the third held out until the next morning when we moved through the front line with orders to capture the German strongpoints without artillery support – stiff orders against which our commanding officers felt bound to protest, but without avail. We reached high ground west of Lesboeufs, when machine guns stationed in the church tower put down an impenetrable curtain of fire. With our ranks sadly thinned we dug in, and held on grimly until a Coldstream battalion relieved us.

Opposite: *Close-
up: Sergeant
Huborn Godfrey
takes a picture
of steering tail
wheels used to
help manoeuvre
the first tanks.
The wheels did
not work well
and were soon
removed.*

Where was the secret weapon? We had been excited by vague rumours of a formidable new machine that would scare the Germans out of their wits, and spread panic all along the line. The first troops to attack had been preceded by a creeping barrage which left gaps 100 ft wide for the terror machine – but none arrived in our sector. It appears that nine were allotted, two had engine trouble and came too late, and the rest lost direction and wandered aimlessly about.

Gunner Alfred
Reiffer, D17,
Heavy Branch,
Machine Gun
Corps

We were a male tank and carried two 6-pdr guns ['female' tanks were armed with six machine guns] with several hundred rounds of ammunition and some Hotchkiss light machine guns. Our tank was full up with stores of all kind – drums of engine oil, gear oil, iron rations, gas masks, equipment, overalls, revolvers, and 'bump your head against the roof of the tank' leather helmets, carrier pigeons in a basket, semaphore signals. We even went into action with ten x 2 gallon tins of petrol (flaming red in colour) on the outside of the tank on either side of the exhaust pipes!

The crew were briefed about their objective, before snatching a few hours' sleep. The village of Flers was our first objective, our second, the village of Gueudecourt. About 5.30 am we were all awake and getting everything ready to go over the top. It was only half-light on this misty September morning when the barrage from hundreds of our guns signalled our start. Four of the crew, including myself, swung the starting handle and the 105 hp Daimler engine of D.17 roared into life and noise and we were off.

Driver Ernest
Reader, Royal
Field Artillery

One tank that I was watching trundled along, having rolled flat a machine-gun post which had been hurriedly set up, and was obviously looking around for new worlds to conquer. Away off his line was the broken stump of a much shattered tree. Without any hesitation the tank headed for it determined to bulldoze it. But sad to relate the stump refused to be pushed and the tank rolled over. A German gun crew were quickly off the mark and over open sights scored a direct hit, which put paid to the tank. …

The ground from High Wood on the enemy side sloped gently down towards Bapaume, Le Sars and Péronne. We could see the tanks leading the way, crushing pockets of resistance whether from machine guns or the few pieces of field artillery which were still manned. Our tanks and infantry were followed by signallers reeling out field cable wire. Most exciting of all were our gun teams who hitched up and brought their guns forward to new positions at the gallop (and to hell with the dictum that says that field guns must never go faster than a trot). The guns would be dropped in new positions, a few rounds blazed off, then 'gun limbers' would be signalled then hitch up and forward again. Meanwhile to keep up with the ammunition requirements firing battery wagons would come charging up to replenish shell stocks immediately available for the guns. In the case of our own battery, our GS wagon which had just reached the wagon line after drawing fresh supplies from the ammo column took part in this wild escapade, charging up flat-out with the best of them and that was a sight for sore eyes to see that enthusiastic team. Why the body did not quit the chassis over that torn-up ground I shall never know.

Inside the tank, the atmosphere was sickening. When you are in action and all the traps are down, the fumes are hardly bearable. There is a thick haze of petrol and gas fumes and the cordite fumes. It was hot. September was hot that year and with the engine running it was incredibly stuffy. The noise was deafening, with our guns going, the German guns firing and the engine running, we had to make pre-determined signals with our hands and fingers. It was impossible to speak to anybody. I had a good stomach, but others were sick, spewing up all over the place and passing out. Eight men cooped up in a tank with no air for hours and the smell awful.

We had two men in the tank at Flers and their nerves gave out and they went funny in the head. They had a glazed look, they didn't know what they were doing and they were unsteady on their feet. We were all on the verge of collapse.

Gunner Archie Richard, D7, Heavy Branch, Machine Gun Corps

There was hell outside alright, but there was such a hell of a noise inside and we were such a tight-packed crew that we just didn't concern ourselves with what was happening outside. Our main pre-occupation was doing our job – keeping our feet and keeping a wary eye out for the rock and roll of the tank.

I was No. 2 gunner to Percy Boult on the starboard six-pounder gun and our day started when Boult excitedly told me he was going to fire at a German observation balloon (spotting for the artillery). We were then about halfway to Flers. Several rounds were fired and Boult claimed a direct hit. The balloon disappeared and this may have had some bearing out the partial success of the tanks attacking Flers.

As we approached our first objective we were stopped by an infantry runner who carried a message from his brigadier asking for our help to clear up a strongpoint near Flers. Lieutenant Hastie refused – saying his orders were to attack Flers. As we came into the village, which was a heap of rubble with (in places) a few of the skeletons of houses still standing, Boult spotted a couple of German machine gunners – at first-floor level – who were firing at us. Four rounds of six-pounder aimed at their only visible means of support, at almost pointblank range, was enough to put them hors-de-combat.

A few yards further on Lieutenant Hastie stopped the tank and told us to strip to the waist on the starboard six-pounder as we were approaching a cross-road in the centre of the village and 100 yards to

Gunner Alfred Reiffer, D17, Heavy Branch, Machine Gun Corps

our right there was a German battery of field guns. As we crossed this road we were to engage the enemy guns with the starboard six-pounder. We stripped to the waist and then the tank lumbered on up the main street of Flers. We were within 50 yards of the cross-road when we were stopped again by a runner who informed us we were in our own barrage and we had orders to retire. The infantry had apparently run into stiff opposition and the second objective had been abandoned. Lieutenant Hastie turned us about and I think all of us heaved a sigh of relief. We retraced our tracks and turned back for Delville Wood. When we were about halfway between Delville Wood and a ridge about 3/4 mile away (on the Flers side) Lieutenant Hastie stopped the engine and said he was going over to see the tank lying under the ridge (Lt Head's, I believe). For the first time since the action started our engine was silent and we then realized there was indeed – hell to pop outside. We were sitting – rather helpless – in the middle of one of the fiercest German barrages of the whole war. Within five minutes we had received a direct hit on a track and we were ordered to abandon the tank.

Gunner Albert Smith, D I, Heavy Branch, Machine Gun Corps

We stood by the tank waiting for orders, but we got none, so late afternoon we took some food and made our way back across shell holes and trenches, there were dozens of dead from previous fighting, we got to a road and found a hole in the side and stayed the night, the following morning we were on the road, some sidecar machine gunners were passing so we stopped them and told them to report where we were.

Later Captain Hastie asked for volunteers to go to a tank that was in no-man's-land, a general had been to see Hastie and they were afraid that the machine guns would be used against the King's Liverpool Infantry who were going over the top the following morning. I and Reiffer went at midnight, they said the barrage would be lifted between 12.00 and 1.00 am. We crept to the tank and entered and found all guns useless.

Although the tanks had mixed fortunes, the attack had been a success and the Germans had, in places, been pushed back several thousand yards. A tank was even reported driving up the main street in the village of Flers, and many Germans

A Mark I tank ditched in a former German trench to the west of the village of Flers.

either fled in panic or surrendered before these large, cumbersome but effective steel beasts of war.

16 September: The second day was similar to the first except that one had more funerals to take. I started a cemetery near one of the dressing stations with burying three officers and forty-five men, one of whom was Raymond Asquith. The division came out of the line that night. We were able to have an evening service on the next day, just a voluntary one with a celebration afterwards in the open, to which forty-five officers and men stayed. Of the 3rd Battalion Grenadiers who went into the line, only two officers came out unwounded; John Hopley was one, though as a matter

Chaplain William
McCormick,
Army Chaplains'
Department
attd Guards
Division

of fact he was wounded but stayed on, the biggest man in the battalion, and Worledge Gordon, the smallest. Rogers, Crawley and Head were in a dugout, and Head bent down and put his head on the pillow to say his prayers with his posterior sticking up in the air. The other two at the end of twenty minutes wondered at the length of his devotions, so Rogers pushed him and finally knocked him over as they realized he had gone to sleep in that extraordinary position.

Lieutenant
Edward Tennant,
4th Grenadier
Guards

Thank Heaven I have come safely out of this battle after two days and two nights of it. It started properly at 5.00 am, 15th, and the artillery fire was terrific. We were in support and went up about 7.45 and sat down again further up just the right side of the German barrage. Then I was sent across to the Guards to go with them, find out where they proposed going, and lead the battalion up beside it. Off I went, and joined the ___ Guards, and went forward with them. When we had skirted G[inchy], the further of the two Gs, and were going through a little dip in the ground, we were shot at by Boches on the high ground with rifles, there must have been about twenty shooting at us. I was walking in front with their CO and adjutant, and felt sufficiently uncomfortable, but didn't show it. Bullets scuffed up dust all around with a wicked little 'zump', but they were nearly all short and none of us, at least who were in front, were hit.

Thus we went on, and they took up their position between two of these huge steel tanks on the near side of the ridge. Then they lent me an orderly, and I started back to bring the battalion along; it was an unpleasant journey of about half a mile over nothing but shell holes full of dead and dying, with any amount of shells flying about. Several whiz-bangs landed very close to me, but I got back to the battalion and explained the position to them, and then we all went down there and took up a position on the right of the … the CO, the Adjutant, the doctor, and I spent that afternoon, evening, and night in a large rocky shell hole. We were severely shelled on and off the whole time, and about four men were done in in the very next shell hole a couple of yards away. That night was one of the coldest and most uncomfortable it has ever been my fortune to spend with the stars to see.

Meanwhile most of the battalion had gone up to support the ___ and ____ Brigade, who had done the attack at five that morning, and had lost heavily. At seven or eight next morning we moved our Batt Headquarters to the line of trenches in front which had been dug the night before. This was safer than our shell hole, and as we had the worst shelling I have ever experienced during that afternoon and evening, it was probably a very wise move.

An attack took place at 1.15 pm that day, and I will tell you more about it when I see you. My worst job was that of taking messages down the line of trenches to different captains. The trenches were full of men, so I had to go over the open. Several people who were in the trench say they expected every shell to blow me to bits. That night we were again shelled till about 8.00 pm and were relieved about midnight. We got in about 2.30.

The original graves that now form Guillemont Road Cemetery. On the far right is the grave of Lieutenant Raymond Asquith, the son of the Prime Minister, Herbert Asquith. The grave of Lieutenant Edward Tennant, possibly with the white picket fence, is also seen in Sergeant Huborn Godfrey's photograph.

I was dog-tired, and Churchill, who now commands No. 4 Company, was even more tired. Soup, meat, champagne, and cake, and I went to bed till about 2.00 pm. That is the time one really does want champagne, when one comes in at 3.00 am after no sleep for fifty hours. It gives one the strength to undress. …

Darling Moth', I am so thankful to be alive; I suppose you have heard who are dead? Guy Baring, Raymond Asquith, Sloper Mackenzie, and many others. It is a terrible list. Poor Olive will be heartbroken and so will Katherine. Death and decomposition strew the ground. …

20 September: Tonight we go up to the last trenches we were in, and tomorrow we go over the top. Our brigade has suffered less than either of the other two brigades in Friday's biff (15th), so we shall be in the forefront of the battle. I am full of hope and trust, and pray that I may be worthy of my fighting ancestors. The one I know best is Sir Henry Wyndham [severely wounded at the Battle of Waterloo], whose bust is in the hall at 44 Belgrave Square, and there is a picture of him on the stairs at 34 Queen Anne's Gate.

We shall probably attack over about 1,200 yards, but we shall have such artillery support as will properly smash the Boche line we are going for. And even (which is unlikely) if the artillery doesn't come up to our hopes the spirit of the Brigade of Guards will carry all resistance before it. The pride of being in such a great regiment! The thought that all the old men, 'late Grenadier Guards', who sit in the London Clubs, are thinking and hoping about what we are doing here! I have never been prouder of anything, except your love for me, than I am of being a Grenadier. Today is a great day for me. That line of Harry's rings through my mind, 'High heart, high speech, high deeds, 'mid honouring eyes'.

I went to a service on the side of a hill this morning, and took the Holy Communion afterwards, which always seems to help one along, doesn't it? I slept like a top last night, and dreamed that someone I know very well (but I can't remember who it was) came to me and told me how much I had grown. Three or four of my brother officers read my poems yesterday, and they all liked them very much which pleased me enormously. I feel rather like saying, 'If it be possible let this cup pass from me,' but the triumphant finish 'nevertheless not what I will but what Thou willest' steels my heart and sends me into this battle with a heart of triple bronze.

I always carry four photos of you when we go into action, one is in my pocketbook, two in that little leather book, and one round my neck, and I have kept my little medal of the Blessed Virgin. Your love for me and my love for you, have made my whole life one of the happiest there has ever been; Brutus's farewell to Cassius sounds in my heart: 'If not, farewell; and if we meet again, we shall smile.' Now all my blessings go with you, and with all we love. God bless you, and give you peace.

Eternal Love,
BIM.

Bim was sniping when he was killed absolutely instantaneously by a German sniper. His body is buried in a cemetery near Guillemont. The grave is close to that of Raymond Asquith, and we are placing a cross upon it and railing it round today. Forgive this scribble, we are still in action, and attack again tomorrow morning. Bim was such a gallant boy.

Lieutenant Colonel Henry Seymour
4th Battalion Grenadier Guards.

From Tennant's Commanding Officer

Overleaf:
German soldiers of the 180th Infantry Regiment hunt for lice amongst their clothes, Thiepval, early 1916.

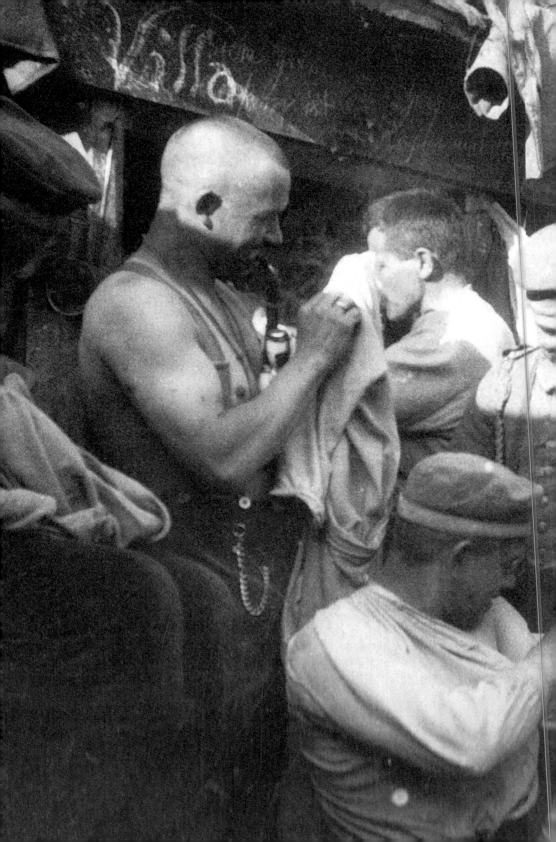

6 Nut Cracking

'I suffer mostly from the fact that I share a dugout with sixty men, without any ventilation. The air is indescribable. When one comes from above, one gasps like a fish. It is so hot that after two hours, one wakes up in a bath of sweat.'

Lieutenant Kimmich, 2nd Battalion 180th Infantry Regiment

The British line north of the Albert–Bapaume road, between the villages of Pozières and Courcelette, had taken sufficient ground that the Thiepval spur, so long a thorn in the British side, had become a salient poking into the British line and dangerously exposed to British enfilade fire. Haig was persuaded that the Germans were beginning to crack and, at the end of September, an opportunity presented itself for Thiepval to be stormed successfully. Four divisions, two British and two Canadian, would make the assault over a 6,000-yard frontage, with a heavy artillery bombardment in support. The following are extracts from the diary kept by a German officer, Lieutenant Kimmich, from July to 25 September. They vividly evoke the pressure that German soldiers were placed under by almost incessant attacks, and their increasingly desperate endeavour to hold the Thiepval spur. It is not known what happened to this officer, but the diary was recovered from a dugout and translated by Army Intelligence. Kimmich's diary is illustrated with images taken from early to mid-1916 inside Thiepval village and at Mouquet Farm, another German strongpoint close by. The German photographer belonged to the regiment holding Thiepval but his identity is unknown.

Since 21 July we have been in line north of Thiepval. The position was quickly put in order and strongly wired but doing this we attracted the attention of the English to such an extent that they turned a battery onto us which by night and day at irregular intervals fired several thousand rounds of shrapnel shells at us. For hours, one round of shrapnel followed another but does no harm to the dugouts.

Lieutenant Kimmich, 2nd Battalion, 180th Infantry Regiment

Opposite: Two British shells that have failed to explode are displayed in a German dugout at Thiepval.

August 8: In the afternoon about two hours shrapnel fire in my neighbourhood. But then they begin a heavy bombardment of the 9th Coy 180 at about five o'clock with heavy 28 cm shells, the fire moves towards our sector. I could see the things for the last 50 metres of their flight. Every two minutes one round. ... A gigantic explosion, everything that is not nailed down flies onto the floor. Immediately after comes the second. I now ordered my platoon to move off to the right, I myself went to the 1st Coy in order to report by telephone. The shells cause all the beams to break and sag, the earth falls down. I look up at the roof and think, 'If another one comes then you are buried.' Ten minutes previously I had a support put in under the crossbeams that saved our lives. The third round hit the communicating dugout, right of where I was standing and penetrated into the dugout, fortunately I had not waited for that one. I had moved to the left wing where Lt Kapp lived. Formerly I had difficulty in imagining what was the matter with a man who lay motionless in hospital, if one asked, the answer was he has been buried. Certainly that is the most horrible death. How many have suffered it? I was incapable of at once returning into the dugout, rather be killed in the open than be buried alive here.

August 9: Owing to necessity a passage has been made. By day it is the 'position of the dead'. Not a movement. The English airmen rule the air to such an extent that we dare not show ourselves. A shell has hurled a dead man of TR 99 into the trench.

How are we ever to make the place habitable?

August 10: I was wakened at 4.30 with the report that Corporal W. has taken a shell splinter – pierced his chest. He was on duty trying to establish communication with the 1st Coy 180 and was taking shelter in the old dugout at the same moment as the shell exploded and he got a splinter through the shoulders and heart. The whole section wept, he is the 3rd man killed in the same section and all of them old soldiers. He had been a war volunteer of two years' standing. It is a crying pity. The strength of my nerves is approaching exhaustion. It is impossible to sleep and the fleas do not make it any easier, reading is out of the

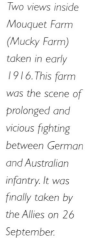

Two views inside Mouquet Farm (Mucky Farm) taken in early 1916. This farm was the scene of prolonged and vicious fighting between German and Australian infantry. It was finally taken by the Allies on 26 September.

question, by making a round of the position I am at last somewhat quietened. Every night at least one attack between Fme du Mouquet, Pozières and Martinpuich. One gets gradually accustomed to the constant thundering of the guns.

August 12: ... at 10.30 at night the whole horizon blazes, the most awful intense bombardment (drumfire) which I have ever experienced commences. The earth continually trembles. Lights go up, white ones, strained with expectation, everyone awaits the coloured artillery signals,

Overleaf: Relaxing times: German soldiers enjoying themselves before the Somme offensive and the hell that was to be exacted in Thiepval.

everyone fires a light over no-man's-land. Each time a hurried look in front of us, everything is clear. There is in fact no pause. What is the [guns'] report and what is the burst, no one is capable of deciding. Three red lights go up like anxious calls for help. Our artillery fires as if possessed. To survive in this cauldron of hell is out of the question. They are firing in every direction. Some shells from the Russian howitzers burst in front of our sector – this has a cheering influence – then the sharp tac-tac of the German machine guns begins, they want to mow down the first wave of the enemy as they get out of their trenches advancing for the attack, the infantry get hand grenades ready.

After an hour the fire dies down. Some guns still continue after the others, like the last rumbling of a heavy thunderstorm. Now a field battery with renewed zeal commenced again to bombard our sector, as long as the heavies were speaking they did not dare to do so. Evidently they have got up some 21 cm shells for them (the heavies). Thus the whole night passes. I get the men busily working on the damaged dugouts, the gigantic shell craters on the top of the dugouts must be filled in again.

At last at four o'clock I go home in order to lie down for a couple of hours. Then the fleas come in columns of fours and drive all sleep away. I jump up out of the dugout and scatter naphthalene everywhere about – useless – the inner enemy does not allow himself to be driven off.

August 13: As early as 6.00 am an English airman comes along, the artillery bombards the communication trench, result four killed belonging to the 1st Coy 180. I saw a wonderful aeroplane fight. A German biplane attacked two British machines, he attacked them [until] one swayed full from right to left and glided down near Pys; the other English machine went off. It is a pleasure to have seen so skilful a German airman. Towards midday the weather cleared up so that from fifteen to twenty airmen are playing about in the air and twenty-five observation balloons are to be seen. It is all right for them while no living being may show himself in the trench because these devils see every movement (literally every rat jumping).

I myself have started a campaign against the inner enemy and during one raid found eight, of whom seven were taken, no wonder one is driven half mad. It is a perfect hotbed of fleas, all large sized ones. …

Opposite:
Pictures taken from an album belonging to an unknown officer in the 180th Infantry Regiment serving at Thiepval. Top right are the ruins of Thiepval Château.

Paradise appears to me to be a bath, a clean bed, and to sleep uninterrupted for eight hours. The feeling of dirt dampens one's spirit. Today was Sunday and as a finale the Germans fired three rounds of heavies into the wood so that the whole geography shook. Tonight it is my turn on duty. A delightful feeling!

August 14: The weather brings about a pause in the fighting. With mixed feelings we notice that it is raining. If only a little rain falls it is all right. But the decomposing corpses are smelling more strongly again, and the clay becomes more heavy. During the night there was [*sic*] a certain number of German attacks, one sees the change in the battle line by lights that go up.

August 16: In the morning we drive in the staff coach of the 1st Bn 180 to Biefvillers to the *flammenwerfer* [flame-thrower] demonstration. What extraordinary means are adopted to send men from life to death! A stream of burning oil sets the entire garrison in a trench on fire. The smoke has a great morale effect. It is very suitable to clear up an English nest. …

August 17: In the morning I saw two English airmen fall down in flames, a horrible fascinating spectacle. I saw the bodies falling out separately like black spots.

The English are using a new kind of shell. They are fire shells, they hurl out flaming bullets and an enormous flame. Very beautifully coloured smoke, as yet I don't know anything about their effect – very active air reconnaissances and enormous air activity behind our lines. We must expect an important attack tonight, probably against Thiepval. Since I have seen the gigantic mass of munitions, I don't believe the English will break through. …

August 22: A counter-attack by T.R15 in the neighbourhood of Fme du Mouquet, they reached their goal, but at heavy cost. The English have also gained experience. They only fire on our position with the heaviest guns; in June they used to fire for days with field guns, now they carry out intense bombardments with heavies. We identify 15 cm, 24 cm, 28 cm, and 38 cm. We are not afraid of any of these as they all have flat trajectories; they only have a morale effect but do not penetrate our cover. Thus yesterday's bombardment of Thiepval caused no casualties. There are craters of gigantic size, the splinters fly more upwards. The most loathsome gun is the 18 cm howitzer. It fires a delay action fuse, that is to say they only explode after they have penetrated 6 feet or so down. There is no crater as all the force of the explosion is downwards. Today our left wing and Thiepval is continually under fire of the heaviest calibres, so there is going to be another attack tonight. You can easily watch the last 200 metres of their flight, how the shining black cylinder whistles into the ground. They attach great importance to Thiepval because we are sitting like a mouse in a trap.

The French communiqué intimates with victorious glee, 'We have dug out four machine guns.' We have got at least two-three English machine guns in every Coy. We don't tell a soul about that, on the contrary, they shall assist us to receive the English properly.

This morning I was outside in the fog in order to have a look at the fellows by day. Now their flesh is almost dried up, how a human leg becomes when it is lying there all alone. The English are so covered up in the grass that one can hardly notice them. ...

Diarrhoea is rampant among us, practically everyone is suffering from it, some to such a degree that they can hardly drag themselves along, the vast quantities of flies take care that it is always spread further. Many of the men look like corpses. ... Yesterday a sentry collapsed from sheer weakness and died. ...

August 25: Thiepval and Hill 141 represent a hell which no imagination can picture. Shelters are destroyed and uninhabitable; trenches no longer exist. One lives in shell holes, which change hourly, no, every minute. The heaviest shells come whistling in and cover in the living and unearth the dead. All communication is above ground, for that reason our losses are stupendous. In two or three nights at most a company is wiped out. Wax yellow, without emotion and unconcerned, the stream of wounded passes to the rear. Warm food is not to be thought of; one takes iron rations which the stomach can hardly digest. As for water, we only get a few bottles of mineral water; hand grenades, cartridges and light rockets take precedence. ...

How ironical is the sentence used in the English Communiqué of the 21st inst: 'Today the German aviators showed a livelier activity. Some even dared to cross our lines.' The bitterness is that it is perfectly true. All these visible signs strengthen the British morale. Every piece of trench is to be taken. 38 cm shells have been falling all around for fourteen days and nights. Every quarter of an hour the earth is turned over. If a fortnight does not suffice, then they take four weeks over it or eight weeks as on Hill 141. They do not need to be sparing with ammunition, accordingly firing continued until the captive balloons and aviators report that all the garrison is buried. If they have got one piece, then they treat the next piece in the same manner. How many infantry have been buried is immaterial.

And that is what nations do who want to civilize Africa and Asia, it is enough to drive you silly – and we have to battle with these inwardly

German positions on the edge of the Thiepval spur that dominated British positions.

hollow Englishmen and only outwardly polished French, who stand miles below us in intellect. It is a mockery of history.

August 27: Early this morning a beautiful rainy Sunday morning. So peaceful that one would think there was no such thing as an offensive. It is true that shrapnel whistles, but these are part of one's life. Today I changed over to my new quarters; as soon as I had arrived I was buried by a large shell. The bombardment continues. Another dugout destroyed. One bears everything. It borders on desperate gaiety and apathy.

August 28: The bombardment begins punctually at ten o'clock. Any wood that was still there was quickly made into props for between eleven and twelve o'clock 197 heavy shells were counted. One sits there and waits for the shell that is to bury us. Spades are there to clear the entrance in order that one may be able to get out. If they come and all goes well then they will have a nasty nut to crack. Only the English are in a hurry, and the bombardment can quite easily last another fortnight or a month. By that time the dugouts will be destroyed, there are no longer any trenches. One is always looking at one's watch but it is a long way to Tipperary. The first Coy moves off away from the bombardment, the line is scarcely occupied. Continuous earthquakes. My eardrums are painful caused by the violent airwaves, for that one talks as long as possible otherwise one

Inside the village of Thiepval. These buildings were reduced to dust between June and September, when the village was finally taken.

tries to pass time by playing a mouth organ, for sleep is quite out of the question.

August 29: The bombardment continues gradually, one despairs, the front line is completely obliterated. How the line is to be held is a puzzle to me. A fresh joyful hurricane bombardment is a pleasure compared with this steady accurate, every shot counted, dead sure bombardment. We are gradually from day to day approaching nearer to the centre point of this bombardment. Yesterday and the day before they fired a 24 cm shell exactly 3 metres in front of the entrance to my dugout. Now there is a crater there where one could ride round in a ring. Always one keeps on thinking if only they don't bury us, for the Thuringians say 'we would not bury a bailiff so deep down'. Just as it comes to my platoon the bombardment ceases. One has to screw up all one's moral courage not to lose one's energy. At 5.30 a thunderstorm broke loose, just as if the Creator wished to have a joke about the entire bombardment for such thundering and flashes the poor humans cannot emulate with all their raging and all their wits they are after all miserable dwarfs.

August 30: The rain continues. It is a bit more like November weather. Storms and rain and fairly cold besides, so that you have to have a fire going. The trenches are bottomless, the bottom, all shot to pieces, eagerly sucks up the water, so that one always has to wade in mud up to one's knees. Now the fearsome time of fatigue parties begins. To get through without any burden is a slow, painful process. Now one has to drag up coils of wire, all kinds of obstacles, beams and above all, food. The whole region through which once the communication trench used to run is kept continually under fire. The men are so exhausted that sweating and soaked they all but sink down, and in addition every day there are some who do not return. What hardships the troops who have to lie in the trenches without any mined shelter have to endure, the foxholes dug with great pains, but without supports fall in and men are buried. Standing in the mud up to one's knees we have got to hold out. The only good thing about the weather is that the heavy artillery has ceased as no observation balloon or aeroplane can show itself; accordingly one can make up long arrears of sleep.

September 1: The English are taking their time over their attack. They are going to make certain, absolutely certain, the destruction must be complete, and we can't defend ourselves. It is impossible to rebuild what is daily destroyed.

Behind their lines the harvest is being gathered in, a large herd of cattle is pasturing. Long English columns pass by, relieved infantry are marching along, people are walking peacefully about. And all this within range of our artillery. Our communications are all cut, so there is nothing to be done. It pains and revolts me to such an extent that I have no longer heart to observe. In the evening gas with its smell of fruit.

September 4: At last, relief from suspense. Yesterday at five o'clock I lay down, at six o'clock, I am wakened. 'Sir, there is an intense bombardment on our position.' So it is an attack, the bombardment increases in intensity. I immediately jump up to the OP; there is nothing to be seen. Down again, up again, then I see an Englishman in front of the wire.

One of the German Maxim MG08 machine guns that caused havoc amongst the British infantry as they attempted to storm the seemingly impregnable Thiepval defences.

'Out with you, they are coming!' He came alone, there is no one else.
I remain up there in the raging sea, my ears tingle. The shells burst so
near that it hurts my eyes. But still it is a glorious feeling one pays no
heed to the dangers. One stands like that at the bow of a ship in a stormy
sea. My eardrums nearly burst. After ten minutes' intense bombardment
I see the English breaking in on the right. Immediately we man two
machine guns and turn the fire on the right flank, mowing them down.
Then the English turn their heaviest artillery onto us, one of the best
lance corporals is killed and five others wounded. I lie with the gun
(an English one) at the ready. Then some more come on and it mows
them down very nicely. Then the alarming news comes that the 2nd
line behind me is in English hands, everyone is retiring. Accordingly we
are being taken in the rear. I send forward a patrol but it does not get
through the English barrage. I remain sitting on the mound and watch
where the shells are falling. It is impossible for the English to advance.
Another platoon comes to reinforce me. I have lost seven men. There is
nothing to be done but observe. Towards four o'clock I send out a patrol
with the orders to definitely ascertain what is in the trench. It comes
back and reports that with the exception of dead and wounded, there is
no one there.

Two battalions of the Duke of Wellington's Regiment [1/4th and
1/5th] made the attack. Owing to an extraordinary coincidence they were
annihilated. There was a relief going on on the Ancre. The machine guns
were to be there at 6.15 am but arrived up early at 5.05 am. The relief was
interrupted by the bombardment and instead of four machine guns there
were eight there. These mowed down the two battalions. An advance by
the second and third wave of attack is no longer possible, as the artillery
is working in great style, thus the attack had been driven back and the
position has been cleared. In the evening, 10th Coy occupies the shell
holes, the German wounded are brought in. I am dead tired and my head
aches. I only desire sleep.

At four o'clock in the morning the English wounded arrive, they are
bandaged and sent on. It is fairly quiet. I have just been out, at the same
moment an intense bombardment with shrapnel was opened on the
sector, but no infantry action followed. I think it was to ascertain if the

Granatloch b/ Thiepval

German casualties buried in and around the many shell holes at Thiepval.

position was held. Now the bombardment by heavy artillery continues. It is only twelve o'clock; that means a long afternoon.

The groaning of the wounded last night was terrible to listen to, and we had no men to carry in the severely wounded. If the line is weakened like that again, they will break in.

September 5: … the neighbourhood itself looks absolutely indescribable. It is like this. I picture the desert, the entire country without one green blade of grass, everything ploughed up by shells. The trees consist of scarred stumps, always more shells. In the line itself no one knows who the other is, neither we nor the English knows for certain where the nearest opponent is. Every foot of ground is prepared for battle. One cannot move without a gas mask, everywhere smells of rotten apples to such an extent that one's eyes water and one's nose also in sympathy is affected.

September 9: One gets accustomed to everything, even to this position. I suffer mostly from the fact that I share a dugout with sixty men, without any ventilation. The air is indescribable. When one comes from above, one gasps like a fish. It is so hot that after two hours, one wakes up in a bath of sweat. …

September 21: Now we are again sitting on the top of a volcano. We are the garrison of Thiepval. It seems strange after eight days of rest. …

And here I am again, once more covered with lice and feel as uncomfortable as possible, we are between two millstones and being slowly ground to pieces, then you have the inflexible rule 'no trench is to be vacated, every inch of ground must be disputed'. When you consider the fact that our line forms a small sharp salient and that the trenches are completely destroyed, owing to which one platoon is entirely separated and with whom we have completely lost touch, that we have no defences, without any means of communication, that one platoon has to man a company front, one realizes that it is a gambler"s last throw. I am anxious to know what will happen.

September 22: I have had a look at the position. It is all over. We can see exactly that any progress the English make in the direction of Le Sars and more especially in the direction of Miraumont allows Thiepval to fall like ripe fruit into their hands. The superiority of the English airmen and owing to them, of their artillery is crushing. It is the airmen who make this offensive what it is, and they are really worthy of all admiration. But

in spite of all we must and will conquer. Today they carried out a relief in broad daylight. I watched it and could only clench my fists in vain. Most disheartening!

September 23: I am endeavouring to vacate the position at once. We have dug a new trench, which makes a flanking fire possible, in the event of their making an attack on the south-east corner of Thiepval. Yesterday we had a four-hour bombardment of our trench with every kind of calibre. It is uncanny, the air that has been displaced does not seem to return; the report seems to break itself on the few remaining tree stumps. …

Today is 24 September and six o'clock in the evening. I am writing with my gas helmet on, the gas is becoming continually more dense, everybody is shouting, the mucous membrane of the nose is affected, there is a continual irritation in one's throat. It became so strong that illness supervened.

Part of the German trench system, badly damaged by British artillery.

Private Sydney
Fuller, 8th Suffolk
Regiment

24 September: Paraded at 9.30 am, in 'battle order', and with rolled overcoats, and marched off via Bouzincourt towards the trenches. We marched through 'Blighty' Valley, past a 12-inch howitzer (beside which was the wreck of one of our aeroplanes), through 'Blighty' Wood, over our old front line trenches, and into the captured enemy trenches before Thiepval. I was attached as a signaller to D Coy, with Bobby Ruegg. We got settled about 6.25 pm in a deep German dugout, in which were several well-made iron beds. The troops we relieved here gave us the cheerful reassurance that we should 'never take Thiepval', and also gave us terrible descriptions of the amount of artillery and machine guns which the enemy had on his front. This, together with the knowledge that several divisions had tried to take the position and failed, did not cheer us up very much. The old enemy trenches we were in had been shelled so much that they were no longer trenches in the ordinary sense of the word, but merely chains of shell holes. We had a phone line to our front line, which was in the old German third line trench. This forward line was cut by 5.9" shells during the night. I went out to repair it, and repaired nine different breaks, but even then I was unable to get the line through. Our men were busily digging assembly trenches, the foremost of which was in front of our front line – in no-man's-land.

Lieutenant
Kimmich, 2nd
Battalion,
180th Infantry
Regiment

September: Our Coy Commander, Lt Lindemann, has reported sick suffering from gas poisoning; accordingly I as next senior take over command of the company. It is a dangerous position to be in, when taking over command to hold the most threatened outer defence of Thiepval, which is being flattened out by every means and from every direction. They bombarded the trenches with every calibre of gun they possess, from the lighter shells to the heavier trench mortar torpedoes, which tear craters 4½ metres in depth. During the entire weary afternoon they have been bombarding the 2nd line, every three or four minutes the lights go out, the dugout trembles, and one is expected to sleep through that sort of thing.

*Opposite: An
officer waits for
the attack on
Thiepval, 26
September. His
arm is resting on
a box of Stokes
mortars.*

To go out and have a look at how things are going on the right is impossible. One only sits and waits until either the dugout is destroyed or until the evening comes. One often thinks, 'O Lord, if possible, let evening come,' and this during the morning. Beside me the orderlies are singing folk songs with enthusiasm rather than with ability.

The assault would begin at 12.35 pm with Canadian troops attacking east of Mouquet Farm and pushing forward from Courcelette village. To their left the 11th Division would attack what remained of Mouquet Farm, while the 18th Division, including the 8th Suffolk Regiment and the 11th Royal Fusiliers, were tasked with attacking Thiepval itself.

Private Sydney
Fuller, 8th Suffolk
Regiment

26 September: Got ready, and moved up towards the front line at dawn. Each man carried on his back, affixed to his haversack, a lozenge-shaped piece of bright tin (cut from a biscuit tin) about 8 x 6 inches. These were worn so that our artillery observers could accurately observe the extent of our advance. There was much delay, and we waited in 'Joseph' Trench and again in 'Hindenburg' Trench for some time. In the latter trench we were stopped for some time opposite the half-buried and putrefying remains of an English soldier – very nice too, just before going over the top. Also very suggestive. We eventually reached the forward assembly trench about 10.00 am.

It was a lovely day, bright and warm. Our guns were fairly quiet all the morning, only an occasional shell going over us. A very big howitzer (probably the 12-inch in 'Blighty' Valley), was firing into Thiepval, and huge splinters from the shells kept buzzing over our trench, which, being a newly dug one, was very good 'cover'. We were just beside the remains of a solitary hawthorn bush. To the right of us we could not see much, but to the left the ground rose rather sharply and we could see many of our men in the continuation of the trench we were in. We were informed that the barrage would commence at 12.35 pm., and we were not to fix our bayonets until then in case the enemy saw them glitter in the sun, and rumbled us – we wanted the attack to be a surprise one, if possible. The rum was issued. The guns remained very quiet, and only a few enemy shells came over, dropping some distance over us. Our watch was a very interesting object to us, especially as 12.35 pm drew near. A few minutes before that time, the order was passed along the trench – 'Fix your bayonets'. Then, at what was, according to our watch, half a minute or more to 12.35 pm, four 18-pounder guns fired, – one – two – three – four, and in a few seconds all the hundreds of guns behind us were firing. The barrage dropped just in front of us, so close that the

18-pounder shells seemed to only just skim our trench, and for a few minutes I found it difficult not to keep ducking.

The first wave went over immediately, then the second, then the third, all at a few seconds' interval, and then – the fourth, which included D Coy Hdqrs and ourselves. The noise made by the guns was a continual thundering roar, very different to 1 July. A minute before, we could have whispered to one another – now we had to shout in each other's ears if we wanted to speak. The barrage was like a wall of smoke and dust, topped by the white smoke from the shrapnel bursts. It was now 200 yards away, (approximately), and was slowly creeping forward in front of our first wave. A slight wind was blowing the smoke away from us, very nicely. Away we went, at a steady walk, carrying our rifles at the 'high port' – bayonet pointing upwards and to the left – so as to avoid accidentally spiking one of our own men.

Just before zero: British artillery pulverize enemy positions on the Thiepval spur.

Lieutenant
Adrian Stephen,
D Battery, 1/4th
South Midland
Brigade, Royal
Field Artillery

Above: *Both of
these pictures were
taken by Lieutenant
Patrick Koekkoek
minutes before the
infantry advance on
Thiepval.*

The trenches were silent and motionless. Then suddenly, at the appointed minute, the slopes of Thiepval seemed to move with small brown figures, like a field alive with rabbits, and the guns swept down on Thiepval and the country to the right of it. At first the men advanced in disordered masses, but gradually taking their own time they opened out like a stage crowd falling into their allotted places. I could see the first wave walking towards Thiepval, and then a second wave sprang up and spread out behind them, then the last wave took shape and followed up in artillery formation; small bunches of men, with an interval between each bunch, or more often six men advancing in single file with a stretcher-bearer in the rear. It was a wonderful sight. Never have I seen such a calm, methodical and perfectly ordered advance. It seemed incredible that this parade could be marching on Thiepval, the most sinister of German strongholds, yet hardly a man fell. The barrage was as perfect as it was terrible. The white

smoke of shrapnel ran like a rampart along the trenches that were the first objective, as clear as though it were made of tape carefully placed and measured.

Indeed, the barrier of white smoke, broken now and again by a black puff from an enemy gun, might have been an ermine fur with its little black tufts.

From my vantage point I could even look over the barrage onto the trenches beyond, but it was hard even for a moment to drag one's eyes away from the little brown figures that were slowly but steadily drawing upon Thiepval.

We hoped to disturb the Boche in the middle of his dinner. Our assembly trench was shelled rather heavily at about 12.15, and we thought at first that we had been discovered. However, no one in our company was hurt, and after about ten rounds of 5.9s [shells] we had peace. Our shelling had been merely normal, but at 12.35 the biggest barrage ever used was to open out.

With the first shell we were over the top, and had gone several yards before the barrage had really started. When it did start – my word! It came with a fearful ear-splitting crashing and rending, thousands of shells bursting almost simultaneously. We met Boches running about, scared out of their wits, like a crowd of rabbits diving for their holes. Men were rushing about unarmed, men were holding up their hands and yelling for mercy, men were scuttling about everywhere, trying to get away from that born fighter, the Cockney, but they had very little chance.

I had the pleasure of shooting four of them before I was wounded in the wrist. After this everything seems blurred. I found myself in a shell hole with one of my men who was also wounded. We patched each other

up, and then went on. I have visions of excited men tearing after the Boches, visions of men sitting over dugout entrances waiting to shoot the first Boche that appeared.

I saw men stop, light a cigarette, and walk on again as if walking down a street. There did not seem to be many bullets flying about us, but no doubt the noise of the guns prevented us hearing them. We had not got far when a huge shell, or *minenwerfer*, burst about 15 yards behind us, and to the right. I did not hear it coming, owing to the noise made by our guns, although it must have been about 11-inch calibre. We were almost knocked down by the explosion, but were unhurt. A man just in front of me was hit by one of the splinters, which entered his right side, and stopped just under the skin in the centre of his chest, making a big lump there, like a large boil. Paused in a shell hole to bandage him up, as well as we could. In the same shell hole was another man who had been shot through the calf of a leg – a nice, 'cushy' one.

We went on again, over the enemy's front line, which had been taken away easily (first objective). Shortly afterwards we had to stop again – a party of the enemy were putting up a desperate resistance in a piece of communication trench, around a dugout. They were firing away at our men who had passed them. Our Support Coy (B), came up, and soon cleared them out, shooting the riflemen first, and then bombing the dugout, down which the survivors had bolted. We forgot our own Coy for the time being, and watched the fight, waiting our chance to take a hand. Two of the enemy were lying dead on the top of the dugout entrances, wearing their steel helmets and equipment, and with their rifles under them, just as they had died, riddled with bullets. Another was lying, buried almost to the neck by a shell which had dropped near, but still alive. I shall never forget the expression on this man's face – ghastly white, his eyes staring with terror, unable to move, while our chaps threw bombs past him down the dugout stairs, and the enemy inside threw <u>their</u> bombs out. The explosions of the bombs in the dugouts could be felt rather than heard – we could feel the shock of the explosion, but the sound was deadened by the depth of the dugout. One little German popped out, wearing his steel helmet, holding both hands

Private Sydney Fuller, 8th Suffolk Regiment

Opposite: A German sentry lies dead in the trenches at Thiepval, the day after capture. Above him, top right, is a trench periscope still in position while lower down two German stick grenades sit in a box.

above his head, and crying 'Mercy, mercy!' He was shot at once, and dropped like an empty sack.

Lieutenant Adrian Stephen, D Battery, 1/4th South Midland Brigade, Royal Field Artillery

Sometimes a wave of men would dip and disappear into a trench only to emerge on the other side in perfect line again. Now they are into Thiepval! No, the line suddenly telescopes into a bunch and the bunch scurries to right or left, trying to evade a machine gun in front, and then with a plunge the first wave, broken now into little groups, vanished amidst the ruined houses. What desperate resistance they encountered in the dark and mysterious passages beneath those ruins, only the men who fought will know, but the other waves swept on up to the slope, till they too were lost amidst the village. Farther to the right, where the barrage had lifted, more brown figures streamed across the open. A black dog ran out of a dugout to meet them; a man stooped down and fondled it. When they drew near to a line of chalk heaps I saw black masses emerge and march towards our lines. Prisoners were giving themselves up without a fight. Prisoners were pouring in from all sides, sometimes in black batches, guided by a brown figure and a shining bayonet, sometimes a single Boche would race, hands above head, panic-stricken till he reached our lines. Thiepval was now a closed book, though runners would sometimes emerge and dash stumbling to our trenches.

Private Sydney Fuller, 8th Suffolk Regiment

We suddenly realized that we had lost touch with our (D) Coy, which was now several hundred yards in front. We at once started off to catch them up, as they might require a signaller at any time. We could see our men swarming over the ruins of the village, and they seemed to be going well. On the right, I saw a long line of men running towards our rear, and for a moment I thought it was the beginning of another repulse. Then I saw that they were holding their hands above their head – Germans. They had surrendered, and left their trench like one man. On we went, keeping our eyes and ears open for any of the enemy who had possibly been left behind alive. On reaching the Thiepval–Pozières road we stopped for a rest, in one of the huge shell holes. Our 'moppers-up' were busily bombing the many dugouts in and around the ruins of the village, shooting most of the occupants as they came out. I saw one German rush out, in his shirtsleeves, with his hands full of watches and other things he had collected from his comrades. He offered them first to one of our men, then to another, but no one touched the things – they were too busy with the more serious business. Then, on our right, two of the enemy suddenly appeared, and began to run towards their own lines. We were just about to open fire on them, when they turned, and began to run up the road towards us. One was an elderly man, wearing a Red Cross armlet. The other was a young chap, very tall. They seemed to be mad with fear, and were sobbing and crying. For some reason they appeared to want to get into the village. Two of our men got out in the roadway and called on them to stop, but they were too terrified to be reasonable, and dodging past the bayonets, they ran on until they were shot by a party of bombers.

A piece of shell struck my mess tin, which I was carrying on my back, making a huge dent and a small hole in the lid of it. On we went again, to the second objective, (Zollern Trench), where we found the Coy halted, as per the programme. Our barrage had halted too, some distance in front of the trench. One of our 18-pounder guns was firing short, just on our right, and I saw one of its shrapnel shells burst directly over one of the RAMC,

The Thiepval–Pozières road. Private Sydney Fuller reached this road and rested here during the fighting.

seriously wounding him. Our OC Coy ordered us to keep a short distance from the enemy trench, as it was, quite possibly, mined. We therefore got out, and sat down among the shell holes just outside.

Looking back, we saw a tank (the first I had seen) moving slowly about on the edge of the village. It fired several small shells at the trench we had just left. I suppose the commander of the tank, seeing us come out of the trench again, thought we had been driven out by the enemy, and so tried to assist us. The shells all hit the top of the trench, but did not appear to explode – they merely threw up a little earth. The tank got stuck in a big shell hole soon afterwards, near the spot where we had crossed the Thiepval–Pozières road. We waited where we were for the scheduled time, which was over an hour. At the appointed time, our barrage lifted once more and we went on for our final objective – (Bulgar Trench).

Second Lieutenant George Cornaby, 11th Royal Fusiliers

On the left, D Company had very hard fighting along the old Boche front line. They were eventually held up on that line about level with the chateau, having got on well, but with very heavy losses. Captain Thompson was hit in the head, but continued fighting until hit again and killed. Of the three platoon commanders, one was killed, one wounded, and one (Hawkins) stunned by the explosion of a trench mortar shell, but kept on with the company.

C Company killed a great many Boches in a trench about 250 yards west of the chateau, and running north and south. Along this same trench Major Hudson, of A Company, was hit through the shoulder, but continued until the final line was taken and consolidated. On his way down he got a bullet through the thigh, breaking the bone, and died a few days later.

Battalion Headquarters in the Leipzig Salient had had no news of the fight, so at about 1.15 Colonel Carr took Headquarters forward. There was still an intense barrage, and a number of men were hit going up. On getting to the chateau ruins, which were merely a heap of broken bricks, we found that Colonel Maxwell, commanding 12th Middlesex, had just arrived there. As there was no doubt as to what was happening on the left (D Company's sector), Colonel Carr and Captain Cumberlege, the Adjutant, proceeded in that direction. A machine gun immediately opened on us from very short range, and Colonel Carr got three bullets through various parts of him – fortunately none of them serious – and Cumberlege was also hit. …

The line eventually held was about 300 yards in front of the chateau. The Boche shelled the whole area, and particularly the trench from which the attack had started, until dark, but slacked off during the night.

The next day I went up to look for Captain Thompson, and found him. We buried him at the cemetery at Black Horse Bridge, Authuille. He was probably the best company commander the battalion ever had.

The Boche retaliation was feeble and badly placed. His barrage fell behind all our men, and very few shells had burst among them, and even then never did they cause a man to turn his head or swerve out of place – unless he fell. At this stage a tank crawled onto the scene and crept laboriously, like a great slug, towards Thiepval. It disappeared among the ruins, puffing smoke. Subsequently it caught fire. Thiepval now became as stony, as devoid of life, as it was before the attack. Away to the right, however, a fresh assault was being launched. A new barrage opened, and our men swept forward to another objective, wheeling slightly as the trench in front ran diagonally across their path. Suddenly, as though spirited away, they vanished, sank into the ground. Watching carefully we could distinguish a movement among the long grass and wire, and sometimes a man would leap up, dash forward, or run backward. It seemed they were playing at hide and seek. Probably they were. It is certain they were held up by something, and the bitter fighting which continued the next day for Hessian Trench – the trench in question – made one wonder how they ever got as far as they did. Yet all this time men were streaming backwards and forwards to the Zollern Trench just in the rear. How astounding, this careless movement across the open! Even during my exploration I had found myself strolling about in places where I could sometimes see Boches running along their trenches. It makes one smile to remember the old corps dummaries of 'peace time' warfare. 'Our snipers shot two of the enemy today.' Slaughter now has become so wholesale that one is careless of the mere individual.

When the light failed, our men were still playing hide and seek. We had taken the Zollern Redoubt, part of the Stuff Redoubt on the right, and part of the Schwaben Redoubt on the left. Above all, Thiepval had fallen. Thiepval, the proud fortress garrisoned by one regiment since September 1914, had at last, after three big attacks, yielded.

Lieutenant Adrian Stephen, D Battery, 1/4th South Midland Brigade, Royal Field Artillery

Debris left behind by the Germans in the Thiepval trenches while (right) evidence of the power of the British bombardment is clear to see.

Private Sydney Fuller, 8th Suffolk Regiment

Several of the captured enemy dugouts were burning fiercely, having been set fire to by the bombs. Many of these dugouts evidently had in them stores of enemy bombs or ammunition for from time to time one or another would 'blow up' like a small mine, hurling timber high in the air. After lying out for about two and a half hours, we began to get back to Zollern Trench, going one at a time, because of the sniping of the enemy. I found that my companion, Bobby, had gone to sleep, and I had to awaken him by prodding him with the toe of my boot. I went back to the trench first, and arrived safely – Fritz was a bad shot, and only hit the ground. I then watched Bob make a bolt for it. He started off all right, but before reaching the trench he was attacked by cramp in the legs, and had to stop in a shell hole, coming in later.

The dugouts were explored, many with enemy dead at the entrances or lying on the stairs. Down below were all the paraphernalia of an enemy garrison who had hastily evacuated their position; reels of telephone wire, German telephone equipment, clothing, food. On a table Fuller saw 'freshly opened tins of some evil-smelling stuff', which he was told was horseflesh.

The casualties in the battalion were 'surprisingly light', averaging forty-five per company. In Fuller's company only one officer had been killed and one wounded.

For the first time [at Thiepval] I saw Germans surrendering in droves before putting up a fight. For the first time his hitherto faultless military machinery failed to swing reserves where they were wanted. On 26 September I felt our moral ascendancy. It was as obvious, also, as the map at my elbow or the ground under observation. It was not pronounced, but it was there. … We must push on-on-on without rest and without mercy, even towards ourselves. Our moral ascendancy, however slight, makes one feel like that. It fires one with fresh enthusiasm.

Lieutenant Adrian Stephen, D Battery, 1/4th South Midland Brigade, Royal Field Artillery

27 September: D Coy moved back to Thiepval, our trench too crowded. Found Batt Hdqrs in a big dugout beside the Thiepval–Pozières road. It was fairly quiet, so we had a look around the village. There were scores of dead Germans about, especially in the road. Most of them had a device like a double crown on their shoulder straps. Nearly all were the 180th Wurtemburgers. The village was completely smashed, hardly a wall standing. Saw a well, which had apparently been used by the enemy, there being a windlass and rope at the top of it. Near this well was a large dugout which was evidently the food store of the enemy garrison. In it we found some raw meat, scores of cases of soda water, bottles of beer, a small keg of good cognac, many boxes of cigars, etc., etc. The cigars were the kind issued to enemy troops, and were very good. The only living things in the dugout were one cat (unharmed) and thousands upon thousands of large houseflies. The beds in the dugout appeared to have been left in a hurry, judging by the way the things were left. On the floor at the foot of the entrance steps lay a bag of German mail, the seals unbroken, as if it had been dragged into the light to be opened. We opened it, and found letters and parcels addressed to the late garrison. Many of the letters contained photos of families, girls, etc., in Germany – wives, children, and sweethearts no doubt. Some of the parcels contained underclothing, some eatables of various kinds – jam, butter, etc., which were not at all bad. I found some good pastry in one parcel. In another (addressed to a major, commanding a 'Kompany'), we found some eggs, quite fresh. I took some of the boxes of cigars along to the Coys nearby – no use hoarding them – eat, drink, (smoke) and be merry, for tomorrow or the next day we should probably die.

Private Sydney Fuller, 8th Suffolk Regiment

Overleaf: The increasingly squalid conditions of the Somme battlefield are obvious. Note the rifle used as a makeshift tent peg.

7 Mud and Guts

'No one could struggle through that mud for more than a few yards without rest. Terrible in its clinging consistency, it was the arbiter of destiny, the supreme enemy, paralyzing and mocking English and German alike. Distances were measured not in yards but in mud.'

Captain Sidney Rogerson, 2nd West Yorkshire Regiment

In the dusk of a leaden afternoon we march away from Trônes Wood through Guillemont and Ginchy. On the eastern side of the tiny village of Ginchy we are suddenly confronted with a wide, rolling, open plain over which there is no road but only a single 'duckwalk' track. Slowly the battalion stretches itself out in single file along this track, and one by one the men follow each other, till the trail extends like the vertebrae of an endless snake. On either side lies the open plain.

Not a sign of life is anywhere to be seen, but instead there appear, in countless succession, stretching as far as the eye can pierce the gloom, shell holes filled with water. The sense of desolation these innumerable, silent, circular pools produce is horrible, so vividly do they remind me of a certain illustration by Doré to Dante's *Inferno*, that I begin to wonder whether I have not stepped out of life and entered one of the circles of the damned; and as I look upon these evil pools I half expect to see a head appearing from each one. Here and there the succession of pools is broken by what appear in the fading light to be deep yawning graves, and over these our duckwalk makes a frail and slippery bridge.

On and on we go. Jog, jog, jog behind one another, till slowly the merciful darkness shuts out all sight of this awful land of foreboding. But now the difficulty of our march increases, for many of the laths of these duckboards are broken, and in the darkness a man trips and falls, pitching his sandbag of rations or box of bombs into the mud that lies deep on either side of the track. Whenever this happens, the rest of the battalion

Lieutenant Max Plowman, 10th West Yorkshire Regiment

Opposite: *Lieutenant Patrick Koekkoek called this 'Lone Tree'.*

behind him has to halt while he picks himself up, recovers his load and steadies himself on the track again before trying to make good the gap between himself and the man in front. Despite the cautions passed along the file a hundred times: 'Look out' – 'Mind the gap' –'Hole there', these mishaps constantly occur, till we in the rear wonder why in the name of Heaven long halts should be needed when those in front must still be miles from the trenches. At last the men in front move, and on we go again. On and on, till it seems we must be seeking the very end of nowhere, for still the Very lights, which will show us the line of the trenches, do not appear. Every now and then shells drop, sometimes near enough to spatter us with mud and make us shudder to think what kind of death we should meet if one dropped near enough to lift us into the watery, muddy depths of a shell hole. But even the shells seem to be wandering, for they come fitfully, as if they were fired from nowhere and had lost their way.

On and on we go. It is getting towards midnight now. The duckwalk ceases and we come out on high grassland, where the going is good so long as we keep to the crest of the hill and pick a careful way between the shell holes. Now we are turning and gently descending the hill. The waspish flight of whiz-bangs is heard quite close. We must be near the line at last, though it is still out of sight. Now we drop into mud ankle-deep. A man shouts it is up to the knees where he stands. New voices are heard. The company is no longer extended. There is Rowley. We have arrived.

Across 20 yards of quagmire rough trenches are dimly visible. They are the reserve trenches – ours. The men clamber into them and wrap themselves in their groundsheets. We have reached the mud.

There had been evidence at the end of September that perhaps the ferocious fighting of the month was remorselessly wearing down the Germans so that they were showing signs not just of cracking, but of actually breaking. Even though autumn was fast approaching, the Commander-in-Chief was determined to continue the offensive into October, as a halt to operations would let the enemy recuperate and stiffen their defences. Haig's orders were to press on until winter made operations impossible. Poor weather at the beginning of October temporarily postponed attacks, but a determined onslaught was launched on the 12th along a 4-mile front. Nevertheless, rainy weather made the terrain increasingly difficult and by mid-October, General Rawlinson was already predicting that conditions were such that it would prove impossible to supply enough ammunition to the guns to adequately support the infantry. October would be a month of bloody attrition, with mixed results for everyone. German morale had taken a battering but it did not follow that they would not fight and endure the Allied attacks. If nothing else, the battlefield would be wretched for everyone.

On reaching the front trench line, Lieutenant Max Plowman and fellow company officers made their way down the short staircase into the former German dugout.

The air below is hot and thick: the dugout is not more than 6 feet square, and there are now six of us. The captain of the company we are relieving accepts another drink, and wishing us luck, climbs out. We take off our equipment, but the quarters are too close for anything like comfort. Lilley sits on a case of German soda water which he opens and finds is full. ...

There is little to be done outside, so we talk the night away and discuss civilization as if it still existed for us, dozing between whiles, eating raisins, drinking whisky and taking the air when the fug becomes unbearable. ...

Here, by daylight, outside the dugout, there is nothing within sight to give an inkling of where we are. The front line is said to be over the crest of the sloping ground on our right, about a thousand yards from this spot,

Lieutenant Max Plowman, 10th West Yorkshire Regiment

'The wages of sin are death,' states the caption written by Sergeant Huborn Godfrey. One of the thousands of German dead that littered the battlefield.

but nothing of it is to be seen, and on all sides nothing but open rolling downs. A map is the only guide, and that instructs us we are between Gueudecourt and Lesboeufs, rather nearer Lesboeufs than Gueudecourt, though both villages are out of sight. The map declares a windmill once stood here. There is not a trace of it now. Facing the line, HQ dugout is forward on our left, hidden in a sunken road, and the second line runs somewhere just beyond it. The trenches our men occupy are negligible hastily thrown-up dykes, and as we are practically unsighted there is no harm in moving about on top – indeed there is no alternative. Ploughing through the mud, I find many bodies lying about still unburied. How unreal they look! They merely remind me of the gruesome newspaper pictures of the dead on battlefields. Yet looking on them now I reflect how each one had his own life, his individual hopes and fears. Individually, each one was born: dead, they come back to individuality.

Private Albert Edwards, 1/6th Gloucestershire Regiment

Oh! the skeletons lying about – picked quite clean. One little fellow about 4′10″, I should think, with a small forage cap covering his skull – bones for legs – these sticking down into the knee boots so familiar in the German army. A piece of shell had cut through the right boot, breaking the leg, and the two ends were plainly visible through the boot.

A rifle was clenched in his right hand, bolt open, and at least one cartridge in the magazine. Empty cartridge cases scattered around showed that he had fought from his shell hole, possibly had killed some of the advancing British, and then was laid low.

Oh! what can one think of warfare? Here is one of our enemy's men, perhaps boy would be more correct – killed by us! There are many more of both sides yet to fall, and become as this fellow!

There is some sorrowing mother away in far Fatherland who mourns her son – probably never knows that he lies uncovered in enemy territory – but there is the other side of the question! Think of the *Lusitania*, Louvain, Rheims, London, and heaps of other crimes. Yes, old Skeleton, you belong to a nation of murderers – outlaws – vermin, and as either of these you have met a fitting end!

Come here, and look! In the tumbledown breast work, there are four British skeletons – Scots of the 15th Division, who fell on 15 September.

A shell has burst in their trench, killing three of them outright, I should think, while the fourth has tried to crawl back to safety, and has been hit again and died! (Civilization. Twentieth century!)

We move down through Martinpuich. Before our July attack, civilians must have lived here in perfect safety, as amongst the ruins one can see odd pieces of curtains, tablecloths, sheets, broken crockery and other oddments. The road below Martinpuich is fairly good and with the exception of shell holes, there and here, the road is quite good for wheeled traffic. About three quarters of a mile from the ruins of Martinpuich, one comes to a sharp turn to the right, and there on the side of the road lay two dead mules. Thus the spot was called 'Dead Mule Corner', even in official records.

A few hundred yards beyond this corner one comes to a large tree lying across the road. This was our dump, just on the outskirts of Le Sars, called Fallen Tree.

Having dumped our loads, we mounted and had an uneventful journey back to La Boisselle.

Finding a safe passage across the morass of the Somme was exacting, as the mud slowly subsumed all former landmarks, and the battlefield in October and November became uniformly dull to even the keenest eye. Whether going up the line with rations or simply passing from one stretch of trench to another, the chances of becoming disorientated and lost were very real, as autumn mists descended and the days shortened.

It is dark again. We are waiting for the mules to bring up rations. There has been little enough to do during the day, beside cheer the men up and get them to rub their feet and change their socks, and so, if possible, ward off what is miscalled frostbite. Rain has been falling off and on all day, and once or twice a great silt of mud outside the dugout looked as if it intended to close up the entrance. We dug hard to prevent it, and though the water still runs down the steps, the mud seems to have stopped shifting.

The mules are late: but that's no wonder; what is marvellous is that those small-footed beasts should ever be able to drag their feet through

Lieutenant Max Plowman, 10th West Yorkshire Regiment

the miles of mud that lie between us and Ginchy. No horses could do it. That this is a fact is now borne out by the Quartermaster Sergeant, who, unused to marching, arrives fagged out to tell us that the doctor's horse has slipped into a shell hole up to the neck and had to have his load of rations cut from his back before he could be pulled out. Those rations are now at the bottom of the shell hole. Somebody will have to go short in consequence, and Rowley very properly decides that the company in reserve must be the losers.

The rations arrive and are apportioned: the men loaded up with the bags and old petrol tins filled with water. A priceless jar of rum is given into the charge of an NCO. The business of getting the party off is not made easier by shelling which comes presumably because a lantern carried by the transport party has been observed.

As soon as the ration party has moved off, Hardy and I parade thirty men and two sergeants and set out for Brigade Headquarters in search of sandbags. We have no guide, and after going steadily for about an hour realize we have lost our way. This is not surprising considering the country and the darkness, but we must of course find the Brigade Headquarters if we spend the rest of the night in search. Batteries are firing in the hollow. The men behind those gun flashes will be able to direct us; so we make for the flashes and in time arrive at the gun pits. An Australian battery puts us on our track.

It is no simple path. Time and again we are climbing over deep, waterlogged, disused trenches, tripping over telegraph wire, and tearing rents in our clothes on barbed strands; but before midnight we reach the deep dugouts. There, after waiting some time, we load each of our men with as much as he can carry. Slowly we make the return journey, going well until we pass our own reserve line and encounter the 400 yards that separate us from Battalion Headquarters. Here the mud is often knee-deep. The men are tired and hungry. They get stuck in the mud and have to be pulled out; but after any amount of wrenching and pulling, falling and swearing, we do get the sandbags delivered. Precisely what purpose they are to serve we cannot think, for anyone who has tried to fill sandbags with mud that is like glue knows he is performing the task of Sisyphus.

Opposite: *Two men passing with apparent urgency down a trench at Beaumont Hamel.*

Captain Eric
Whitworth,
12th South
Wales
Borderers

The line was in a valley and frequently, by day and night, thick mists came up and on these occasions, to help the guide, an NCO was detailed to flash backward every few moments an electric torch to show the relief or party the position of the small trench, only 15 yards long, which had to be hit to find Company Headquarters.

A company was entirely in the hands of its guides; a mistake on the part of a guide one night delayed the relief two hours, and such a mistake might have much more serious consequences than this. The front trench was not continuous, in fact only a very small proportion was held, and there were large gaps of 150 to 200 yards. A guide who lost his way might easily find himself in the middle of no-man's-land, and, where the German lines were only 50 yards away, the error might not be discovered in time to prevent the party wandering into the enemy's lines. This type of mistake undoubtedly explained the capture of several German prisoners by our troops. On one occasion a German machine-gun officer was taken with his guide. It turned out that he had come up to see the line on the night previous to the relief and the guide led him by mistake through one of the gaps in their own line.

Captain Sidney
Rogerson, 2nd
West Yorkshire
Regiment

I started out for Battalion Headquarters in the Sunken Road, so confident in my ability to find it that I took no orderly with me. Alas for such presumption. I had gone no more than a few dozen paces when I began to have misgivings. Surely, I should have passed Dewdrop Trench by now. I paused to take what bearings I could, but the night was black as pitch. Landmarks there were none. A shell burst here and there, and I remember thinking what a wrong impression the ordinary war picture gave. They always showed shells exploding with a vivid flash, but all that now happened was a scream, a thud, and a little shower of red sparks as from a blacksmith's anvil. There was not the faintest glimmer to light me on my way. I stumbled on. Doubts became anxiety. I was lost! No matter that I ought to know I could not be far away from someone; I was afraid. Throughout the war this was my worst nightmare – to be alone, and lost and in danger. Worse than all the anticipation of battle, all the fear of mine, raid, or capture, was this dread of being struck down somewhere where there was no one to find me, and where I should lie till I rotted back slowly into the mud. I had seen those to whom it had happened.

So now anxiety passed almost at once into panic. I went forward more quickly, first at a sharper walk, then at a desperate blundering trot. Was it imagination? Or were more shells really beginning to fall, rushing down to sink into the soft earth and burst with smothered thuds? Yes! Little showers of red sparks were all around me. I struggled on, fell once again, many times, tore my coat on barbed wire, cut my hand. When would a bullet from this chattering machine gun strike me in the head or back? The nape of my neck ran cold at the thought. My heart thumped louder than ever, both from terror and effort. I was getting blown. I could go no further. Then I stumbled, pitched forward, slithered down several feet, caught my kit on some signal wires, sank up to my elbows in wet mud. I had reached the Sunken Road!

In such a moonscape, anyone with an intuitive sense of direction was a godsend. Captain Eric Whitworth had 18-year-old Private Knight.

Knight proved a most capable and devoted orderly. At night he had a wonderful sense of direction and instinct for choosing the best path: darkness was perhaps less strange to him as previously he had worked in the mines in South Wales. He always came about with me in the line, following close behind, except when in different places I often told him with perfect confidence to lead on in front. A great deal of work fell to him, owing to his skill as a guide: he was of course constantly taking messages, and on nights when we were to be relieved he always went back to bring in the leading platoon of the new company, but his chief work was coming with me on the ordinary rounds of trench duty every night. In the winter on the Somme, when our line consisted only of isolated posts with long gaps in between and no trench to show the way, it was a great anxiety off my mind to be able to leave the direction entirely in his hands. Sometimes to spare him, on getting back to Headquarters, I would tell him to turn in and sleep. Two or three hours later, I would start out again, not intending to take him, but I always found him waiting when I had clambered out of the dugout; apparently he found out from my servant or the Company Sergeant Major when I was next going out.

Captain Eric Whitworth, 12th South Wales Borderers

His spirit was indomitable. He was of very slight build and appeared to suffer much from the cold and wet, but he never complained or went sick. If his health was weakened, as no doubt it was, nothing could break his spirit. One night of a relief in winter when the wind was at its worst and there was a steady downpour of rain, the incoming company commander told me how Knight had several times gone back and helped out of shell holes men much bigger than himself, and then came up to the front again as a guide, carrying some of their rations in sandbags. The relief was several hours late and but for Knight's efforts it would have been much later still.

Such an orderly as this made the long hours of trench duty in the winter pass with a minimum of trouble and anxiety. Indeed he became also a companion, though quite unconsciously, for we rarely, if ever, spoke of anything to break down the barrier of our official relationship. Nor did he expect or receive any reward, other than an occasional hot drink from the Sergeant Major and some extra socks which had been sent out from my home for him.

The horses and mules upon which the British Army relied so heavily to carry ammunition and supplies as close to the gun line as possible suffered every bit as much as the men. To be tied up in long horse lines and in increasingly cold and bitter weather was a torment, to which could be added ravenous hunger and not unnatural fear. Horses in particular were unsuited to the workloads placed upon them and the conditions under which they served: too often they sank into oblivion still attached to the guns and the limber they pulled.

Driver Rowland Luther, C Battery 92nd Brigade Royal Field Artillery

In this cold and hunger, the horses now developed a new habit – they all started chewing – ropes, leather, or even our tunics. While you were attending to one horse, the other would be chewing at you. So we reverted to chains, a big steel chain for pinioning down, another from the horse's noseband, just like a heavy dog chain. The bags from which they were fed oats and corn had become sodden with rain, and when a harness man was placing this on its head, the horse would swing it up and sideways. Many a driver was hit senseless with such a blow. No man could feed two horses like this, so it was again a case of one man per horse, otherwise the horse not being fed would rear up and plunge in all directions. The horses then turned to chewing at one another, and they soon became hairless, and a pitiful sight. This was war, however, and no inspector from the Society for the Prevention of Cruelty to Animals came that way.

Have you ever watched a flypaper full of flies? If so you have an idea what the Somme was like. It was just like a human flypaper. Six big strong horses could not pull an empty ammunition wagon weighing about 5 cwt through the mud and if a horse fell down it, five times out of ten, it had to be shot as it was a terrible job to get it on its feet again. We have tried for as much as twelve hours to get one horse up. Can you imagine being pinned under a horse in thick sticky mud? Of course you can't even imagine the mud. I had one of my legs pinned down by a horse and a few shells dropping round about to make it more pleasant. The other fellows tied a rope round me and another round the horse's neck and legs; previously they shot the horse so that it should not kick. There were between thirty and forty men pulling on the ropes and it took them over two hours to get me out of it. On another time a fellow was pinned more securely than me. We tried every way to get him out. We even tried about twenty horses hooked together to pull the horse away but that couldn't budge it an inch; they even broke the harness on the job. The poor fellow underneath was giving instructions how to act. Several times he told us to leave him until it was daylight, but of course we couldn't do that. We eventually freed him by digging away all round him and propping the horse as we dug. After all this and a good stiff dose of rum he was all right again. There were dozens of these cases on the Somme and after a time we took it as a matter of course.

Driver Percival Glock, 281st Brigade, Royal Field Artillery

To me, one of the beastliest things of the whole war was the way animals had to suffer. It mattered not to them if the Kaiser ruled the whole world; and yet the poor beasts were dragged into hell to haul rations and gear over shell-swept roads and field paths full of holes to satisfy the needs of their lords and masters. Bah! many a gallant horse or mule who had his entrails torn out by a lump of shell, was finer in every way than some

Private David Polley, 189th Machine Gun Company, Machine Gun Corps

Heavy draught horses pull some 'elephant iron' as weather conditions deteriorated.

of the human creatures he was serving. I believe I might normally be described as a peaceful, easygoing sort of chap, but the sight of a team of horses, hitched to a limber, on a road in the forward areas, screaming with fright at a shell burst in the ditch beside them, turned my mind in such a direction, and instilled a desire to wipe out those responsible for the poor brutes' presence.

Private John Mortimer, 10th York and Lancaster Regiment

We got relieved. Our five days of action behind us – we were traversing a road called the 'Devil's Mile' – it was a quagmire of a road. The mules were waiting just down the road to carry the magazine panniers to the rear. We loaded the mules and I put the canvas jacket on the Lewis gun, then we continued down the road. I had to carry the gun until we got to the point where transport wagons were waiting with the Lewis gun boxes. The road was like a ploughed field and we had not got far down the road when Jerry opened out with his guns and believe me – he had the range of the 'Devil's Mile' to a nicety. The Lewis gun officer, Lieut Ayres, shouted to us to get down the road as best we could. 'We'll meet at the old German dump at the other end of the road,' he instructed. As we struggled along a shell dropped close by, the mules increased speed, as I tried to keep up with them I found myself sticking in the mud. As one of the mules was passing me I grabbed hold of a strap on the pannier carrier on its back and from that moment I travelled the most terrifying half-mile I ever experienced in my life. I clung to the carrier on that mule's back like grim death. On two occasions I was dragged along but I managed to get back on my feet. When we reached the old German dump my feet were sore and I was caked in mud and just about exhausted. How the gun remained undamaged I shall never know.

On our front there were seventeen divisions or nearly half a million men and there was only one road for the whole transport, so you can guess what it was like, seventeen divisions of transport using one road. It was one continual stream of wagons, guns, horses, motor lorries etc. day and night for weeks and months. The ammunition dump was about half a mile from the guns and it took us anything from six hours to thirty-six hours to travel this distance. The reason for this was if any vehicle broke down or was hit by a shell it had to be cleared away before the others behind could move; we couldn't go round as there were trenches and barbed wire all along each side and the out coming traffic was using the other side of the road, and not more than two vehicles could pass at a time it being so narrow. The motor vehicles made it worse for us as they would invariably get two wheels down a trench, which would mean about twelve hours' work to get it on the road again or failing that push it right over on its side, anything to clear the road. On one occasion it took us thirty-six hours to deliver a matter of thirty-two shells one journey and when we got back to our bivouacs the rest of the battery had moved; it took us six hours to find them and another hour to build a new bivouac and have something to eat (we didn't know whether it was that day's dinner or the previous day's) and get to kip. We had been asleep half an hour, when we were called out again and got back again seventeen hours later, for four hours then up again and so on all the time. When we were out for these long stretches we very seldom had any food with us for the simple reason there was none to have, for we might start out at midnight or just after, and the rations not arrived.

Driver Percival Glock, 281st Brigade, Royal Field Artillery

In such conditions it was hard for anyone to find much to laugh about. The fighting seemed relentless, the pressure exerted on the enemy almost continuous. Yet humour was critical to morale and nothing was sacrosanct. Even an encouraging message from the King himself was worth a wry smile.

Driver Percival Glock, 281st Brigade, Royal Field Artillery

We had a very inspiring message – from the King – read to us. Words to the effect that we were on a very hard task, one of the hardest men had ever been called upon to do and he felt sure as everybody at home did, that we would do our very best and if need be sacrifice ourselves to this just and honorable cause and he was certain that we would come out of this battle covered in glory etc. etc. Anyway we came out covered in mud so I suppose we were justly rewarded, we were lucky to come out at all.

Gunner Victor Archard, C Company, Heavy Section, Machine Gun Corps

18 October: I should like you to see a heavy artillery attack from a distance; at night I mean. The attack starts at a definite moment, when hundreds of guns from the 15″ whose message weighs about half a ton, or rather more, to the deadly and quick-firing 18-pdr, break simultaneously into fire. The horizon is lit up with the flashes which dance and move like some Will o' the Wisp, not for a few yards but on a large horizon, while the actual flash of the big guns which stand further back can be seen dotted here and there, and disappearing as soon as seen. And the noise! The whole air is laden with rumbling, broken by the clear boom of the large guns which are nearer to one. Each separate gun along the line cannot be defined, it is merely the air overwhelmingly laden with the sound.

This is at a distance of about xxxx [censored] miles from the big guns; and some xxx [censored] from the smaller ones.

Now suppose yourself between the heavy guns and the trenches, in fact between the field guns and the trenches; the open ground in which are found the communication trenches, first dressing station, etc. Here the snap of the 18-pdr is predominant, a nasty spiteful snap it is, and the shells whistle, still spiteful over our heads. Xxxxxxxx [censored] the heavy artillery, and the shells from them spin high above your heads, sounding slower and more pompous than the smaller fry. It is as the bark of a retriever compared with that of a terrier.

Do you know that the big shells can be seen leaving the guns and flying across the sky? Given a clear sky and bright sun, and stand with your back towards the sun and you can watch the shells quite plainly. I was watching some medium sized shells the other day. They weighed xxx [censored] each, and there were three guns firing. As each left the gun, the shell appeared just like a cricket ball chasing across the sky, and the best sight was when two or three left practically at the same time. I was able to follow them for a very long way, but they go very quickly.

Of course, there are high and low velocity shells; those of which I spoke were from howitzers, a gun which fires at a high angle and so flies over obstacles.

Some weeks ago I was camped at a place which was daily shelled by Fritz; he sent over a few at somewhat irregular hours day and night. Nearly every shell struck the ground 100 and 200 yards from us, so that the fragments came back to us and even beyond us. The best of it was that on each occasion we heard the German gun fired, then saw the shell explode, then heard it whistle over our heads (although it had by then exploded), and lastly heard the explosion. Note the peculiar sequence. This shell, you see, took quite a second longer than sound to travel on a clear day; the result was that we were kindly given notice of the coming shell. The reason for ducking on hearing a shell is not to miss the shell but to miss the fragments and shrapnel.

It is really funny how one is able to stand such things as are experienced under fire; it makes quite a psychological study. My nerves are now better than they have ever been, I believe.

I should like you to see anti-aircraft guns firing at hostile aircraft, on a clear bright day it makes a fine sight. The shells are usually xxxx [censored] which explode in the air, causing a small flash, and leaving a puff of smoke about as large as a bucket at first but gradually spreading out. On a still day these puffs remain in the sky for a quarter of an hour or so; the Germans use xxxx [censored] smoke and we use xxxx [censored] so that sometimes a mixture occurs when the enemy aircraft mix with ours. I have seen some hundreds of these spots in the sky and look pretty as ours are intensely xxx [censored]. I so often wish I could sketch well, we see such amusing things sometimes. Really one of the most amusing pictures I saw, and I laughed and still laugh at it, was the following. We were in a corner one day and it was necessary to fetch a few pieces of timber which were lying on the ground about 100 yards from us. We could not get to it in the trenches,

An anti-aircraft
gun points
heavenward. Most
were manned by
men of the Royal
Garrison Artillery.

but were forced to risk the open which we did pretty quickly. Just as I got
to the heap I saw one of our chaps running back with about 6 feet of wood
under his arm, and as he started, he heard the whizz of a 'whiz-bang' shell,
and bending low he took to his heels; but the face!! Gee-whizz, I laugh
now when I think of it; the comicality of it was too great to allow me to
move quickly for the minute; the chap was by no means afraid, but it was
a warm corner and did not court favour.

An unrelenting north-east wind gripped the battlefield and to a man everyone
shivered and shuddered. The sky was a blanket, grey with quickly shifting clouds. The
vagaries of the weather and the effect of steady rain on the churned-up battlefield
increasingly put paid to further attacks until the ground became firmer. Proposals
to attack and take Beaumont Hamel, that village fortress and one-time first day
objective, slipped and slipped again over the last week of October.

Inclement weather continued to hold up major operations. Despite increasing
unease amongst corps commanders and particularly General Rawlinson himself, Haig
was keen not to end the Somme offensive in a morale-sapping whimper. Securing the
best positions possible before winter was vital, but so was a final uplifting victory and
the opportunity came in the second week of November, when the weather improved:
the ground began to dry although the ambient temperature remained bitterly cold.
Finally a date could be set, 13 November, for the final assault of the campaign. Several

divisions would take part over a frontage of several miles, from the village of Serre to the river Ancre, with the German bastion of Beaumont Hamel at its centre. This heavily defended village would be the primary target of the 51st Highland Division. The ground around the village had one advantage over land 2 or 3 miles to the south: artillery might have pounded specific objectives around Beaumont Hamel, but the sodden earth had not been fought over and reduced to an irrevocable porridge.

Amongst the officers preparing to go over the top was 19-year-old Norman Collins. He had been in France just a matter of weeks.

The night before (12th), my batman, a lad called Grigor, came to see me and asked if I could provide him with the means of buying a small bottle of whisky – quite illegal of course, but I gave him the money to do it. He would be going over the top with me and he was very likely to be killed, as I thought I would be. We had been told that we would go over the top in the second wave at six o'clock, so our watches were synchronized and we waited for the creeping barrage that was to cover our advance.

In the hours before the attack I spoke to two fellow officers, Lieutenants Smith and Mclean. We chatted and joked and I remember Lieutenant Smith telling me one curious thing and that was that he was going to go sick but not until after the attack. He had developed a severe rupture and he wanted the hernia attended to in hospital, but he wouldn't go sick beforehand as he had been nominated for the attack and his absence would seem cowardly. I thought that was very brave of him because he could have gone sick. In the event he was killed.

As the time approaches, you're looking at your watch to see the hours, and then you're looking in front to see when the barrage will open, and then you look to see that your men are equipped and ready to go. Everyone went in with fixed bayonets and as many Mills bombs as they could carry. The officers carried a cane, a walking stick, a .45 revolver and they also carried a few bombs.

At 6.00 am it was still dark and there was a thick fog, then suddenly a mine went up under the enemy line and 2,000 guns opened fire and dropped on their trenches. The whole horizon seemed to go up in flames. It was so loud you could not pick out individual shells; it was just a continuous drumming. A solid canopy of steel went over our heads.

Second
Lieutenant
Norman Collins,
1/6th Seaforth
Highlanders

Then there was dead silence, and the silence was itself stunning; the contrast, and then about two minutes later our artillery raised their sights and dished out their barrage onto their second line. I suppose I might have blown a whistle but it doesn't mean anything, so you sort of shepherded the men over. You are very aware of the example you are setting the men; if they saw you funking it – showing fear – they wouldn't think much of you. I saw men dropping right and left: I've a vision of a Gordon Highlander pitching forward onto his hands and knees. I went up to him and he was stone dead, his kilt raised, showing his backside.

We were working in a very small area; the rest of the front is nothing. When you saw men wandering about, which did happen, because to begin with it was dark, and if they got a bit lost, it was the officer's job to form them into a fighting unit, no matter what regiment they were in. Knowing one's duty took one's mind off the horrible things.

My servant went with me, Grigor, and he stuck with me as far as he could all the time. The Germans were taken entirely by surprise and their front line was captured quite easily with few losses. We had cut quite a bit of their defensive wire beforehand and the main German defensive position, known as Y Ravine, with its deep dugouts, was taken. I was in the second wave that advanced through the first wave towards the German second and third lines where they managed to get their machine guns up. I must say, the Germans were good soldiers, many fought to the end. I saw one machine gun fight to the last round.

A small number of men came up on our right from the Naval Division, led by Colonel Freyberg, and entered Beaumont Hamel in front of us at an angle. My role was to get into their trenches and throw Mills bombs down into the dugouts. A couple of platoons were detached to clear the dugouts and we took some hundreds of prisoners. I remember a young German prisoner coming in, hopping along using a piece of wood as a crutch. I had him put onto a stretcher and taken back with our own wounded, and I could see that I wasn't very popular at all for that. I was seen as using up a stretcher and a valuable service to help a German at the expense of our own.

There was nothing left of Beaumont Hamel. It had been so badly pulverized that effectively it could only have been identified by map references. As I walked around I saw in the mud and bricks a washing

The entrance (left) to a German kitchen in the village of Beaumont Hamel after capture.
On the other side of the door (right), the unappetizing cooking facilities.

mangle, two rollers and a cast iron frame and that was practically the only thing left in the village which showed that human beings had ever lived there. An enormous amount of ammunition and bombs of various descriptions were liberated from the dugouts.

The dugouts were very deep and had flights of stairs down to the bottom and wire beds. There was even a system of brass bells, like you would see in a house, which a batman could ring before entry into the innermost rooms.

Overleaf:
Beaumont Hamel:
a captured 9-inch
German trench
mortar still in
position.

One of the enemy battalion headquarters, marked on a captured map, had been detailed as a special objective to a platoon of the 6th Seaforths led by 2nd Lieutenant G.V. Edwards. In spite of the fog, this officer led his command most skilfully to the point and captured the CO, the HQ and

Anonymous officer,
152nd Brigade
Headquarters, 51st
Highland Division

some 300 prisoners. I was with General Burn when Edwards returned to Brigade Headquarters. His story was that, owing to the thick fog, his party surprised and surrounded the place without opposition. The HQ was in a deep dugout; there was no trouble, the whole of the inmates surrendering tamely when told of the strong reinforcements at hand.

Unluckily these failed to appear, and Edwards' platoon being heavily outnumbered, the German CO told him quite nicely and politely that the position was reversed and that he and his men were now the prisoners. There was nothing for it but to submit and Edwards accompanied the CO down into the dugout. Here he was given a drink, treated with every consideration and even invited to look through the periscope – a huge affair which gave its owners a commanding view of the surrounding countryside.

It was thus, the fog having lifted somewhat, that Edwards spotted the arrival of the long expected reinforcements. Not to be outdone in courtesy by his German hosts he begged them to consider themselves once more as his prisoners and, as such, to accompany him to the surface. This they did, only to find in arrival that they were called upon to surrender for a third time – on this occasion by a chaplain and a party of Dublin Fusiliers.

Edwards went up to him to explain the situation; the chaplain promptly knocked him down and disappeared in the fog with his captives.

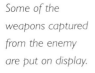

Some of the weapons captured from the enemy are put on display.

In extenuation of this somewhat militant act it should be remembered that Edwards, in common with other platoon leaders, was dressed in the ordinary service dress jacket, with web equipment of the rank and file and with badges of rank only on the shoulder straps; also he was covered in mud. No doubt the chaplain was no more impressed with his story than he was with his appearance; hence his summary treatment of an unusual situation.

The fighting continued the following day with further, much smaller, gains. In all, 5,200 Germans had been taken prisoner, a remarkable haul in the circumstances and a significant success, as had been hoped. Half-hearted German counter-attacks were repulsed. The Battle of the Somme was now spluttering to a finish. On 18 November, operations were ended and the offensive closed.

The work was not over. Around Beaumont Hamel there was a new job of burying the dead, not just of the fighting of 13/14 November but of the fighting on 1 July. The front line had not moved at this village and the dead had lain out in no-man's-land for four months.

Over the course of three days, Second Lieutenant Norman Collins was appointed burial officer to carry out the loathsome job of retrieving and burying the bodies. They worked in full view of enemy observation balloons and were shelled as they roamed across the churned-up ground, causing a few additional casualties. One shell burst within 10 yards of Norman and covered him with mud, but he escaped unharmed.

I was told just to get on with the job of burying the dead. I had a squad of men to help me, carrying picks and shovels, and also stretchers. Of course some of the men they were picking up were their brothers and cousins and they of course were very upset, very, very upset. Their numbers included my two particular friends Smith and Mclean: both had been killed. Lieutenant Smith had been a dentist in civilian life, and Lieutenant Mclean a divinity student; it shows you the waste of life there was in that war.

We took the dead on stretchers back to Mailly-Maillet Wood and dug a long trench and put the dead in there, wrapped in an army blanket, neatly packed in like sardines. They fell side by side and they were buried side by

Second Lieutenant Norman Collins, 1/6th Seaforth Highlanders side. We covered them up and gave them a proper funeral with reversed arms; all the ceremonial of a proper funeral, blowing the Last Post and the pipes playing *Flowers of the Forest*. As an officer you needn't stand aloof, but the best way of comforting the living would be to give them a stroke on the head or a pat on the back or some gesture like that, without words. But it was a horrible thing to do, to have to bury your own cousin or brother.

After burying the dead of the regiment, Norman was then detailed the loathsome task of burying the dead of 1 July, bodies that had lain out in no-man's-land for over four months.

Second
Lieutenant
Norman Collins,
1/6th Seaforth
Highlanders

Nobody knew what to do, we were all fresh, all newcomers to the job. All we could do was remove the paybooks. These were in quite good condition as they were in a sort of oil cloth which protected them. Photographs of mothers and fathers and sweethearts and children were all there, and of course their last will and testament. I don't know how many we collected – hundreds I suppose. We left their identity discs on so they could be identified later, and put the personal items in a clean sandbag. Then we shovelled the dead into shell holes, most half-filled with water, about thirty rotting bodies to a shell hole, and covered them up as best we could. We tried where we could to get a bit of wood and make a mark to identify the place. In the setting sun I saw the green and blue tinge to the shell water, and it looked rather beautiful.

There comes a time when emotion becomes a strange sort of word, you get so much that you become deadened to it, you're bound to. You didn't know men that had been dead for four and a half months, you only knew them as young soldiers and officers who'd gone to war just as you had, and they'd died. You felt in a way horrified to think that there you had, in my case, probably 900 or so young men who had all come over to France to do what they thought no doubt would be a wonderful job of work and in one day – one day – they were destroyed. You thought then, and you saw what happened, and you realized what their aspirations and their ambitions were and that they were going to put the world right, and all they did was to die in a few minutes.

Finally, the loathsome job was finished and with one or two men I took the sandbags full of pay books down a communication trench to Brigade Headquarters. I noticed as we went that the communication trenches had bodies, and parts of bodies, sticking out of the wall for quite a long way. The trench, I suppose, had been dug through the dead where they lay.

After delivering the paybooks, Norman Collins returned to the front line and his men, with whom he felt a heightened affinity.

It was the closest bond because we were both living in the same world. It's extraordinary really, because the association between officers and men as a rule was very short. Neither lived very long, but during that period it became the most intense feeling. Your affection for the men under you – there's no doubt about that. We used to write to their mothers when they were killed, and the mothers used to reply asking for some sort of memento. 'Have you any little thing you could send us to remind us of our dear boy?' which you could never send, of course. It was really quite pathetic. I don't believe we ever replied to these letters, otherwise we would have been entering into correspondence and I believe there was an order forbidding this.

The letters, I'm afraid, had little variation amongst them because sometimes there were about sixty to pen, and you didn't even know who you were talking about. 'Dear Mr and Mrs So and So, I'm sorry to have to tell you that, as you no doubt have already heard by telegram, your dear son was killed on such and such date. He was a fine chap and I was very fond of him and he was a good soldier and you, I'm sure, are very proud of him,' and so on and so forth. As much as you could do, you made her feel that her son was a hero and that's about all.

Second Lieutenant Norman Collins, 1/6th Seaforth Highlanders

By 22 November, the battlefield immediately around Beaumont Hamel had been cleared of the dead, or at least the bodies that were visible. Close to 1,000 Allied dead had been found, and where possible personal possessions collected, before the bodies were buried, including 630 men killed on 1 July.

After such intense action, a division would need to be taken well away from the fighting, into proper rest, perhaps 20 or 30 miles, to refit and recuperate. Otherwise 'rest' rarely meant rest, and men were routinely required for working parties, mending roads, carrying supplies. Accommodation on the Somme was frequently within the fighting zone – a zone, owing to the ferocity of the fighting, that was greater in depth than those encountered in 1915 – and amenities were basic. At Camp 34, where fighting had once raged, the men were left to their own devices to create a semblance of domestic life. Captain Sidney Rogerson's battalion, the Second West Yorkshire Regiment, was going into the line and crossed over with the sorry remains of another battalion going the other way.

The camp was situated on an open space of what had once been grassland between the mangled remains of Trônes and Bernafay Woods. The distance was shrouded by rain and mist from out of which the boom of gunfire came distant and muffled.

'Camp 34' itself was a camp in name only – few forlorn groups of rude tarpaulin-sheet shelters huddled together, as though they shrank from the surrounding desolation. One or two bell tents there were, it is true, here and there, but even they looked as unhappy as if they knew themselves to be but insecurely at anchor in the rising sea of mud. Though even these few tarpaulin-sheets and bell-tents might have been sufficient shelter for the pitiful remnant of the Scottish Regiment [5th Cameronians], they were entirely inadequate for a battalion more or less up to strength. Since no shelter had been prepared for us, necessity forced us to take steps to procure it for ourselves. In other words, we were reduced to looting, or in the more picturesque language of the ranks, 'scrounging' additional cover. With the grim determination of the British soldier, bedraggled men set off with the hearty approval, if not the verbal permission, of their officers to see what they could find. I am not ashamed to confess that, unofficially, I strongly encouraged the more experienced soldiers – who were therefore less likely to be caught! – to scour the dripping countryside for anything likely to improve the company's accommodation, and even gave them permission to leave the camp 'to visit the canteen, Sir.' Needless to say, that canteen was never discovered but other valuable things were.

Captain Sidney Rogerson, 2nd West Yorkshire Regiment

Opposite: (Above) One of the tanks used to support the infantry at Beaumont Hamel is covered with debris. (Below) The remains of the German cemetery in the village.

So far as I was concerned, the first incident was the arrival of the Colonel [Jack], imperturbable as always, though inwardly raging at the lack of organization which subjected men going into battle to such experiences. Behind him, looking indescribably sheepish, stood my young servant, Briggs.

'I congratulate you on your servant,' the Colonel said casually. 'Why, Sir?' I queried. 'Well, as I walked into the very commodious trench shelter reserved for Battalion Headquarters, I saw your man walking out at the other end with the stove. And you hadn't been in camp five minutes! A good boy, that. But I'm sorry I could not spare the stove!' The Colonel smiled, and moved on.

Captain Eric
Whitworth,
12th South
Wales
Borderers

Our destination was Camp 12, close to Chipilly, which was reached at 3.30 pm. The rain did not stop the whole march but we were buoyed up with a vision, if not of billets, at least of a good camp of huts with field kitchens and the prospect of a hot meal and the intense delight, which is not worn away by months of active service, of the English mail. Our arrival, however, was a bitter disappointment; the difficulties of the start in the darkness of the early morning, the utterly depressing half hour after we detrained, the physical effort of the 9-mile march in these conditions were nothing as compared with the empty feeling of all ranks when Camp 12 came into view. Our billeting officer had taken over the camp the same morning from the French. It was situated on the edge of a wood which, in winter, only intensified the atmosphere of cold inhospitality. Half an hour was occupied in getting the battalion from the road into the camp, as each officer, NCO and man struggled across a hundred yards, sinking every step a foot deep in liquid mud. The men's huts were not boarded or raised off the ground. There was nothing to separate them from the damp soil, for the straw left was too filthy to be used at all. Outside the huts no kind of paths had been made and the complete lack of any sanitary organization was evident. The officers' quarters were little better and our company mess was a hut exactly similar with a few wire beds and a wooden table thrown in. …

The absence of billets was due to the depth of country which, during the offensive, had come within the zone of artillery fire, which had desolated all the villages and the countryside. This was a great hardship for the troops when they were not actually in the line, though the hut accommodation was good and constantly improved. ... At Colonne, north of Vimy, when the brigade was holding the front trenches, the battalion in reserve was comfortably billeted in Bully-Grenay, which the inhabitants had not evacuated in spite of the occasional hostile artillery fire. On the Somme, even when the whole division was out of the line, the battalion went back in motor lorries to a camp of huts. The comfort of coming straight from the trenches to a billet where the kitchen fire was always at our disposal for warmth or cuisine could not be compared with the return to an empty hut with a few coke braziers and possibly some canvas partitions to divide up the company quarters and retain some warmth.

Yet something more than material comforts such as these and a real bed were missed; there was nothing to replace the genuine hospitality of our reception, the welcome of the children quick to recognize a second visit, and the friendly half-hour with Madame round the fire before going to bed, all of which contributed to an atmosphere which gave the mental change and recreation so needed during months of continuous warfare. The men suffered similar disadvantages. Pay was of little use to them with only the limited supplies of a divisional canteen. The civilized recreation and companionship of YMCA huts, the bright and cheerful lights of cottages and estaminets were no longer possible. The long winter evenings were spent herded together in huts, with here and there a patch of flickering light from a candle affording the means for a game or nap. Outside no village walks or avenues of trees with happy life and movement for all to see, but only mud with struggling transport going to and fro.

After spending many days in the trenches that November, Sidney Rogerson's battalion was withdrawn to a camp, this time for a supposedly short stop on the way to well-deserved rest much further from the line. The battalion arrived at Grove Town, a camp next to a long-established and busy casualty clearing station. On this occasion there was reason for spirits to rise appreciably as the rain stopped and the men went foraging.

Captain Sidney
Rogerson, 2nd
West Yorkshire
Regiment

*The winter of
1916/17 was
one of the worst
in living memory.
Two Australians
stand in the
snow of Albert.*

Companies quickly set to work to build their own bonfires ... as if in compassionate recognition of our display of self-help, the rain stopped. Thus in an incredibly short space of time the whole scene had changed, and from drooping dejectedly about, talking in undertones or not at all, the men regained their spirits and their energy, and laughter and song rose from the circles round the fires. With still no sign of the missing train, they started wandering farther afield, especially towards the dripping tents of the (Grove Town) casualty clearing station, whence one of my NCOs hurried back to me with the news that he had found behind one of the marquees a big dump of equipment taken from the wounded or dead men. A lot of this equipment was of the khaki webbing type which was the active service harness of the regular army. When the regiment had landed in France in November 1914, every man had naturally been equipped with webbing, but of recent months the new reinforcement drafts had arrived with the unsightly leather belts and cartridge pouches such as were issued to Kitchener's Army, until there were almost as many men with leather as with webbing.

Efforts were constantly being made to discard the leather, for not only was it clumsy, unsightly, and difficult to fit, especially when wet, but it was held to be the badge of the new arrival or the temporary soldier. Any tendency on the part of the war-enlisted man to run down the 'old soldier' must be regarded as a manifestation of an inferiority complex, for imitation is the sincerest form of flattery, and the desire of everyone to possess a suit of web equipment must be put down largely to the desire to resemble as nearly as possible the 'real soldier'.

Here then was a chance, my NCO whispered, to fit out properly the whole of B Company with the converted webbing. Might he have my permission? It was no sooner asked than given, but the news seemed to pass round the battalion, so that, although we had a good start, there was in a few minutes something in the nature of a stampede towards the casualty clearing station. There you have the interesting spectacle under the conditions that prevailed of men jostling and struggling good-naturedly to seize sets of saturated equipment with as much zest and energy as if they had been competing for dips in the bran tub at a parochial bazaar. The discovery of that dump was a godsend, for not only did it enable us to reduce the percentage of leather equipment, but it kept the troops enthusiastically employed.

While the men hunted for kit, or cast around for other forms of salvage, the officers drifted into groups and talked. The satisfaction of food and warmth had so successfully banished all discontent at the non-arrival of the train that it ceased to be a topic of conversation. The casual observer might have been pardoned for thinking we were content to remain at Grove Town indefinitely.

The Somme offensive was officially over. The last knockings had taken place on a day of sleet and with visibility down to just a few yards. Snow too covered the ground, making objectives largely invisible.

Second
Lieutenant
Charles Lloyd,
Royal Field
Artillery

At 6.10 as per programme the show started. However, after the first jar of a few hundred guns going off at once had passed off, I went to sleep again and did not wake up till seven. Got up to have a look at the battle and found snow on the ground, which upset me rather. News very vague all day as to what happened. We hold Ancre trench and part of the Western end of Grandcourt, while the line has been straightened out generally. It started to rain this pm, which will probably interfere with operations. Another ridiculously quiet day. Not a shell this side of the Thiepval Ridge, at least very few.

Major Geoffrey
Hardwick,
57th Field
Ambulance,
Royal Army
Medical Corps

We were up at 6.00 am and were greatly surprised to find the ground covered with snow – it has been very cold during the nights, but snow in November is not common here.

Zero hour was 6.10 am and to the second our artillery started – it was even noisier than that of Monday last, as this time we were amongst the lighter guns whose noise is even worse than that of the 'heavies' – it was a wonderful sight: dawn just beginning to break through, the ground, trenches, shell holes all dead white, a low white mist above the ground and with this the flashes and noise of the guns and in the distance the Boche star signals of red and white. It was the weirdest awe-inspiring sight that I have ever seen – words fail. The gun flashes were wonderful – sometimes battery fire – at others in almost as quick as machine-gun fire. The flashes were of every hue – dull red, yellow, green-yellow, purple and white according to the nature of the explosive. Overhead was the dull swish and clanking of our heavy shells which had been fired off at Ovillers, etc., and immediately above us was that infernal 60-pounder battery that seemed to never stop. No Hun shells came over in reply. The front involved as far as we could see left and right and our little area is practically in the centre. The bombardment lasted twenty minutes only – but it was a terrific one. After that we could hear machine-gun fire rattling like hell – after that we could know nothing until the first stragglers and walking wounded came in – and so we had to ask each other unanswerable questions re the result. That is the strange part of these attacks – that after the men are gone over, those in the back area know very little with regard to how the day has gone.

The guns continued to pound the battlefield, and the men sheltering in freezing conditions would have been unaware that the offensive was over, especially those who fought off a small German counter-attack near Grandcourt on 19 November, or the men of the 10th Royal Fusiliers asked to attack that afternoon to straighten their line. There was one thing, though, that all were too painfully aware of. After five months of fighting, there had been no breakthrough.

The civilians' cemetery of Montauban after the offensive had finally ground to a halt.

23 November: I can't think why Germany wanted war, to destroy homes, and to break hearts, maybe! I do not feel really unhappy, but in me glows a pride – I can feel it as I look at my mud-besprinkled khaki, high boots, and spurs – to think that I have the honour to bear arms against such people as the Germans.

Where is the need for conscription? Oh! Britain, if you could only come to see the devastation, and know what your little BEF is doing, you would never want to introduce conscription! Somehow conscription is repulsive to me. Why can't we go back to those days in 1914, when we had MEN!

My wheel driver has gone off for some vin 'splosh' (white wine) so I still have a few spare minutes to investigate. At the corner of the park under the fir trees there are four beautiful 'girls'! Oh how we do love our 'girls' out here. I stroll over to see the attractive females, and to enquire their names. No. 1 is dressed in deep green, and has a large covering of artificial grass to conceal her from prying airmen. Her name is *Phoebe* – just out from England. No. 2

Private Albert Edwards 1/6th Gloucestershire Regiment

is a little browner, and a little older looking. She is well under the trees, and does not wear a 'veil'. Her name is *Lizzie*. They tell me she is a 'cat' – knocked out four of her German rivals up at Arras a week ago.

No. 3 is grey, with lovely plum-coloured spots over her, together with *Lizzie*, she has been in France eight months. Her name is *Mary*. No. 4, the last, is very 'chic', she is the newest arrival of all, and came from England only four days ago. Her name is *Daphne 2nd*, and when I look at her pretty little figure I quite agree that she was rightly named.

Daphne 1st, unhappily, is 'nappo'. She was knocked out only a week ago, and *Daphne 2nd* was hurried out from 'Blighty' to take her place.

One may think I was a little forward to go over and see strange women! Perhaps I ought to add that *Phoebe, Mary, Lizzie* and *Daphne* are four 9.2 howitzers!

They are going in action tonight to liven up Fritz!

Goodbye, girls! Cheerio!

Second
Lieutenant
Charles Lloyd,
Royal Field
Artillery

25 November: Woke up at about 9.00 after one of the most restless and jumpy nights I have ever spent. My dugout was of the one-sandbag and heaven-help-you order and all through the night 4.2s and 5.9s were

The shattered remnants of High Wood.

flopping about the valley. One fell not 15 yards from my dugout as I discovered this morning. It was very nerve-racking and my nerves – never very steady – went to pot. On several occasions in desperation I tried to make for the mess dugout, not 20 yards away, but in the pitch blackness could not find it and after floundering about in crump holes had to give it up. Eventually fell asleep about 4.00. It rained nearly all day.

16 December

My Dear Abe,

I hope you have not been uneasy not hearing from me for the last few days. We only came out of action yesterday and the conditions under which we have been have made it utterly impossible for writing letters. ...

If I was to recount my experiences since last Friday, I could fill volumes. Of course, what I am going to tell you now is only for you and Harry to read and not to [be] passed on at home, as there is no necessity for them to know I have been anywhere near the line.

Well, last Friday we arrived near the line about 2½ miles from the trenches. We were all put into dugouts, most of them with a few inches of water in. In my dugout there were eight of us, the only entrance was a small hole which we had to crawl through on our hands and knees. It was impossible to stand up, and we sat crushed up till the evening, when I was detailed to carry up ammunition to the trenches. A party of us set out towards the line, guided by a Frenchman, and it was then that I had my first taste of shellfire.

In this part there is no communication trench to lead up to the front line, but we had to advance across country. The whole of this part is one mass of shell holes and mud up to the knees almost everywhere. I cannot describe the state of the roads and fields, but with the most vivid imagination you could not possibly picture such conditions. When we started I put my overcoat on, the bottom of which became thick with mud and clay, and wrapped around my legs. I had two boxes of ammunition each weighing 25 lbs; it gradually pulled me down and I kept falling until I was saturated to the skin. During this time shells were falling all around, the explosions of which were deafening. ... I have been hit by lumps of mud from shells which burst not 50 yards away, and the most remarkable thing, I can honestly say, was that through all this I never felt more cool or self-poised. I feel sure that poor Mother was watching and giving me courage.

Trooper Sam Goodman, Life Guards (Household Battalion)

Overleaf: *French infantry walking down a road on the Somme on Christmas Day.*

We eventually reached the trenches having taken about two hours to go 2 miles. It was on my way back that I gradually dropped back exhausted and suddenly to my horror I found myself sinking in the mud. I was past my waist in it and I hadn't the strength to shout for assistance and there I was stranded, absolutely helpless, not a mile from the firing line, I could not feel my hands and legs, and lost my rifle, and the star lights lit up the sky for miles around. I felt myself sinking in a sleep, and I knew no more until I found myself in a small dugout, and covered with blankets, and a young French soldier was pouring hot rum and coffee down my throat. It appears they found me in the mud and they carried me in their reserve trenches, made me comfortable in their dugout until morning, then they took me back to our headquarters. It is marvellous how quickly one recovers from exhaustion because the following evening our battalion took the line over and spent three days in the trenches. I won't venture to describe these three days, but now we are back about 10 miles, in huts and nice and comfy and I am none the worse except for a slight cold. We have had very few casualties, a good few have been sent to hospital with trench feet and severe shaking. I think I must have a wonderful constitution to have stood it all. I don't know when we go up to the line again, it may not be for some time to come, but I don't mind it. If it wasn't for the mud and cold, I would live in the trenches for duration, but the cold is awful, and there is no way of keeping warm. …

Your affectionate brother, Sam

Major Cuthbert Lawson, 14th Brigade, Royal Horse Artillery

24 December: The Christmas mail has apparently been too much altogether for the post office people and we are getting hardly any letters through these days, even my *Morning Post* failing to arrive and I know that starts off on its travels all right. Of course, only a limited number of supply trains can be run up from the base daily and they fill up with rations and forage first and then take what mails they have room for, and I expect the congestion at Havre is colossal. Anyway, I got a parcel today, a most beautiful cake with almond paste on top, looking most delicious – it will be awfully good and a great help.

It's hard to realize it's Christmas somehow – we are sitting in our little tin shanty, surrounded by mud, trying to persuade ourselves we are warm, while guns of all sorts suddenly break out into crescendos of fury and as suddenly stop – rather a violent form of cracker pulling! Just at present too, to add to the charm, the Hun is 'rocking' (that's the spot expression now) the corner we're in with diabolic persistency with the most evil 5.9" High Explosive – they are from a long range and you hear them coming for quite a long time, a deep sort of whistling sigh, getting shriller and shriller, then a terrific crrrash, followed by a deeper humming like some gigantic bee, as a steel splinter comes sailing in our direction, to flop with a thud in the mud – custom's an extraordinary thing, two years ago we'd all have been terrified, now we really don't worry much – we sort of realize it's just Kismet, and go on with whatever we are doing, but it's a wonderful succession of sounds. ...

The frost has gone and the rain has come, but it still seems very cold, and the mud is frightful – all our little homes leak, and the gun pits are in the most awful state – you want to be a Christian Scientist to see any romance in war these days.

Now the Hun has stopped shelling, and not a gun is firing for the moment – you could almost imagine you were back in England and thinking about dressing for dinner!

27 December: Our Christmas was rather a failure! – we had ordered quite a good dinner and asked a couple of guests. A turkey we got from Paris regardless of expense, and Reynolds had a plum pudding from home, and someone else produced almonds and raisins, but alas our alleged cook became so intoxicated early in the day that the subsequent proceedings interested him no more. – He did make his effort and produced:

(1) Soup – this was Worcester sauce and boiling water and tasted like it.
(2) Fish cakes (I think, but as they were of the consistency of leather and tasted like ink, I'm not sure).
(3) Turkey – raw but not too bad, only not 'pulled' or whatever you call it, so that it was quite impossible to carve – no sausages, and potatoes like rocks.
(4) Plum pudding completely uncooked and ruined, a bit 'ard wasn't it?

Still, we had some port and whisky and made a lot of noise, and that's the main thing.

Overleaf: An abandoned tank from the September fighting near Delville Wood.

8 Fighting Cold

'Shakespeare was never more true than when he said, "Sweet are the uses of adversity". We have learnt to be content with little, to act for ourselves, to do dirty jobs knowing that someone had to do them, to mix with a whole gamut of characters, to find good in a man who at first sight seemed to be little that was good, to work with uneducated and educated alike.'

Private Victor Archard, Heavy Branch, Machine Gun Corps

———————

For months, the Germans had been preparing a new defensive position, the Hindenburg Line, 25 miles to the west of the Somme battlefield. German casualties at Verdun and the Somme had been so heinous that it would be imprudent, indeed untenable, to garrison an extended, meandering front line with its natural bulges and man-made salients; much better to fall back on pre-prepared and shortened trench lines, thereby increasing the number of men per mile of trench held. The British were not privy to such information and so, throughout the winter, the Allies began the arduous task of rebuilding the battlefield infrastructure, with a view to continuing the Somme offensive in the spring, a rebuilding process that would soon be rendered worthless.

As a battalion, we tramped the old duckboards again yesterday afternoon, and now we've two companies in the front line (this time to the right of Lesboeufs) and one in the second, where there is a big new dugout. C Company is back in reserve, doing fatigues at night, salvaging during the daytime and occupying a large dugout, with officers at one end and men at the other, at a spot near Flers called Bull Dump.

Outside it is snowing gently. There is wrath and recrimination within; for, after carrying a rum jar right up here, somebody set it down on a stone and the earth has drunk most of the rum. I think the men would forget the tragedy, only the strong odour pervades the place and

Lieutenant Max Plowman, 10th West Yorkshire Regiment

Opposite: *An officer of the 1st Salford Pals (15th Lancashire Fusiliers) fully protected against the bitter wind near Serre, January 1917.*

they are not philosophic enough to be content with smell instead of taste. ...

The cold turned to rain, and after two days of duckboard tramping, carrying wire, stakes, rations, bombs and duckboards up to the front line, we came out in the rain and just had time to get clean and look round the town of hutments that is now Carnoy, before we were ready to go back to the line.

Last night I had to take a party up and now we're going up again. I am tired: physically and mentally tired. Leave deferred maketh the heart sick. I am sick of the energy of those belching guns firing over our heads as we tramp the never-ending duckboards. I am utterly tired of the mechanical routine of this existence.

Driving snow has semi-hidden the detritus of war.

On 14 January, winter reasserted itself with a vengeance. Temperatures plummeted and the ground froze solid. The land disappeared under a carpet of snow, hiding farm tracks and trenches, shell holes and the minor wreckage of war. Temperatures rarely rose above zero, even during the day, and snow resolutely remained in occupation for the rest of January and into February. The men struggled to cope with the conditions even when issued with extra blankets, leather jerkins and gloves. They huddled up at their posts, sure in the knowledge that the Germans were suffering every bit as much as they were.

16 January: The cold is intense, and the wind of a bitterness indescribable, but still it's better, I think, than the persistent rain and mud – the worst of it is that frost here always means a mist which makes shooting very difficult – things have quietened down all right as far as infantry action is concerned, but both sides still bombard each other pretty hard, and we don't get much rest – in addition of course to fighting by day, we have to shoot from 6.00 pm to 6.00 am every second night, which is a long cold business. The Hun in front of us has his tail down all right, but he's got no end of guns, and his ammunition is absolutely first class.

Major Cuthbert Lawson, 14th Brigade, Royal Horse Artillery

17 January 1917: a gun emplacement belonging to 121 Siege Battery. Six hours after this photograph was taken, the gun took a direct hit and four of the crew were killed or died of wounds.

Got the *Morning Post* of the 13th today and see I have achieved the exalted rank of major! Rather amusing going from subaltern to major without passing any exam – can't say I feel a very senior officer though! I believe they are giving me two more howitzers and so making me up to a six-gun battery, which will be rather nice.

23 January: Too busy to write – hard at work on a completely new position, at the same time fighting hard in this one – everything has to be carried 2,000 yards over the snow, and the ground's like iron.

Incredibly and fiercely cold – about 20 degrees of frost last night – sponge a lump of ice – ditto milk – waders frozen solid and impossible to put on – and a freezing wind and colder than ever today. I never saw such cold – it simply defeats you.

Am awfully fit, but very tired of the open-air life in winter.

26 January: Your letter of the 18th [arrived] today and two parcels, one with a woollen jersey attached – which I put on forthwith! and the other the muffler I wanted so badly which came through awfully quickly didn't it? It is a ripping one and just exactly what I wanted. I am wearing so many clothes now, my buttons will hardly do up, and I look just about as fat as you do! Still I don't sweat much! – 20° of frost we get each night, just think of that, a temperature of 12°F and it never goes above 18° in the daytime, so the cold is really intense.

Lieutenant
Martin Evans,
9th Welsh
Regiment

1 February: The other evening our company had the honour to get one prisoner; I fear this sounds sarcastic, it is not meant. Herbert's patrol was out at 6.00 pm and stopped this crawling prize. We cannot think what he was doing out there, unarmed, aged 19, and now we know the Saxons are opposite. It seems almost a pity to kill these Saxons because whether we like it or not they are our ancestors. Lest I malign the Welsh, it must be added, not ancient Britons' forefathers. This distant cousin of ours was brought into our HQ and fairly wolfed cake and tea, he even tipped the crumbs into his tea lest any be lost. He could not speak English or French and we could not speak German but by dint of signs and shouting we ascertained he was not well fed over there. Later he gave away useful

information that a corps was being relieved. Our artillery was quick to harry and played hell, but their retaliation knocked a battery out, twelve gunners getting killed.

We were billeted in farm buildings, sleeping arrangements being wood frames with wire netting stretched across. These were very cold for sleeping on especially as we were now experiencing severe frost and snow, and all the old buildings were rather open and draughty. As I had only one blanket I took a favourable opportunity to acquire a bread bag and some straw which made a fine mattress and stopped the cold underneath. Being a native of Boston in South Lincolnshire, I had experienced plenty of very cold winters but never before anything so bad as the one we were now up against. Everything became frozen up and water had to be obtained by melting ice and snow. Fortunately several fellows of the original company had small Primus stoves. I had one of the so-called 'pocket' variety, and this enabled us to attend to washing and shaving with hot water, the owner of the stove having the first go, of course. The ice or snow was melted in a cut-open petrol can, and the number that used it after the first turn was surprising.

Everything was frozen practically solid, including tins of fruit. Eggs obtained from nearby farms burst their shells, and one's boots were frozen stiff by morning. This period of extreme cold lasted throughout January and most of February. Road transport was for the greater part of the time at a standstill, except for a minimum of light vehicles, for fear of

Corporal William Dawson, Heavy Branch, Machine Gun Corps

A chance to potter about and search for souvenirs was very tempting but apparently others had been to this tank first.

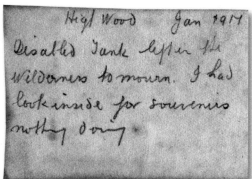

High Wood   Jan 1917
Disabled Tank left the
Wilderness to mourn. I had
look inside for souvenirs
nothing doing

A Holt tractor struggles to pull a gun across the battlefield.

damage to the roads. I somehow managed to get some sleep through this very hard period with my only blanket and the loan of another leather jerkin from my friend Corporal Kennedy who had two blankets. I need hardly say that the rum ration during this period was a real boon and blessing.

Trench raids and small-scale stunts continued to impress upon the Germans that they would be given no extended period of rest in which to recuperate and restore battered morale. These attacks would also continue to improve British positions overall prior to a resumption of fighting in the spring.

In mid-February one such stunt included an advance near the village of Miraumont and an enemy salient that included a position known as Boom Ravine. One of the battalions taking part in this 'bite and hold' operation was the 11th Royal Fusiliers, including a 23-year-old officer, Lieutenant Richard Hawkins. He had been on the Somme for the whole campaign, taking part not only in the advance on 1 July but also, in late September, in the successful storming of that strongest of

German positions, Thiepval, in which he had been stunned by a German mortar, and of his close friends, Captain Tommy Thompson was killed and Second Lieutenant George Cornaby was lightly wounded.

Our forming-up place was just in front of a depression known as the Gully and our target was Boom Ravine, a short distance ahead, seizing the high ground in order to provide observation over the upper Ancre Valley.

Lieutenant Richard Hawkins, 11th Royal Fusiliers

I was commanding D Company and on the night of 16 February we began to move up. There were two routes to the forming-up line; both were very congested and in the dark it was almost impossible to get the men up. The journey was made more difficult by the weather. For at least three weeks it had been freezing hard, indeed, that winter was one of the coldest periods I can ever remember, but this night a thaw had begun to set in. We waded through the mud and slime to be in our positions by 4.45 am and were harassed all the way by artillery and machine-gun fire, causing a lot of casualties just to get my company in position.

At 5.30 am I went round the line with some rum and gave all the men a good tot, chatting to them as I did so. I finished about 6.00 am. The only thing I could do then was to establish my headquarters at the top of a small ravine that ran at right angles to the main objective, Boom Ravine. At 6.20 I clambered to the top of the ravine, which was 25 or 30 feet high. I just managed to see from my watch that it was 6.25 am; it was still dark. The time went on, 6.26, 6.27, 6.28. It was 6.29 when the biggest bloody barrage I had ever been through suddenly descended on us. It was obvious that the Germans had wind of our attack. Captain Collis-Sandes, who was commanding B Company, turned up at my side. 'I think this is going to be a pretty awful show.' 'Yes,' I replied, 'I think I am going to get myself a rifle and a bayonet,' and I collared one from a fellow who was dead.

At 6.30 our barrage opened with a blinding flash behind us. We were still bogged down with the German barrage when there was another flash and Collis-Sandes fell dead and I was hit in the shoulder. It was like being kicked by a mule. As the force spun me round, I lost my balance and fell right down the ravine, crashing into some barbed wire at the bottom. I lost consciousness for a while. I awoke as it was beginning to get light, to hear a Cockney voice say, 'Cor blimey, 'ere's Lieutenant Hawkins, the poor so-and-so is dead.' 'No, I'm not,' I replied, 'but I shall be if you don't get me out of this lot.'

I'd lost a lot of blood but they helped me to my feet and took me back a couple of hundred yards and there I met dear old Doctor Sale, from Australia. He stripped my tunic and put some dressings on before he called over three German prisoners, 'Here, come and get hold of the end of this stretcher.' He needed a fourth man and, looking around, he saw a German officer. This man was a good-looking young fellow with a ginger moustache and he explained in fairly good English that it was not the job of an officer to grab hold of a stretcher with three private soldiers. Dr Sale was a pretty busy man, and he hadn't time to argue, so he just repeated himself. The German said, 'Nein'. Dr Sale was a very good rugby three-quarter and he stuck his boot into this fellow's behind and he took off. They started to go round in a very big circle, down in the shell holes, and up the other side, the doctor launching a kick at this officer every few yards and missing practically every time because of the impossible state of the ground. In the end, old Sale caught him and kicked his backside several more times, after which the officer decided he would take the end of the stretcher after all.

When you get up on the shoulders of four fellows, it's a long way down to the ground and we were walking on a very muddy slippery duckboard, with not really room for two people abreast. I looked down into the shell holes and didn't like what I saw. I said, 'Oy, I'm getting off.' I didn't want to get tipped down into one of these shell holes, so I walked out, weak though I was.

The fighting was particularly hard and the line swayed one way and then another before Boom Ravine was eventually secured, although the village of Miraumont, an objective, remained in enemy hands. Nevertheless, once again the Germans were reminded how untenable their position on the Somme had become.

19 February: I am afraid there will be a gap between my last letter and this, but the fact is that we don't seem able to send back letters from the trenches, or at any rate don't have it done. Out now, after a fairly peaceful time, though we were lucky too, I think. The cold first, and then mud later, when it thawed, were pretty bad – not so much for us, who had a dugout (Boche) to retire to, as for the men who hadn't.

Second Lieutenant Robert Vernède, 12th Rifle Brigade

I found that two hours' standing about over the ankles in icy water in ordinary boots froze me up, but was nothing like so cold as last time, when we spent all the time in the open trench. The Boche is very sensible in that way. The whole front, however, is extraordinarily desolate in this weather: pock-marked with frozen shell holes, every kind of abandoned material lying about, and bodies in ghastly attitudes, just as they fell and were constricted to the ground by the frost immovably until the winter chooses to give up its dead. I think if everybody could see these scenes,

Above: Walking wounded ready to catch an evacuation train at Grovetown Casualty Clearing Station.

Left: Wounded men awaiting their medical treatment in a pre-operation ward at Sailly-Saillisel.

the general horror would somehow find the way out, which ordinary mortals and intelligence don't seem to. The time the men have while they live is bad enough; it's pathetically absurd to see them plunging about in the mire, laden to the teeth, falling into shell holes in the dark, getting stuck fast, cursing and patient, and half of them ill enough to be in bed or hospital in peacetime. I pulled one little man ahead of me eight times out of mud holes into which he had fallen in the course of about 200 yards, as we came out.

Towards the end of February, the Germans began the first stage of their controlled retirement from their front lines to the Hindenburg Line. The first night of the withdrawal took the Allies entirely by surprise.

Major Cuthbert Lawson, 14th Brigade, Royal Horse Artillery

26 February: Great excitement here – the Hun has done another 'midnight flitting' and evacuated Serre and Miraumont, and we haven't quite re-established touch with him yet and found out where he's gone to – it's defeated our Staff altogether – for weeks now they've been planning the capture of Serre, an enormously strong fortress we've already failed badly at twice, and now the Huns have calmly walked away and given it to us, so all our plans are a washout and we'll have to start on some fresh ones.

It's really a pretty big thing, as Serre in addition to being tremendously strong, is on a ridge which commands Puisieux, and as we also have the ridge north of Grandcourt which commands the valley of the Upper Ancre, we should make it pretty uncomfortable for the Boche.

1 March: We are all on tiptoe with eagerness and curiosity – the Boche is fairly hopping it, no one knows quite why, and of course no one has the foggiest idea where they will stop. The prevailing theory is that they will stand on the line Bucquoy, Achiet-le-Petit, Loupart Wood, Grevillers, Le Transloy – fight a delaying action there, and then withdraw by successive lines until they reach the famous Hindenburg Line, which covers Cambrai and St Quentin, and where they hope to fetch up by the end of March.

Meanwhile I have been careering over the country looking for new [gun] positions, and inspecting my late targets with great interest – the Hun gun pits are a wonderful sight, they have been absolutely wrecked, and there's hardly a dugout left that hasn't been blown in – our counter-battery work has been jolly fine. I've been in Miraumont, and Irles, and Puisieux and walked over miles of muddy country – lots of dead Boches about, Beaucourt and Ten Tree Alley especially fairly stink with them! Nice and warm, but always every day a mist which quite ruins observation.

A patrol of the 1st Salford Pals 3 miles in front of the old front line, assessing the extent of the German withdrawal.

The Boche has done his retirement with amazing skill – he must have shifted his heavy stuff during the frost, and we never spotted a thing. He's left all our staff guessing. … Meanwhile I reckon the Hun must be preparing an offensive somewhere, as he simply can't be done in yet, and he'll probably give us all a very nasty shock one of these days.

Mud everywhere, rather of the putty variety and the roads all destroyed, so an advance will be a fearful and wonderful thing.

Lieutenant Martin Evans, 9th Welsh Regiment

3 March: So much news I hardly know where to begin. At the end of my last letter or on [the] envelope I put 'We are moving tonight.' The order came through suddenly, was cancelled and reordered. The staff were losing their heads with this enemy retirement … could not write earlier as where we were communication trenches did not exist, and hardly any communication with the rear, so a letter miraculously got up; there are just miles of water-filled shell holes, one vast desert defying description. The wagons got stuck in the mud, dud shells or gas came over as we were eating, making the food come up the way it had gone down – nearly; we were too tired to mind anything. It took us six hours to get to the new line, passed a crashed plane – ours (on coming out two days later a lone dog was in the cockpit). Had to negotiate the watery craters as they are a veritable deathtrap when men slip into them. Reached the line at 7.00 pm and took over from the Worcestershires, who could give no information whatsoever.

Private Sydney Fuller, 8th Suffolk Regiment

17 March: Parade, 9.30–10.30 am. Very quiet – no guns heard, but scores of wild rumours. At night, we noticed big glows in the sky, as if from fires. One was in the direction of Bapaume, and there were three others at different points. Heard that Fritz was retiring, and burning the villages as he went. Also heard that Bapaume had been taken by us.

18 March: Had a look round the old trenches near Ovillers. In the old no-man's-land there still lay scores of our bombs, just as they had been dropped by killed or wounded men on 1, 2 and 3 July 1916. Just beyond the old German front line, I saw the remains of many French soldiers, with fragments of red trousers and dark blue tunics. These, no doubt, were the

French soldiers who were killed there in 1914, during the 'settling down' period. Noticed a map displayed outside our orderly room hut, on which map was marked the extent of Fritz's retirement.

The Padre asked me if I would accompany him to visit our old front line and no-man's-land, which was littered with British dead. Ours were in lines where they had fallen. They were just skeletons in khaki rags and their equipment. We walked up to the old German wire – the Padre had brought a friend with him – and the three of us turned back to look towards our lines. Then the Padre said a prayer for the dead and we sang the hymn, *For All the Saints*. Next morning the dead were buried by an overnight fall of snow. It was some weeks before no-man's-land was cleared when V Corps began to make new cemeteries to finally lay our pals to rest.

Private Reginald Glenn, 12th York & Lancaster Regiment (Sheffield City Battalion)

The scenes were indeed terrible, and I doubt whether there has since been any stretch of land so crammed with horror as the stretch of no-man's-land from Gommecourt to below Beaumont Hamel.

Numerous skeletons lay there in long rows, with their equipment on just as they had fallen in their waves in the fights of 1 July and after. Dead 'Boche' were around, and here and there remnants of bewildered cattle shot in the early days.

The gaunt, spiritless trees of Gommecourt Wood on the left had been silent witnesses of slaughter. The bodies lay in all kinds of positions – some very straight, some doubled up, some with arms folded, some with legs doubled under them, some with legs crossed. Heads were loose, and some had rolled from their trunks.

It was strange how we soldiers looked on with a callous, detached air. Probably no one blenched at such a mass of disaster and suffering. In his dairy one of the men wrote thus:

'I visited the old no-man's-land today, and afterwards was alarmed at my callousness. I found that my mind had noted the fact of rats having fed on the bodies without the slightest feeling of sentiment. I found I had noticed that the teeth in the skulls gleamed in the sunshine. I found I had noticed that some of the skulls still had patches of hair, red hair and black hair, adhering to them. So matter of fact! I had remarked how the trousers

Sergeant Richard Sparling, 12th York & Lancaster Regiment (Sheffield City Battalion)

and boots looked as if packed with sawdust, and how one man's crumbling thigh bone resembled the brown, musty edges of a century-old volume. Such is the effect of war.'

Major Cuthbert Lawson, 14th Brigade, Royal Horse Artillery

20 March: These are great days aren't they? and something to have been in at – if only it was not so cold! Just think today I have been into Bapaume, the place we have been trying to take ever since 1 July last, and which has cost such thousands of lives – I used to think we would never get there, and could hardly believe it when I heard we'd got it. Just at present we aren't doing any fighting as the Hun is far out of range. He has gone back to his Hindenburg Line covering Cambrai and St Quentin, and we can't get up to him until we have remade the roads and relaid the railway. He has laid the country absolutely waste as he's gone back and taken all the unfortunate inhabitants with him.

The villages, great and small, he has demolished, putting a dynamite charge in every single building and blowing it up, and finally setting the ruins on fire. He's blown great mine craters in all the roads, making them impassable, and not only made the railway useless, but bodily removed all the rails and carted them off into Germany I suppose. The line up the Ancre Valley is the main Paris, Amiens, Arras, Lille, Brussels, Berlin, St Petersburg line, so the French are rather annoyed about it. Cavalry have gone on, but there's too much wire, and they haven't got into the Huns, and meanwhile the feet are hung up by the roads – so nothing much will happen for a bit. …

It's extraordinarily interesting going over the re-conquered territory – I've been to Achiet-le-Petit, Achiet-le-Grand, Bucquoy, Gommecourt, Courcelles, Ervillers, Irles, Grevillers and Bapaume.

The first thing that strikes you is the enormous use the Hun makes of light railways – he runs them everywhere, and supplies all his batteries with ammunition by rail, saving an infinity of work to men and horses. Horses apparently he has cut down to a minimum – I saw no signs of horse lines anywhere.

The other marvellous thing is the way the Hun digs. He has trenches everywhere, mile after mile of them – he must be a cross between a mule and an elephant!

And then his barbed wire – he often has three belts of it in front of a trench – sometimes five – each belt 30 yards wide, and 5 or 6 feet high – just think of having to cut that – the more I see of his lines, the more I marvel that we have ever turned him out of them. No power on earth would shift the British Army entrenched like that.

It's difficult to say what will happen now, as our Great Offensive, which has been being prepared for months, now finds most of its objective gone – so entirely new schemes will have to be worked out, and the masses of heavy howitzers moved, all of which will take a long time and greatly shorten the period for major operations this year – which looks as if the war might be prolonged.

I rode with two officers across the river and down the east side to Péronne to look for billets for the sappers. All the inhabitants had been removed. Churches, public and private buildings of all kinds, bridges and roadways had been blown up; water supply sources and communications destroyed. There are few signs of the town being shelled by the French or British. The almost complete ruin of the buildings in the principal streets has been brought about by the Germans blowing out of the fronts or setting fire to them. The underlying mentality of the Hun is boastfully shown by a large signboard, high up on a wall of the ruined Hôtel de Ville – a Renaissance building on a fine corner site, '*Nicht ärgern, nur wundern*' (Do not grow angry, only wonder). Fires were still burning in many directions, with occasional explosions as booby-traps and delayed-action mines exploded.

We quickly learned that the most innocent-looking object, such as an apparently discarded steel helmet on the ground, might cover a bomb arranged to explode if the helmet were picked up. Everywhere the debris of war and discarded equipment lay around. For any souvenir hunter the choice was unlimited. For my part, with my promised leave so far holding good, I watched my steps with the utmost circumspection and took no risks. I permitted myself one reminder of Péronne. It was a prominent notice posted on a wall and printed in French and German. Translated it reads: 'It is forbidden to throw sweepings, kitchen refuse, or any other rubbish into the stream. Offenders will be punished.'

Lieutenant
Victor Eberle,
2nd Field
Company, Royal
Engineers

21 March: Hundreds of cavalry (the majority being Indians), came through the village going forward. There were 17th and 19th Lancers, some of the Suffolk Yeomanry, the 6th Dragoon Guards, and some RHA [Royal Horse Artillery]. Some of the cavalrymen were inclined to be sarcastic – no doubt they did not like leaving their nice, safe billets after all this time. (It was a shame really.) One shouted, 'What, have you lost him, then, and now we've got to find him for you?' We assured him that he would 'find' Fritz all right, and advised him not to worry, as he would have plenty to worry about when he did find Fritz.

Private Sydney Fuller, 8th Suffolk Regiment

For so long, the men who fought on the Somme had seen the battlefield through a trench periscope or a risky look over the top. Safely released from their confined environment, they were finally able to see the ground for what it was, and they were profoundly shocked. After recovering from injuries, Second Lieutenant Geoffrey Fildes crossed the Somme on his return to France in the spring of 1917.

Setting forth once more, by a route that passed through the heart of the Somme country, we had been gradually confronted by a terrible panorama. From the open door of our goods van, we were able to realize more than ever before the magnitude and fury of the struggle of the previous autumn. In every direction, as far as the horizon, stretched a desert of brown shell-ploughed slopes and hollows, and scattered upon the face of this landscape, clumps of splintered poles, gaunt and blackened by fire, marked the sites of former woods and copses. ...

Such a region as this, exceeding the limit of our vision in every direction, presented a scene surpassing human imagination. It haunted one like a nightmare. Neither of my companions accompanying the draft had served in France before, but, like most people, they had read newspaper accounts of the Western Front. Now, however, they were amazed. Seated beside them in our van, even I was enthralled by the passing spectacle, but it did not prevent me from noting their murmurs of astonishment. Their feelings were hardly to be wondered at, for, though familiar with the Somme, I, too, had not realized until now the

Second Lieutenant Geoffrey Fildes, 2nd Coldstream Guards

A farmhouse set on fire by the Germans as they retreated to the Hindenburg Line in March 1917.

degree and extent of its awful ruin. Life – human, animal, and vegetable – had been engulfed; not a leaf, hardly a blade of grass, no sound of bird, greeted us; all was done and finished with. Here indeed was the end of the world. …

Everywhere around us a wild confusion seemed to have upheaved the land, leaving behind it an ocean of rubble heaps. French helmets battered to shapeless lumps, and Lebel rifles red with rust, lay in the stiffened mud, scattered among the countless refuse of the British and German armies. In many craters lay great pools of bright-yellow water, whose stagnant surface disclosed many a rotting corpse. Coils of wire, like bramble thickets, ran in and out of the sun-baked hummocks, fluttering bleached tatters from their barbs. Close at hand, the mangled fragments of a machine gun protruded from a reeking mound, and beside it lay a human skull, picked clean by birds. Everything was encased by a monotone of mud. Here, as we turned from side to side, odours assailed us at every breath, while a profound silence intensified the dreadful melancholy of the scene.

As Lieutenant Fildes reached the limits of the 1916 battlefield, he climbed a low ridge. What he saw on the other side was little different from countryside he had seen in England or from the train that had brought him from the Channel ports, but in comparison with the battlefield he had just crossed, the sight of nature, or rather normality, undisturbed and seemingly peaceful, was almost unreal. It was to all intents and purposes the same unsullied rural vista that had greeted the men who left the battlefields of Ypres and Loos to march down to the Somme just over twenty months before.

Second Lieutenant Geoffrey Fildes, 2nd Coldstream Guards

Now we had arrived upon the summit. The skyline before us lurched lower at every step; still all that we could see was a wide expanse of blue sky. Then the ground fell away, and the distant landscape confronted us. For an instant the prospect held one spellbound, so thrilling was its revelation, so placid its majesty. At first I was only conscious of the exclamations of those nearby, for even the attention of the men was centred on what lay ahead. Stretching for miles, bounded by the far horizon north and south, a glorious vision rose to greet us, a riotous pageant of shimmering colour. The low ridges opposite blazed under a mantle of sunlit grass, and scattered upon them, trees, flecked with vivid shoots, spread forth a lacework of slender boughs. Wheeling in a multitudinous swirl in the middle distance, a flock of crows flapped slowly on its way, while at the foot of our slope, a group of mottled roofs was half concealed by branches. Behind all these, displaying a widespread carpet of unblemished pasture land, glowing in the full radiance of the sun, the country undulated into the distance, luxuriant with verdure, scattered spinneys, and a patchwork of fields, and revealing at every point the freshest tints of an awakening world.

Greedily we feasted our unbelieving eyes, scanning the far perspective of the land until baffled by the distant haze. So suddenly had it appeared that it seemed at first only a mocking mirage. But no – still it lay there inviting contemplation. There lay spring in all her vastness and all her splendour.

Below: The old German line at Gommecourt, now entirely safe to cross.

Overleaf: The road to Peronne after the Germans had laid waste to the ground. Trees were cut down to block the advance of the Allies.

Acknowledgements

I would like to thank the staff at Pen & Sword Books, who have been particularly generous in their support for this book, especially Jonathan Wright, who completely understood the ambitious nature of this project and has been a great help and support. I'd also like to thank Charles Hewitt for backing the book and Tara Moran, Matt Jones and Heather Williams, who have also worked exceptionally hard; to them all, I am very grateful for the great team effort of bringing *The Somme* to publication. I would also like to express my gratitude to Jon Wilkinson, for the book's cover design, Linne Matthews, for her careful and insightful editing of the book, picking up a number of small errors of consistency that I had overlooked, and to Mat Blurton, for his exceptional layout design and creativity, and also my thanks go to Katie Noble.

I would like to make especial mention of my friend Fiona Gell in Special Collections, Leeds University. Her help has been much appreciated. Fiona and all the staff have always been very supportive of my searches through the Liddle Archive. My thanks too to Richard Davies, who, although he has officially retired from the University's Special Collections, still points me in the right direction and offers knowledgeable advice.

As always, I am indebted to my fantastic agent, Jane Turnbull, who is a very good friend, generous both with her time and with her considered thoughts and advice. Thank you yet again, Jane.

My warmest thanks must go to my family: to my wonderful mother, Joan van Emden, who, as ever, has apparently unlimited time to offer when the pressure is on, giving me the benefit of her unparalleled expertise in the English language. My huge thanks go to my wife, Anna: she helps to keep everything calm and on track, despite her own work commitments. And thank you too to Ben, our son, who is a delight in every way.

I am grateful to the following people for permission to reproduce photographs, extracts from diaries, letters or memoirs: Michael and Ann Brock, for permission to use photographs from the album of Lieutenant Patrick Koekkoek; Mrs Hazel Kentish, for her permission to use an extract from the memoirs of Lance Corporal George Brown, 21st Northumberland Fusiliers (2nd Tyneside Scottish); Kevin Varty, for his permission to use images from the private photographic collection of Lieutenant Richard Hawkins; Richard Hills, for letting me borrow the remarkable collection of photographs taken by his grandfather, Huborn Godfrey; Robert Bagley, for the image of Captain William Morton Johnson; Tom Yuille, for the image taken by his father, Captain Archibald Yuille, 8th East Lancashire Regiment (p.75); Nik Racine, for extracts from the memoirs of Private James Racine, 1/5th Seaforth Highlanders; and the Nash family for kind permission to use extracts from the diary of Lieutenant Anthony Nash.

My gratitude for help and advice also goes to Stephen Chambers, David Empson, Jeremy Banning, Peter Barton, Jon Cooksey, Paul Atterbury, Stuart Arrowsmith, Stephen Barker, Ian Collins, Mrs Willcock, Michael Stedman, Alan Fidler and Malcolm Brown.

I have sought whenever possible to obtain permission to use all illustrations and quotations in this book. When this has not been possible, I would like to extend an apology and would be glad to hear from copyright holders.

Sources and Permissions

Published Memoirs

Adams, John Bernard Pye, *Nothing of Importance*, R.M. McBride & Co, 1918

Bidder, Harold F., *Three Chevrons*, John Lane, The Bodley Head, 1919

Bloor, William Henry, *War Diary of*: privately published, undated

Brownlow, Cecil A.L., *The Breaking of the Storm*, Methuen & Co, 1918

Buxton, Andrew, *The Rifle Brigade, A Memoir*, Robert Scott, 1918

Clayton, Rev Philip, *Letters from Flanders*, The Centenary Press, 1933

Cliff, Norman D., *To Hell and Back with the Guards*, Merlin Books, 1988

Collins, Norman, *Last Man Standing*, Pen & Sword Books, 2012

Cornaby, George, *The 54th Infantry Brigade: Some Records of Battle and Laughter in France*, Gale & Polden, 1919

Crozier, F.P., *A Brass Hat in No Man's Land*, Gliddon Books, 1989

Eberle, Ellison, *My Sapper Adventure*, Pitman Publishing, 1973

Evans, M. St Helier, *Going Across*, R.H. Johns Ltd, 1952

Eyre, Giles, *Somme Harvest*, London Stamp Exchange, 1991

Feilding, Rowland, *War Letters to a Wife*, Spellmount Classics, 2001

Fildes, Geoffrey, *Iron Times with the Guards*, John Murray, 1918

Fraser-Tytler, Neil, *Field Guns in France*, Naval & Military Press, undated

Gosse, Philip, *Memoirs of a Camp Follower*, Longmans, 1934

Housman, Lawrence, *War Letters of Fallen Englishmen*, Victor Gollancz, 1930 (incl. letters from 2nd Lt William Dyson, 2nd Lt John Engall, Lt Headley Goodyear, Pte James Parr, 2nd Lt Adrian Stephen, Lt Theodore Wilson, 2nd Lt Arthur Young)

Howell, Philip, *A Memoir by his Wife*, George Allen & Unwin, 1942

Hutchinson, Graham Seaton, *Footslogger*, Hutchinson & Co, 1933

Longley, Cecil, *Battery Flashes*, John Murray, 1916

Lyon, Thomas, *More Adventures in Kilt and Khaki*, The Standard Press, 1917

Mark VII (Max Plowman), *A Subaltern on the Somme*, The Battery Press, 1996

Nash, T.A.M., *The Diary of an Unprofessional Soldier*, Picton Publishing, 1991

Roe, F.P., *Accidental Soldiers*, privately published, London, 1981

Rogerson, Sidney, *Twelve Days*, Gliddon Books, 1988

Vernède, Robert, *Letters to his wife*, W. Collins, 1917

Published Books

Barton, Peter, *The Somme, A new Panoramic Perspective*, Constable, 2006

Brown, Malcolm, *Somme*, Sidgwick & Jackson, 1996

Cooksey, John, *Pals*, Pen & Sword, 1986

Glenconner, Pamela, *Edward Wyndham Tennant: A Memoir*, John Land, 1919

Hart, Peter, *The Somme*, Cassell, 2005

Jolliffe, John, *Raymond Asquith, Life and Letters*, Collins, 1980

Middlebrook, Martin, *The First Day on the Somme*, Penguin, 1984

Orr, Philip, *The Road to the Somme*, The Black Staff Press, 1987

Pidgeon, Trevor, *Boom Ravine*, Pen & Sword Books, 1998

Stedman, Michael, *Manchester Pals*, Pen & Sword Books, 1994

Stedman, Michael, *Salford Pals*, Pen & Sword Books, 2007

Winter, Denis, *Death's Men*, Allen Lane, 1978

Unpublished Memoirs

Cole, V., *An Englishman's Life*, 1973

Interviews conducted by the author with the following Great War veterans:

Lieutenant Richard Hawkins, 11th Royal Fusiliers

Private Frank Lindley, 14th York and Lancaster Regiment (2nd Barnsley Pals)

Sergeant Walter Popple, 8th King's Own Yorkshire Light Infantry

Gunner Archie Richard, D7, Heavy Branch, Machine Gun Corps

Private Joe Yarwood, 94th Field Ambulance, Royal Army Medical Corps

Archives

Durham Record Office, Durham

By kind permission: 'My Part in the Battle of the Somme', by Sergeant Herbert Moss, 18th Durham Light Infantry: D/DLI/7/478/4

The Fusiliers Museum of Northumberland, Alnwick Castle

By kind permission: Diary and letters of Lieutenant A.O. Terry, 23rd Northumberland Fusiliers (4th Tyneside Scottish)

Soldiers of Gloucestershire Museum, Custom House, Gloucester Docks, Gloucester

By kind permission: Private A.G. Edwards, 1/6th Gloucestershire Regiment. Ref: 3083

The National Archives, Kew

Cab 45/188: Lieutenant Colonel Francis Bowen, commanding 14th Royal Irish Rifles

Cab45/166: Lieutenant Kimmich, 2nd Battalion, 180th Infantry Regiment

Cab45/137: Lieutenant Eric Sheppard, 1st Lancashire Fusiliers

Imperial War Museums, London

By kind permission of the Department of Documents, and with grateful thanks to Tony Richards: private papers of:

Private Robert Cude, 7th The Buffs (East Kent Regiment). Ref: Documents 129

Private Sydney Fuller, 8th Suffolk Regiment. Ref: Documents 2607

Driver Percival Glock, 281st Brigade, Royal Field Artillery. Ref: Documents 9632

Trooper Sam Goodman, Life Guards (Household Battalion). Ref: Documents 6408

Major Geoffrey Hardwick, 59th Field Ambulance, Royal Army Medical Corps. Ref: Documents 7835

Private Edward Higson, 16th
Manchester Regiment. Ref:
Documents 11596

Lt Col Frederick Johnson, 88th Field
Ambulance, RAMC. Ref: Documents
248

Major Cuthbert Lawson, 14th
Brigade, Royal Horse Artillery. Ref:
Documents 7834

Lieutenant Charles Lloyd, D Battery,
81st Brigade, Royal Field Artillery.
Ref: Documents 7830

Driver Rowland Luther, C Battery,
92nd Brigade Royal Field Artillery.
Ref: Documents 1325

Rifleman William J. Lynas, 15th Royal
Irish Rifles. Ref: Documents 278

Chaplain William McCormick,
Army Chaplains' Department. Ref:
Documents 12745

Private John Mortimer, 10th York
and Lancaster Regiment. Ref:
Documents 7449

Signaller Cyril Newman, 1/9th London
Regiment (Queen Victoria Rifles).
Ref: Documents 12494

Sergeant Arthur Perriman, 11th South
Wales Borderers. Ref: Documents
4860

Private David Polley, 189th Machine
Gun Company, MGC. Ref:
Documents 4825 (one very short
quote)

Private Henry Russell, 1/5th London
Regiment (London Rifle Brigade).
Ref: Documents 7312

Private William Thomas, 14th Royal
Welsh Fusiliers. Ref: Documents
7110

Lieutenant Alex Thompson, 1/6th
Northumberland Fusiliers. Ref:
Documents 6703

Private Frank Williams, 88th Field
Ambulance, Royal Army Medical
Corps. Ref: Documents 13573

**The Liddle Archive: Special Collections,
Leeds University Library, Leeds**
By kind permission and with special
thanks to Richard Davies: Second
Lieutenant George Webb, 1st Dorset
Regiment – Liddle/WW1/GS/1697

**Royal Engineers Archives, Brompton
Barracks, Chatham**
By kind permission: Royal Engineers
Library: Captain Stanley Bullock, 179
Tunnelling Company, Royal Engineers
Royal Engineers Museum: Second
Lieutenant John Godfrey, 103 Field
Company, Royal Engineers

**The Regimental Museum of the Royal
Welsh, The Barracks, Watton, Brecon**
By kind permission: Captain Eric
Whitworth, 12th South Wales
Borderers

**The Tank Museum, Bovington Camp,
Bovington**
By kind permission:
Gunner Victor Archard, C Company,
Heavy Section, Machine Gun Corps:
WW1/ArchardVS
Gunner William Dawson, C Company,
Heavy Branch, Machine Gun Corps:
WW1/DawsonWT
Gunner Alfred Reiffer, D17, Heavy
Branch, Machine Gun Corps:
WW1/ReifferAHR
Gunner Albert Smith, D1, Heavy Branch,
Machine Gun Corps: WW1/SmithAS
Driver Ernest Reader, Royal Field
Artillery: WW1/ReaderER

A NOTE ON THE AUTHOR

Richard van Emden has interviewed more than 270 veterans of the Great War and has written seventeen books on the subject including *The Trench* and *The Last Fighting Tommy*, both of which were top ten bestsellers. He has also worked on more than a dozen television programmes on the Great War, including the award-winning *Roses of No Man's Land*, *Britain's Boy Soldiers*, *A Poem for Harry*, *War Horse: the Real Story*, *Teenage Tommies* with Fergal Keane and most recently, *Hidden Histories: WW1's Forgotten Photographs*. He lives in London.

Gallipoli
Tommy's War
Meeting the Enemy
The Quick and the Dead
Tommy's Ark
Sapper Martin: The Secret Great War Diary of Jack Martin
The Soldier's War
Famous 1914–1918
The Last Fighting Tommy (with Harry Patch)
Boy Soldiers of the Great War
Britain's Last Tommies
All Quiet on the Home Front (with Steve Humphries)
Last Man Standing
The Trench
Prisoners of the Kaiser
Veterans: The Last Survivors of the Great War
Tickled to Death to Go (reprinted in 2014 as Teenage Tommy)